The 1957
Francisco S

The 1957 San Francisco Seals

End of an Era in the Pacific Coast League

P.J. DRAGSETH

Foreword by Ken Aspromonte

McFarland & Company, Inc., Publishers
Jefferson, North Carolina, and London

LIBRARY OF CONGRESS CATALOGUING-IN-PUBLICATION DATA

Dragseth, P. J.
    The 1957 San Francisco Seals : end of an era in the Pacific
Coast League / P. J. Dragseth ; foreword by Ken Aspromonte.
       p.   cm.
    Includes bibliographical references and index.

    ISBN 978-0-7864-6545-3
    softcover : acid free paper ∞

    1. San Francisco Seals (Baseball team) — History.
    2. Pacific Coast League — History   I. Title.
    II. Title: Nineteen fifty seven San Francisco Seals.
GV875.S353D73 2013
796.357'640979461 — dc23   2013007177

BRITISH LIBRARY CATALOGUING DATA ARE AVAILABLE

On the cover: *artwork* "Seal Stadium" by Dan McHale, 2007,
www.danmchale.com; *foreground* detail from the 1957 San
Francisco Seals Yearbook (courtesy of the author's collection)

Manufactured in the United States of America

McFarland & Company, Inc., Publishers
  Box 611, Jefferson, North Carolina 28640
   www.mcfarlandpub.com

For my grandchildren,
Taylor, Rylie, Joey, and Danielle,
with love

Table of Contents

Acknowledgments

There is one man ultimately responsible for this book, my dad, for coaxing and cajoling to lure me to my first baseball game. That was in 1953 and "everything baseball" in my life, including three previous books published about the game, have evolved from that first adventure. Thanks for taking me out to the ballgame, Dad!

At age nine in 1954 I wrote a fan letter to Sal Taormina, my favorite Seals player. To my surprise and delight he answered and thanked me for my loyalty to him and the team. Just as he motivated ballplayers he mentored, including Hall of Famer Willie McCovey, he motivated me to always try hard and do my best no matter what the endeavor. We had a unique friendship until his death, and this book is one of the products of his kindness. Thank you, Sal, for being such a wonderful man.

To Ken Aspromonte, Chip, watching your 1956 and outstanding 1957 seasons then following your major league career as both player and manager left an indelible impression. Sal Taormina was my first favorite on the Seals team, and you were my hero. That plus your kindness and generosity over the years made you the perfect person to write the foreword for this book. It's appreciated so much. Thank you.

To the other members of the 1957 Seals team, it was a particular privilege and honor looking back and sharing memories of that unique season with you as you graciously interviewed with me. It was such fun talking with you, especially since you have held a special place in my memory all these years. Sadly, some were too ill to participate and others had passed away before this project began, but they are not forgotten.

I'm most fortunate to have photos from the collections of Mark Macrae, David Eskenazi, Doug McWilliams, and Ray Saracini plus the Irwin Herlihy photo of the Seals statue and plaque located at the entrance of the Giants' AT&T Park in San Francisco. The book would not be complete without your contributions. A sincere thank you.

To others who answered questions or clarified conflicting research along the way, especially baseball historian Ray Nemec, and Seals Stadium visitors' clubhouse man Bill Soto, thank you. And a big thank you to Sal Taormina, Jr., who was a very young fan in 1957 and knows how much that team means to me.

And especially to my husband, Rich, who understands my lifelong love of the San Francisco Seals and the need to present the story of their final season, thank you for making it possible. I love you.

Foreword by Ken Aspromonte

It's an honor to be asked to do the foreword for a book about the 1957 Seals by P.J. Dragseth, an old friend and president of my fan club during my playing days. She began as a Seals fan in the third grade in 1953 and always says she grew up in Seals Stadium following her team through the last game in 1957. That season was memorable for all of us.

For me, 1957 was a pivotal year in my career. I got married on February 16, and my bride and I went to San Francisco to play baseball with the Seals. We had a good ballclub and that's always a big help to individual players. I know it helped me a lot. And we played under a good man, Joe Gordon, who was my favorite manager. That year I won the Pacific Coast League batting title with a .334 BA, led the league with 35 doubles, and was called up to the major leagues by the Boston Red Sox when it was over. You just can't describe it when you're at home plate and feel good swinging the bat and everything seems to fall in line. I saw the ball better and made a lot of good contact, close to 180 hits, I think. And it was good knowing that I was helping the team as well as myself.

The fans were probably the best minor league fans any of us had ever run across. When they found out they were going to get a major league team they still stayed with us. I think part of that was because the team was so much improved from our 1956 team that struggled along the entire year. But in '57 we were in contention, at or near the top the entire season.

It was quite an experience for the younger players like myself to play the style of baseball in the Pacific Coast League. The competition was at a high level. We did well and won the pennant. Over all, it was a great time in San Francisco and we loved it there.

Ken Aspromonte played for the San Francisco Seals in 1956 and 1957 before spending six seasons in the major leagues with the Red Sox, Senators, Indians, Braves, Angels, and Cubs. After a brief stint as a player in Japan, Aspromonte returned to the United States and, from 1972 to 1974, managed the Cleveland Indians.

The 1957 Seals. Front row (L–R): Tommy Hurd, Sal Taormina, Bill Abernathie, Manager Joe Gordon, Coach Glenn Wright, Nini Tornay, Harry Dorish, Ken Aspromonte. Second row: Trainer Leo Hughes, Bill Prout, Jack Spring, Leo Kiely, Frank Kellert, Haywood Sullivan, Bill Renna, Eddie Sadowski, Albie Pearson. Third row: Grady Hatton, Riverboat Smith, Bert Thiel, Jack Phillips, Marty Keough, Tommy Umphlett, Bob Chakales, Harry Malmbreg (Don Falkner Photography, David Eskenazi Collection).

Preface

Writing this book was a baseball journey I have been destined to take since the end of the 1957 season. My beloved-and-never-forgotten team was the San Francisco Seals, whom I followed day by day for the final five years of the Golden Era of the Pacific Coast League, 1953–1957, when I was aged 8–12. My memories of that entire experience still linger and elicit emotion after all these years: the team, the players, the league, and games at Seals Stadium with my family are the best memories of my childhood. It was all such fun: those Sundays when Dad drove us 80 miles round-trip from our home in Martinez to San Francisco for doubleheaders; night games when we braved the cold; the trek to Edmonds Field in Sacramento, 90 miles away, when the Seals played there. In those days fans were allowed to get up close and personal with the players, as we were admitted to the park early enough to watch batting practice, talk with those on the sidelines, and get autographs.

Oddly enough, over 50 years later in the course of my research for a book about veteran baseball scouts I met Gary Hughes, longtime scout and special assistant to the GM of the Chicago Cubs at the time of this writing, who shared my love of the team. We joke that we "grew up together"—a few rows apart at Seals Stadium. He and his friends sat in the first row behind the home dugout while my family and I sat in the front row next to the Seals batrack near home plate. We probably saw each other hundreds of times during those years, yet never met. He had many fond memories of those days:

> I became a Seals fan in 1947 at age six when my uncle took me to my first game. I distinctly remember walking into the stadium and seeing all that green and just being overwhelmed by it. For the next few seasons I went to a few games every year until I was old enough to have friends with cars and then we went to games every day the team was in town and it was wonderful. We always sat in the cheapest seats and worked our way down closer to the action as the games progressed. We always sat on the third base side behind the home dugout so we could talk to the players. The 1957 season was glorious! We had more darn fun. I attended sixty games believe it or not. My favorite was Haywood Sullivan, a larger than life catcher, a bonus baby with Boston who eventually ended up as part owner of the Boston Red Sox. He was a gentleman. On

3

Seals Statue at the entrance to the Giants AT&T Park. The accompanying plaque honors the history of the San Francisco Seals as follows: "This statue stands as a tribute to the San Francisco Seals, a charter member of the Pacific Coast League and the team that established San Francisco as a market for Major League Baseball. The Seals were one of the most celebrated minor league franchises in the country. They won eleven championships and produced many star players who went on to distinguished careers in the Major Leagues. Hall of Famer Joe DiMaggio hit safely in 61 consecutive games as a rookie for the Seals in 1933 establishing what is perhaps the most impressive record in the history of the Pacific Coast League" (photograph courtesy Irwin Herlihy).

the last day of the season he gave me his cap and I treasured it for years. And the night games were so cold we bought cups of bouillon to keep our hands warm. It was cool watching the Hamms beer stein across the street as the lights filled it up to overflowing then emptying it out. Once I start thinking about those days the memories flood back. Being a Seals fan was wonderful, and the beginning of my life in baseball.

Although I didn't know it at the time, those adventures and memories of them were the beginning of my own lifelong love of the game as well as the initial research for this book. Of course, all of it was seen through the eyes of an idealistic kid with limited knowledge, at best, of baseball and the Pacific Coast League, and colored by all the biases and sentimentality one would expect. (I thought Seals players *chose* to play for my team, for instance. So when in 1955 shortstop Leo Righetti was traded to Seattle, I assumed he had abandoned us. The next time the Seals hosted the Rainiers, I called him a traitor!)

Official research for this book began when I located and interviewed many former members of the team who are now in their late seventies and eighties. Sadly, many have passed away. Those who visited with me said they were thrilled to be remembered. Most stated up-front that their memories were not what they used to be, but once we got to talking, recollections flowed like water. That season was exciting for all of us and has become part of baseball and San Francisco history.

ONE

Play Ball! The Birth of Pro Baseball on the Pacific Coast

The colorful 54-year story of the San Francisco Seals and what is now called the Golden Era of the Pacific Coast League, 1903–1957, occupy a unique place in baseball annals. The history of the league is recorded in two separate and distinct eras: the first is from its inception through the 1957 season when it was known for tough, competitive, exciting baseball all played on the Pacific Coast, and the second is from the westward migration of the Giants and Dodgers in 1958 to the present as the league expanded to 16 teams divided into four divisions scattered throughout the United States.

During the earlier era, the league earned a reputation as the best pro baseball west of the Mississippi while all 16 major league teams played half a country away east of that boundary. The Seals, a team remembered for its heroes, characters, and tenacious efforts to survive, were a vibrant part of it all.

Baseball has been documented in the Pacific Coast Region, especially Sacramento and San Francisco, since the 1849 California Gold Rush. Some sources say it was brought west by many easterners who made their way west in search of fortune in the Sutter's Fort. Others suggest that the initial 49ers had neither the time nor the inclination for baseball, and the sport arrived in the region with subsequent waves of eastern transplants who came west as "tradesmen, artisans, and mechanics, many of them baseball fans, who emigrated to service this booming area"[1]*

Historians agree that information about the exact beginnings of the game in California is sketchy and the source of numerous tales and legends, but there's a general consensus that the game went west during the Gold Rush Era. One story credits William and James Shephard, brothers who had played with the New York Knickerbockers before they were among the troops sent to keep the peace during and after the Gold Rush.[2] Another indicated that base ball (two words in those days) was played as many of them traveled as

*Notes begin on page 38 at the end of the chapter.

7

loosely organized teams from mining camp to mining camp in covered wagons in what was called the stagecoach league.[3] San Francisco legends insist the first San Francisco Base Ball Club was formed in Dan's Oyster Saloon on Montgomery Street in 1858 when owner Dan Driscoll and his regulars created the club, elected officers, and had regular Tuesday night meetings, but never played a baseball game![4] Yet another claims the Sacramento Base Ball Club was established in late 1858, which was an impetus for an insulted San Francisco, the most populated city at that time, and the San Francisco Base Ball Club was officially founded and played games in 1859.[5]

The game became popular in small towns, but took an unofficial hiatus during the Civil War when soldiers on both sides of the Mason-Dixon Line played for relaxation until games were interrupted by the call to battle or the ball was lost. Afterward a popular sports paper of the day, *Wilkes' Spirit of the Times* (September 26, 1869), estimated 2,000 clubs were created nationwide during the 1860s, and at least twenty-five of those were in the San Francisco Bay Area.[6]

The Pacific Baseball Convention first appeared on the scene in 1866. It created intense competition and rugged play that attracted a large fan base. The bulk of the games were played in South San Francisco at the first fully fenced baseball park on the West Coast, called Recreation Grounds, built in November 1866, and later replaced in 1884 by the larger Recreation Park that eventually seated approximately 15,000 fans. Over 3,000 patrons flooded into the park for the Convention's first championship game on Thanksgiving Day, 1868. No one knew it then, but more than a title was at stake. When the San Francisco Eagles Club defeated the Oakland Wide Awakes, 37–23, it was the beginning of an intense rivalry between the San Francisco and Oakland teams that was well known throughout the game and sparked Pacific Coast baseball for 90 years!

Another benchmark was the completion of the Transcontinental Railroad in May 1869, which paved the way for teams in the west to have exhibition games with the more established teams from the east who went on barnstorming tours in the offseason and to be seen by fans in the west for the first time. The perfect opportunity came that same year when player-manager Harry Wright of the champion Cincinnati Red Stockings, the first professional baseball team, accepted an invitation to include a series against some of the best teams of the Pacific Baseball Convention as part of its inaugural national tour. The Bay Area promoters had a field day! The games were billed as the most important happening to date for Pacific Coast baseball, the first matchup between a pro team from the east with teams in the West.

Everyone looked forward to the great competition that included seven games. When Cincinnati arrived in San Francisco on September 23, 1869, the area was booming with anticipation. Excited fans turned out in droves to see the ten-man traveling roster comprised of pitcher Asa Brainard, catcher Doug Allison, first baseman Charles Gould, second baseman Charles Sweasy, third baseman Fred Waterman, shortstop George Wright, left fielder Andrew Leonard, right fielder Calvin McVey, center fielder/manager Harry Wright, and substitute Richard Hurley.

However, anticipation quickly turned to frustration and disappointment as the more experienced Red Stockings easily humiliated the locals, who were no match for their skill and experience. In the first two games they defeated the Eagles 35–4 and 58–4, then dashed the Pacifics twice (66–4 and 54–5), the Atlantics 76–5, and ended with two victories over the California All-Stars (46–14, and 50–6).[7]

It was a rude awakening for Bay Area baseball, which the local newspapers labeled amateurish and inferior by comparison. Once they witnessed the quality of eastern baseball, the passionate and determined San Francisco fans wanted players on teams as good as the Red Stockings and clamored for "play for pay" stars of their own. They wanted players who would work harder and find ways to win ballgames because baseball was their job rather than their hobby.

The gauntlet had been thrown down and from that point forward the bar for Bay Area baseball had been significantly raised. The game remained an exciting part of the San Francisco landscape while teams and leagues came and went for over 30 more years. One, the Pacific League (1878), consisted of four teams that played on weekends in San Francisco. Another was the California Baseball League of Professional Ball Players, which would eventually become the California League in 1898. They offered top wages and attracted top local players plus players from more prestigious teams, which resulted in a larger, more stable, and loyal fan base for minor league baseball.

Meanwhile, the thirst for baseball was again expressed in the *San Francisco Examiner* on June 3, 1888, with the publication of Ernest L. Thayer's trademark poem "Casey at the Bat," subtitled "A Ballad of the Republic, Sung in the Year 1888," for which the paper paid him five dollars, the only money he ever received for that effort.

The Pacific Coast League was finally established in 1903 in the first years of a century characterized by national growth and change. Theodore Roosevelt was president. The Ford Motor Company had produced its first 1,708 cars. Construction of the Panama Canal was under way, and two brothers named Wright made history at Kitty Hawk, North Carolina. The Boston Pilgrims, led by their star pitcher, Denton True "Cy" Young, defeated the Pittsburgh Pirates five games to three in the first-ever National League vs. American League World Series. Professional baseball had entered the Deadball Era that lasted from 1900 to 1919, when "pitching and defense" was the name of the game. San Francisco and Los Angeles thrived and were quickly established as the big market teams in California.

At its inception it was a fragile union of six charter teams, each with 14–15 players, some from the Pacific Northwest League and others from the California State League.[8] The Los Angeles Looloos played in Chutes Park, and won the first 15 games of the 1903 season; the Oakland Recruits, named for players recruited to replace others who had left for greener pastures with other teams, played at Freeman's Park, where the outfield grass was managed by a small herd of sheep; the Portland Browns played at the old Vaughn Street Grounds and had one of the first fan favorites in the league, starting pitcher Sammy Morris, a power-hitting Nez Perce Indian from Idaho who caught their eye early when he homered in his first outing, then completed 62⅔ innings in seven starts for a 3–4 record in his only season with the team; the Sacramento Senators, generally called the "Blues" for their blue uniforms, played in Oak Park, which had the usual grassy infield "skinned" down to the dirt for the new season; the San Francisco Stars (later renamed "Seals"), formerly known as the Wasps in the California League, played at Recreation Park at 8th and Harrison before the 1906 earthquake. The new team, the Seattle Siwashes, named after a local Indian tribe, was organized and assembled by team manager Parke Wilson, often called a sly old fox, and played at Recreation Park in Seattle through 1906, when they left the league following the earthquake and didn't return until 1919 as the Seattle Indians. Before the league played its first official game in 1903, all the ballparks had been improved to accommodate more fans and the quality of play.[9]

Good weather on the Pacific Coast permitted eight-month playing seasons of roughly 200 games until 1931, when the pace was dropped to 180 games. However, in an effort to increase attendance the 200-plus-game schedule was reinstated in 1950 for one season, then reduced to 166 in 1951, and back to 168 in 1957. In the early years an enigma that rarely occurs in today's game was commonplace: due to the length of the seasons, make-up games due to rainouts or other events were generally not played unless the final standings were at stake.

Over the years teams relocated and changed names while others came and went. But when all was said and done, the original six charter teams of Los Angeles, Sacramento, Portland, Oakland, Seattle, and San Francisco eventually became a stable eight-team league with the addition of the San Diego Padres (1937) and Hollywood Stars (1938). The next significant change occurred when the Oakland Oaks moved to Vancouver, British Columbia, Canada, after the 1955 season and remained in the league as the Vancouver Mounties (now the Vancouver Canadians). The league wasn't the same without the thrills of the heated Bay Area rivalry. Actually, only three PCL teams were in continuous operation from 1903 to 1957: Los Angeles, San Francisco, and Oakland/Vancouver.

In its time the PCL was populated by players with such creative nicknames as Cactus, Gavvy, Sloppy, Buzz, Babe, Dolly, Ike, Brick, Ox, Hack, Cack, Jigger, Ping, Spider, Sleepy, Wheezer, Sea Lion, Dutch, Sailor, Dazzy, Big Poison, Truck, Fuzzy, Irish, Dolly, Moose, Swede, Kid, Lefty, Red, Sheriff, Rube, Jumbo, Hod, and False Alarm, to name a few.

Sportswriters of the day created a specific jargon for the game that was just as colorful. Pitchers were "twirlers," and those warming up were preparing for "slab service." Home plate was "the pan." Fans were "rooters." The ball was "the sphere." Good curves were "twisters" or "benders." Screwballs were "outshoots." Batters who got hits "connected with leather," and fielders "got their mitt on the horsehide," "hooked in a pop fly," or "hauled in old gentleman Spalding." A good umpire was a "first class handler of the indicator." Pop-ups were "dinky," and the "sphere was slammed" for good hits or "bingles." Batters having a bad day were "filled with wrath," and strikeout victims "wrenched their vertebrae out of joint." The mound was "the box," and the bases were "bags" or "sacks." Fans expected their home teams to give the visitors a "hard rub."[10]

A closer look at the adventures in the league decade by decade is the best way to appreciate the sentimental allegiance to the 1957 San Francisco Seals as the organization thrived, struggled, evolved, and survived in conjunction with the dictates of its environment, the Pacific Coast League.

1903–1909

The first two decades were marked by franchise movement and instability. Before the first game was played, the PCL was in trouble, as it faced an obstacle of its own making.

The National Association, formed to maintain order among teams and leagues, declared the league an "outlaw" league because it encroached into a territory already occupied by the California State League and the Pacific Northwest League Its very presence enticed players from those leagues to jump their contracts to join new PCL teams. But it was not uncommon for leagues to begin as outlaws. Undaunted, the PCL dropped out of the National Association, much to the delight of the fans expecting local teams, and functioned as an independent league. In an attempt to block the success of the new league, the California State League and the Pacific Northwest League both placed teams of their own in San Francisco and Los Angeles, but they folded within a year. The Pacific Coast League survived its first season and was accepted back into the National Association for 1904 with an A-League classification.[11]

Opening Day of the Pacific Coast League was Thursday afternoon, March 26, 1903, when the San Francisco Stars faced the Portland Browns, frequently called "Portlands."[12] Although the Stars won that game, 7–3, the inaugural year saw them off to a lackluster start as they finished in the lower division, in fourth place. Los Angeles, on the other hand, quickly established itself as a league powerhouse when they won the pennant, finishing 27.5 games ahead of second-place Sacramento, and the Seattle Siwashes earned third place thanks to their 19-game winning streak late in the season. From the get-go, Los Angeles put the rest of the league on notice that they were the team to beat in the Pacific Coast League.

One of the reasons for their early domination was pitcher Eustace "Doc" Newton, a former dentist, who led the league in wins in 1903 (35) and 1904 (39). On November 18, 1903, he chalked up the first no-hitter in PCL history when he shut out the Oakland Oaks, 2–0.[13]

Another was outfielder William Hoy, who started with Los Angeles at age 41 after he had played 15 seasons in the major leagues with a career batting average of .287, led the National League in steals his rookie year in 1888 and led the American League in runs in 1901. According to baseball lore, Hoy, nicknamed "Dummy" because he was a deaf-mute, is one of those credited with umpires' adoption of the use of hand signals. When this veteran spent the last year of his pro career in Los Angeles it was the beginning of a unique and significant element of the Coast League, the practice of including older, more experienced veterans still able to play quality baseball but not at the major league level. As time passed, older veterans not only looked forward to playing in the Coast League, but preferred it to the majors.[14]

In 1904 a record was set by the Portland Browns that still stands. Their 79–136 record not only landed them in the basement, 46.5 games behind winning Tacoma, but it was the most single-season losses by any team in league history.

April 18, 1906, was a monumental day for San Francisco as a community as well as for PCL baseball when teams found themselves on shaky ground in more ways than one! Some franchises were in such monetary distress that missing even one game could have resulted in financial collapse, which would have put the entire league in jeopardy. And San Francisco's home baseball field, Recreation Park, was left among the rubble.

However, thanks to the business acumen and generosity of J. Cal Ewing, owner of the Oakland Oaks and one of the PCL founders, all that was avoided. He saved the league from the economic disaster of a lost season by pouring his own money into failing franchises. As a result, the league lost just a few weeks before play resumed on May 23. League offices were temporarily moved from San Francisco to Oakland, and the Seals played in Oakland's Idora Park until Recreation Park was rebuilt.[15]

Despite the obvious havoc resulting from the quake, community leaders believed the continuity of baseball was a solid first step in the return to normalcy in the region. In 1907 the team returned to the rebuilt Recreation Park.

During the 1907–1908 seasons, the league was reduced to four teams: Portland, San Francisco, Oakland, and Los Angeles. But less competition didn't help San Francisco. After slipping to third in 1906 (91–81), they came in a distant second to Los Angeles in 1907 with a 100–99 record, 17 games behind. In 1908 they again won 100 games and dropped to third by 18 games while Los Angeles won the flag for the fourth time. That same year the PCL classification was elevated to AA, where it remained through the 1945 season.[16]

Although weak team batting averages were common during the heart of the Deadball Era, the Seals posted a .245 average that was the lowest ever by a PCL pennant winner. At the same time they set records as a team: runs scored (836), hits (1,685), doubles (292), and stolen bases (349). Individual players stacked up records, too: Henry Melchior led the league with his .298 batting average and 206 hits; Rollie Zeider, nicknamed "Bunions," batted .289 and led the league in runs (141) and stolen bases (93). Two of the starting pitchers combined for 63 wins: LHP Frank Browning (32–16) whose 16 consecutive wins set a league record that still stands, and RHP Clarence "Cack" Henley (31–10), who would go on to compile a lifetime 212–171 league record during his 11-year career in the PCL.[17]

One of the earliest stars of the league, Seals outfielder Ping Bodie, led the league with ten homers as he became a darling with the fans. He was a fun-loving and affable player born in 1887 who wove nine seasons of major league baseball into a pro career that stretched from 1905 to 1928. In 1910 the San Francisco native was the first player in PCL history to hit 30 homers in a single season. Part of his persona was his confused identity. Born Francesco Stephano Pezzolo, he is said to have taken the name "Bodie" from a town where his father was a miner, and later nicknamed himself "Ping" because of the ping sound made when his bat hit the ball.[18]

His popularity was not as great when he played 1,050 games with the Chicago White Sox, Philadelphia Athletics, and New York Yankees. One roommate with the Yankees, Babe Ruth, later recalled, "I'll never forget how Ping Bodie was booed by fans all around the American League circuit. Bodie was always a natural hitter, but just because he struck out several times and was a little awkward in his way, the fans started to boo him every time he came to bat." Sports writers and other sources agree that Bodie was the inspiration and model for the narrator in Ring Lardner's popular "You Know Me Al" baseball stories.[19]

One highlight of the season was the pitching duel on June 8 between Cack Henley and Oakland's Jimmy Wiggs, as they went the distance in a 24-inning marathon that has since been described as "the greatest game ever seen west of the Rockies." The press of the day agreed that "for twenty-three innings before an ever-growing mob of howling fans," the two threw shutout ball. Henley gave up nine hits and a walk. Wiggs relinquished 11 hits and six walks while striking out 13. Finally, in the 24th inning, the nothing-to-nothing tie was broken when the Seals scored an unearned run to win the game.[20]

Baseball at that time was a different game than we see today. The crowds were composed primarily of a rowdy and drunk batch of roughnecks who gambled, fought, and otherwise blew off steam at the ballpark. It was the Deadball Era where the pitchers were in control, the long ball generally got a batter to second base, and the home run was a rarity. The players were tough and scrappy, and every run scored was a hard-fought victory against the opposition. During the first seven seasons, 1903–1909, only 21 batters in the entire league compiled a batting average of .300 or better, and only three were repeaters: Oakland native Charles "Truck" Eagan, who led the league in homers three times with his best being a resounding 25 in 1904; Ernest "Kid" Mohler, a left-handed second baseman who also sparkled in the field and was later player-manager for road games with San Francisco; and versatile catcher-infielder Cliff Blankenship, who split three seasons between the PCL and the major leagues.[21]

San Francisco never found itself in the cellar during the first decade, though the team spent the first two seasons, 1903–04, in the second division. The Tacoma Tigers took the pennant in 1904 in the first of only two seasons in the league until they returned in 1960. Things improved in 1905, when the Seals finished in second place just a half-game behind Los Angeles. According to league statistician William J. Weiss, the Seals' 230 games played set the all-time PCL record. They finished third in 1906. During the next two seasons, the league was reduced to four teams: Portland, San Francisco, Oakland, and Los Angeles. But less competition didn't help San Francisco as they ended up a distant second place, 17 games behind Los Angeles, in 1907, and third in 1908.

The Seals ended the decade on a high note in 1909 as they won their first PCL pennant with a 132–80 record, 13.5 games ahead of second placed Portland. After a name-the-team contest in a local newspaper, the team originally called the Stars, then the Young Americans, was finally christened "Seals" in honor of thousands of Pacific harbor seals that live on Seal Rock, a landmark near the San Francisco shore. Coincidentally, the Oakland Recruits, renamed the Commuters, 1904–1908, became the Oakland Oaks in that same season, and the Seals-Oaks rivalry was official. Baseball historians Bill Weiss and Marshall Wright later ranked that team as number 71 on their list of Top 100 Minor League Baseball Teams of all time.

That same season the league expanded back to six teams with the addition of the Sacramento Sacts and the Vernon Tigers and eagerly prepared to face the century's second decade.

1910–1919

During the ensuing ten seasons the league found its "sea legs" so to speak. In spite of turmoil, scandal, and excitement on and off the field, the PCL gave notice to pro baseball that it was here to stay.

The Seals hoped to win a second pennant to begin the new decade but ended a disappointing third, nine games behind Portland, now called the Beavers, who came into their own when they won two sets of consecutive championships, 1910–1911 and again in 1913–1914. One of the reasons for their success in 1910 was future big league LHP Sylveanus "Vean" Gregg, who pitched a PCL record 14 shutouts, including three one-hit games.[22]

Across the Bay, the Oaks ended just one game behind Portland in second place in 1910, and third in 1911. Though the team was much improved and prospects for the future were good, dissatisfied owner Cal Ewing was frustrated at the lack of a pennant. He blamed their home field, old and dilapidated Freeman's Park, which was the reason the team played home games in such other towns as San Jose and Sacramento in 1905–1906 before returning in 1907. But the Oaks took the pennant in 1912 in their final season in Freeman's Park. Ewing decided to build a new home for his team at the corner of Park and San Pablo avenues in Emeryville, a suburb of Oakland that was the center of many sports activities of the day. He promised it would be ready by the start of the 1913 season. In the meantime, the Oaks had a great season, battled the Vernon Tigers to the end and won the pennant by one game.

Oaks Ball Park was a state-of-the-art facility built in the new horseshoe seating shape. It was considered an "intimate park" with seating close to the field and the players that gradually became one of the trademarks of Pacific Coast League baseball. It seated 11,000 fans, more than twice that of typical minor league parks at that time. In addition to the ballgame on Opening Day 1913, an overflow crowd was entertained by "the regulars in the right field stands who bet loudly on virtually every pitch, and by the booming voice of 'Mush the Ragman,' who heaped abuse on Oakland's opponents."[23] The Oaks played in that park 43 years, until 1955, when they moved to Vancouver, British Columbia, and remained in the league as the Mounties.

Despite the hype and initial excitement, Oakland fell from first to worst that season, 26.5 games behind first-place Portland; the Seals finished fourth, 11 back but 4.5 games ahead of the slumping Angels. San Francisco fans were frustrated with fourth place and the fact that only one player from the team captured a league title (James Johnston, 124 stolen bases).

By that time Cal Ewing had become a major owner of the Seals and considered the Bay Area rivalry crucial to the league. With that in mind he decided to relocate the Seals from Recreation Park, where they'd played since 1907, to a new park in the Richmond District for the 1914 season. He invested over $100,000 (a fortune for that time) in the construction of the "most modern minor league park in the country," Ewing Field, with a seating capacity of 17,500. The only apparent drawback was the well-known cold, damp, and foggy weather there.

In the offseason, while the park was under construction, Ewing sold his interest in the Seals to the Berry Brothers, who also owned the Los Angeles Angels. They hated the weather and didn't want the team to play there. After intense negotiations and a reported "big money deal," it was decided the Seals would try Ewing Field for the 1914 season as an experiment. On Opening Day, May 16, 1914, the Seals faced Portland in front of an overflow crowd. But it wasn't long until players and fans alike complained about the weather. After an unsatisfactory third-place finish the Seals returned to Old Recreation Park in 1915, where they remained until Seals Stadium was completed at the corner of Sixteenth and Bryant in 1931.[24]

But 1914 was an even worse year in Sacramento, as the team that had been moved to Tacoma for the 1904–05 seasons for lack of fan support, changed the configuration of the league again when they went broke in September. In order to sustain play and complete the season, the league assumed their operations, moved them to the Mission District in San Francisco, and renamed the team the Mission Wolves for the remaining 56 games. After the season they were purchased by businessman Bill Lane and moved to Salt Lake City, where they played as the Bees through 1925 before returning to California as the Hollywood Stars in 1926. In the interim, a new team, the Sacramento Senators, was established in time for the 1918 season.[25]

"Out of the fog and into the sunshine" easily described the 1915 season for the Seals. Owner Henry Berry had an informal working agreement with the Detroit Tigers, which sent players who helped the Seals post a 118–89 record to win their second pennant. The most notable among them was outfielder Harry Heilmann, a Bay Area native who began the season as a rookie in Detroit for 69 games, then ended it in San Francisco where he hit .364 in 98 games. He went on to a 17-year major league career which many say established him as one of the five best right-handed hitters in American League history. He was elected to the Hall of Fame in 1952.[26]

Across the Bay things were far from bright for Oakland fans as their team struggled to fifth place in the standings, 24.5 games out, in 1915. The baseball moments that did occur for them belonged to team captain Jack Ness. The slugging first baseman hit safely in 49 consecutive games, a streak that shattered minor league records as well as the 44-game major league record set by Willie Keeler in 1897. However, in 1933 this record was broken when a young Seals player named Joe DiMaggio made his own statement with a record still unbroken: a 61-game hitting streak.

If 1915 was disappointing for the Oakland Acorns, 1916 was dismal, as they ended up deep in the basement, a miserable 52 games out. They didn't have a single pitcher with a winning record. One of them, a lazy pitcher called Sleepy Bill Burns who was traded from Los Angeles to Oakland at age 35 midseason, later went on to national infamy. After spending two more losing seasons with the Oaks (1916–1917), he left the game as a player until he actively returned in 1919 as liaison between gamblers and the Chicago Black Sox in 1919.

Although it may have been unintentional, Oakland did make history in 1916 when, still desperate for pitching, they hired a young LHP named Jimmy Claxton, who made his first appearance on May 28, pitched 2⅓ innings against Los Angeles. Though a bit wild on the mound, it was thought the young man of American Indian heritage had potential and possibly had a future in the league. Press accounts differ, but it seems some former Negro League teammates recognized him. One story says that once Oakland discovered his mixed American Indian–Negro heritage, team manager Rowdy Elliot promptly fired him, explaining he wouldn't be able to help the team after all. Another version is that Oakland knew full well about Claxton's background and hoped the fans didn't. Either way, Jimmy Claxton is in the record books as the first black player in organized baseball (in the PCL), 30 years ahead of Jackie Robinson. According to the records of the Collins-McCarthy Candy Company, which also produced baseball cards, he was also the first black player to have his own card. Claxton returned to the Negro Leagues and played on semi-pro teams until he was well into his fifties.[27]

World War I affected both the 1917 and 1918 seasons. When President Woodrow Wilson announced the entry of the United States into the war on April 2, 1917, the future of baseball that year was uncertain. With the attention of the fans diverted to things related to the war, many leagues faced financial ruin and folded. When well-known players left the game to join the military, they were replaced by unknown high school stars and semi-pro players, and fan support fell even more.

The PCL struggled through and completed the 1917 season. In 1918, when poor attendance forced all teams in the league to cut costs, the rosters were cut from 20 to 16 players. One of those on the Seals roster was a young LHP named Francis Joseph "Lefty" O'Doul, on the first step of his journey to becoming a baseball legend. On May 23, U.S. Provost Marshall Enoch Crowder put out an edict that all draft-eligible men must either work to support the war effort or be drafted. After that the PCL decided to shorten the season, which ended on July 14. That year went into the books as the "work or fight season."[28]

During that time Seals owner Henry Berry found himself too deep in debt to continue and sold the team to three equal partners: George Putnam, Dr. Charles Strub, and former major league catcher Charlie Graham, who would manage the team for four seasons. The new owners advertised the 1919 season as a time of transition and rebuilding, and fan expectations were not high. Good thing, too, because the Seals finished dead last (84–94) and failed to lead the league in any category. But all that seemed unimportant in relation to overall scheme of events that year.

During that time the rivalry between San Francisco and Oakland was nurtured as a centerpiece of the league. On April 20, 1919, one of the greatest promotions began when a Seals-Oaks Sunday doubleheader was split and each team got one home game out of it as fans attended an afternoon game in one park then took the ferry across the Bay for the nightcap in the other. Over the years the rivals competed in multiple heated and popular trans-bay games.[29]

Meanwhile, the Vernon Tigers endured a topsy-turvy decade plagued by moves, changes, and scandal. After playing in Vernon, a small suburb in Los Angeles County (1909–1912) without satisfactory fan support or a pennant despite two second-place finishes (1910–1911), owner Edward Maier of the Maier Brewing Company decided to move his team to nearby Venice, another small town, where he invested $12,000 in upgrades that included parking spaces for fans with automobiles. It received press coverage as the first "drive in" ballpark. The press insisted his primary reason for moving from one small suburb where he lost money to another in the same county was simple: Vernon and Venice were the only towns in the county where fans could buy alcohol. Nevertheless, the team continued to lose money.

Before the start of the 1919 season, the league had expanded to eight teams: Los Angeles Angels, Oakland Oaks, Portland Beavers, Sacramento Senators, Salt Lake City Bees, San Francisco Seals, Seattle Purple Sox/Rainiers, and Vernon Tigers. In May a disenchanted Maier sold the Tigers to a longtime fan, silent movie star Fatty Arbuckle, who bought the team on a lark, filled the stands with Hollywood celebrities of the day, and had fun barnstorming with his players. However, as explained in an October article in the *Los Angeles Herald*, he knew nothing about operating a team and his basic function was signing checks. The Arbuckle saga continued through his highly publicized trial and acquittal for the murder of Hollywood starlet Virginia Rappe, and he finally sold the team to businessman Herbert Fleishacker, who moved the team to San Francisco as the Mission Reds for the 1926 season with the intention of creating a mid-town rivalry between his team and the Seals.

In the meantime, under manager Bill Essick the Tigers took the first of three consecutive pennants, 1918–1920. In the first nine-game "Little World Series" that was held in Washington Park in Los Angeles in 1919 between the Tigers and the American Association's first-place St. Paul Saints, the series stood at 4–4 when Vernon pitcher Wheezer Dell bashed a home run to break a 1–1 tie in the eighth inning, giving Vernon the title.[30]

During the same three seasons, the Seals endured two second division finishes and one on the cusp in fourth.

On the "up-side," Babe Ruth had established himself as a bona fide power hitter, which signaled the end of the Deadball Era and the beginning of what was called "the era of the lively ball."

1920–1929

Despite distractions about the Black Sox scandal that came to the fore and marred the 1920 season throughout the game, the Roaring Twenties was a great decade for the Seals and the Pacific Coast League.

Even though the "Chicago Eight" were acquitted in a court of law, many think as a result of the loss of valuable evidence, baseball's first commissioner, Kenesaw Mountain Landis, banned them from the game for life. But the baseball industry from top to bottom considered this a major public relations debacle and feared for its image as well as its financial future, and attempted to clean house from top to bottom in all leagues.

The PCL didn't escape unscathed. It was tainted in 1919 by rampant rumors concerning gambling by its players. When league President William H. McCarthy got wind of it he initiated a thorough investigation followed by immediate and decisive action. He publicly named accused players, including many with league leading statistics, then brought criminal charges against most, and expelled all from the league. "Prince Hal" Chase, who had a shady reputation involving fighting-gambling-stealing-off the field, was implicated and ultimately banned from PCL parks and suspended from major league play. Vernon was accused of bribing opponents to lose against them. That investigation cleared manager Bill Essick and some of the players of having knowledge of those events, while a few others were found guilty and expelled. The Los Angeles Grand Jury failed to issue indictments against the players, but a clear message was sent. And in April 1921, California Governor William Stephens signed a bill making corruption in baseball a felony, in an effort to prevent future shenanigans.[31]

Though the memory of the scandals left a mark on the game that lingers nearly a hundred years later, it didn't put a damper on the decades of the 1920s and 1930s, which have been called the heyday of minor league baseball. Competition was fierce. Bonds between the players and the hometown fans were strong as fans avidly supported their local teams and vehemently challenged visitors. This was particularly true in the San Francisco Bay Area, where the rivalry between San Francisco and Oakland was recognized as the core of the league. The excitement attracted more fans than ever; some of the greatest teams were fielded, and more runs were scored during the 1920s than in any decade in league history.

Rule changes and the emergence of Babe Ruth contributed to the era of the Roaring Twenties when power, power, and more became the order of the day. After Cleveland shortstop Ray Chapman died after being hit in the head by a doctored fastball pitched by Carl Mays of the Yankees, the rules committee announced at the baseball winter meetings in Chicago that it "banned all trick deliveries (e.g., the emery ball, mud ball and licorice ball) including the spitter." In 1920 the spitball was officially banned at the major league level with the stipulation that pitchers who relied on it to make their living prior to the ban were grandfathered in and continued the practice.[32] The pitch remained legal in the minor leagues, and, as we all know, is still illegally used by some pitchers in the majors.

Writers frequently refer to specific games that were typical of those times, such as the game played May 11, 1923, when the Salt Lake City Bees hosted the Vernon Tigers in the biggest slugfest in PCL history. When the dust settled on the 48-hit, 46-run game, Vernon came out on top of the 35–11 score. Pitcher turned right fielder Pete Schneider, back from a seven-year stint in the majors, was a one-man army that day. In eight at-bats he hit a double and five homers (a sixth missed by inches), including two grand slams, and collected 14 RBI.[33]

The American Olympics champion Jim Thorpe graced the league when he did a 35-game stint with the in Portland Beavers in 1922 and posted a .308 batting average after his six-year major league career with the Giants, Reds, and Braves.[34]

Players enjoyed outstanding games that landed many of them in the record books. Oakland games were well represented. One of them occurred on July 4, 1929, in Oaks Park. Roy Carlyle, the Oaks' slugging outfielder, hit what was called by many "the longest homerun in baseball history." The story goes that the ball was still climbing when it soared over the right-center field fence, over the rooftops of two houses across the street, and landed in the rain gutter of a third house where it was found by one of his teammates the next day. They measured the distance at 618 feet![35]

If ever a player characterized the times in which he played it was Russell "Buzz" Arlett, an uninvited 19-year-old walk-on who made the Oakland squad in 1920. The tenacious, handsome youngster with a roaring fastball and complete repertoire of unhittable pitches that included a spitter became an instant fan favorite and achieved a reputation as "the Mightiest Oak of them all." As a pitcher he had three 20-win seasons, including 29 wins in his rookie year, when he led the league in innings pitched with 427, then repeated the feat with 374 in 1922. Because the switch-hitter had a lively and powerful bat, he was moved to the outfield on days when he wasn't pitching, and led the PCL in career home runs (231) and RBI (1188). On two occasions he hit four homers in one game. He was later elected to the PCL Hall of Fame, and voted *the* outstanding player in minor league history by the Society for American Baseball Research (SABR).[36]

Baseball historians agreed that four minor league dynasties emerged during this decade: Fort Worth in the Texas League, Baltimore in the International League, St. Paul in the American Association, and the San Francisco Seals in the Pacific Coast League.[37]

As for the Seals, well, they gave San Francisco reasons to roar with pride. They were the darlings of the fans and sports writers alike as they took four PCL championships and fielded four of the all-time best minor league teams: 1922, 1923, 1925, and 1928.

The decade began as a sort of enigma with owner Charlie Graham in his fourth year at the helm. After winning the first ten games, they played well throughout a hard-fought season and were 6.5 games ahead of the pack at the end of August when the tired pitching staff gave out. At the same time, Los Angeles went on a 12-game winning streak that turned the standings upside-down. The Seals ended up with a 12–20 record for the month and third place (106–82) in the final standings, two games behind first-place Los Angeles and one-half game behind second-place Sacramento as the entire first division was separated by 3.5 games. Despite the exciting baseball they had enjoyed all season, San Francisco fans were disappointed.

Former National League infielder Dots Miller took the helm in 1922, and the Seals rebounded to take the flag, four games ahead of Vernon with a 137–72 record in a league that was almost unrecognizable from the previous year. Only three teams played .500 baseball, the first division was separated by a whopping 33 games, and Sacramento (second place, 1.5 games back in 1921) held up the pack from the cellar, 51.5 games behind. One bright spot was that Vernon pitcher Jakie May accrued a 35–9 record and was the only 30-game winner of the decade. There were numerous 20-game winners, three of whom were part of the 1922 Seals staff: Ollie Mitchell (24–7), Jim Scott (25–9), and Bob Geary (20–9). On May 22, on the recommendation of former Seals manager Danny Long, the Chicago White Sox purchased agile third baseman Willie Kamm for $100,000 in a deal that made national headlines with one critic claiming that kind of money set a dangerous precedent for baseball's future. The cancelled $100,000 check paid for Willie Kamm was framed and hung in a place of honor on the wall of the Seals business office until the final game in 1957. He was a great third baseman who had a long major league career with the White Sox and Cleveland Indians during the 1920s and 1930s and helped Chicago forget Black Sox third baseman Buck Weaver as he led the American League in fielding eight times and sported a career .281 batting average. Kamm, beloved by Sox fans, was later voted their all-time third baseman.

Following the 1922 season, the New York Giants paid $75,000 for young Jimmy O'Connell, who had joined the Seals at age 18 in 1919. The deal turned out to be a better one for the Seals than for the player. O'Connell swung a big bat and was a fun-loving fan favorite often described as naïve. Although his weak defense earned him the nickname of "the $75,000 bust" from New York newspapers and fans, that actually turned out to be the least of his problems.[38]

Two weeks before the end of the 1924 season, on September 27, he offered a $500 bribe to Phillies shortstop Heinie Sand, asking him not to bear down on his team in the game. Baseball was still shaking from the impact of the sellout by the Black Sox, and Sand refused. He reported the incident to his manager, who immediately contacted the Commissioner. O'Connell admitted offering the bribe, explaining that he was told to do it by Giants coach Cozy Dolan, and that the rest of the team knew it. Upon questioning, Dolan said he couldn't remember the incident. O'Connell said he didn't understand all the fireworks since the bribe was refused, the game was played "on the square," and the Giants beat the Phillies anyway. Commissioner Landis banned both O'Connell and Dolan from organized baseball for life.[39]

Though the Seals took a second consecutive pennant, 1923 was a difficult season due to the serious illness which forced popular Dots Miller to relinquish his managerial tasks to Bert "Babe" Ellison, who took on the role of player-manager. The leadoff hitter, speedy center fielder Gene Valla, continued to spark the team as he batted .334 in 829 trips to the plate. A new face appeared in right field, 20-year-old Paul Waner, later dubbed "Big Poison," who helped the team score runs with his speed and hefty .369 batting average.

The Seals finished 11 games ahead of second-place Sacramento and 46 games ahead of last-place Vernon, which had opened the decade on top. Enthusiastic fans turned out in droves (365,845) for what turned out to be the best attendance in the league that year.

The hard-fought 1924 season found them finishing a disappointing third, one percentage point behind Los Angeles and 1.5 games behind winning Seattle. Returning skipper Bert Ellison led the team in more ways than one with his .381 batting average in 805 at-bats, while Waner and Valla continued to shine as fan favorites.

The Seals rebounded in 1925 with what many experts called the best team ever fielded by the organization. After splitting their first series with Seattle three games each, they went on a 14-game winning streak that landed them in first place, a spot they retained for the remainder of the season. As they logged a 128–71 record, won 24 series out of 27 played, four pitchers compiled a total of 81 wins (Guy Williams, 21–10; Bob Geary, 20–12; Ollie Mitchell, 20–8; Doug McWeeny, 20–5), and Paul Waner batted .401, the first in league history to surpass the .400 mark. But it wasn't easy for the 5' 8", 140-pounder. He battled Frank Brazill of Seattle and Lefty O'Doul of Sacramento toe-to-toe all season. During the home stretch O'Doul fell out of the running, and in August Waner was weakened by a mysterious illness, but he attempted to play through it, risking everything as his average dropped. As it turned out he had been shot in the face in an off-season hunting accident and some of the buckshot was left in his jaw. Once that was diagnosed and rectified he became a terror on the diamond, and won the PCL batting title.[40]

Before the 1925 season, Cubs owner William Wrigley, Jr., had a new ballpark built for their AAA farmhands in Los Angeles christened Wrigley Field, so named a year before Cubs Park in Chicago was renamed Wrigley Field. Modeled after the Chicago park, the concrete, double-deck, horseshoe-shaped park that seated 22,000–25,000 (depending on the source) was immediately dubbed a bandbox because of its batter-friendly short fences.[41] The visiting San Francisco Seals faced the hometown Angels in the first game at the park on the afternoon of September 29, when players on both teams showed their appreciation of the facility as they slammed a combined 29 hits, including the park's first home run, hit by Paul Waner as the Angels won the game 10–8. The park would later be a factor in the league's quest for recognition as a third major league.

In a nutshell, the season was a mixed bag. Sports writer Ed Hughes of the *San Francisco Chronicle*, whose beat had been the Coast League since its inception, said umpiring that season was the worst he'd seen in all those years.[42] In contrast to prior seasons that consisted of tough battles in down-to-the-wire pennant races, the Seals established dominance over PCL competitors early and sustained it through the last game. However, their very success turned out to be the source of the organization's first heaping spoonful of financial pressures: interest in the team waned, press coverage diminished, and the organization suffered at the gate as fans turned to other sports in the region.

There was some hope to rectify things to some degree after the season when the Junior World Series was scheduled between the three AAA champions, the Baltimore Orioles (International League), Louisville Colonels (American Association) and the Seals. Owners George Putnam, Charlie Graham, and Dr. Charles Strub and manager Bert Ellison resisted being slated to play the winner of phase one between Baltimore and Louisville rather than playing the first set of games, because a loss to the winner would relegate the Seals to third-best minor league team status. After Baltimore defeated the Colonels in eight games, the Seals even paid most expenses involved in having the games in San Francisco, hoping the series would go the full nine games and gate receipts would yield some profits. However, though the team won it in eight games, the owners' gamble not only didn't pay off, it backfired. Attendance averaged just 6,000 per game. Even worse, the renowned best team in minor league baseball ended that year swimming in red ink.[43]

In August 1925, another good thing happened for the Seals when the name "Smead" became a household word for San Francisco fans who went to the ballyard in droves to get a look at 23-year-old Smead Jolley. The sturdy, 6'3" LHP/outfielder purchased from Corsicana in the Class D Texas Association quickly established himself as a hitter and never batted less than .346 in a Seals uniform (1925–1929), including a booming .404 in 1928 when he helped the team take the flag before he moved to the majors for four seasons.[44]

The Seals' 1926 season can best be described as a disaster. Not only did the team fall from first to worst, ending in the cellar 36 games behind first-place Los Angeles, they struggled through the season with three managers: Bert Ellison, owner Doc Strub, and Nick Williams combined for a 84–116 record. The organization prepared for the future and brought young Roy Johnson to join Earl Averill and Smead Jolley in the outfield. The hard-hitting trio patrolled the outfield, garnered a fan base all their own, and earned a reputation as one of the greatest outfields in PCL history. The Angels did well on all fronts and took the pennant ten games ahead of second-place Oakland, as Buzz Arlett had the best season of his career.[45]

Led by George Boehler (22–12), who pitched a league high 296 innings, skipper Ivan Howard took Oakland to its first pennant in Oaks Park in 1927 with a 120–75 record, 14.5 games ahead of the pack, leaving the Seals in second. The Missions struggled to seventh place under three managers (Bill

Leard, Al Walters, Harry Hooper) and still failed to create a cross-town rivalry with the Seals. And even Wrigley Field couldn't help the Angels as once again the league flip-flopped, leaving the previous season champs in the cellar, this time 40.5 games behind.

To hear the fans or read Bay Area papers, the Seals-Oaks rivalry was as hot as ever during these years. It seemed as if their personal competition and need to one-up each other was more important than their battles with the six other teams in the league, with resultant capacity crowds and great fervor in both parks whenever the two teams faced each other.

Sports writers agreed that 1928 was "the year of the Seals" as they took their fourth championship of the decade. With Nick Williams at the helm, the team earned a 120–71 record and three pitchers combined for over half of the victories: Dutch Ruether (28–3), Elmer Jacobs (22–8), and Walter "Duster" Mails (20–12). But domination on the mound was often overlooked as the Seals overpowered the league at the plate, plus their individual accomplishments littered the record books. In addition to a .308 team batting average, they slugged 173 homers, 68 more than the closest competitor, Sacramento. The excitement they generated attracted more than 414,000 fans to lead a league that surpassed the two million mark for the second time.

Before the season ended Indians Seals owner Charlie Graham refused a $100,000 offer for the entire outfield by Cleveland owner Alva Bradley. But, true to form, when the season ended Graham refilled the team's coffers and made a killing when he broke up the outfield and sold the players individually: Earl Averill to Cleveland ($50,000); Roy Johnson to Detroit ($50,000); and Smead Jolley to the White Sox ($35,000). Averill and Johnson began their major league careers in 1929; Jolley played in the majors from 1930 to 1933.[46]

The Missions headed for the 1929 season with high hopes of finally capturing their own Bay Area fan base that would establish a sustainable and solid cross-town rivalry with the Seals. For this quest manager Red Killefer was bankrolled with $25,000 to purchase some of the best players available, which he did. After losing nine consecutive games in early April, the team bounced back with players like former major leaguer Ike Boone, who collected a league record 553 total bases and 55 homers, and logged a .407 batting average. The Missions were declared first-half winners on July 4, but later lost the end-of-season playoffs against Hollywood. The Seals ended nine games back. It was the only time they finished the regular season ahead of the pack.

Meanwhile Seals ownership looked forward to the next decade with talk of a new ballpark for the team. They invested $300,000 to purchase property in the Mission District where, ironically, the land claim filed on the site 75 years previously was in the name of the Home Plate Mine. At an estimated cost approximating a million dollars plus rent for the five years remaining in their contract at Recreation Park, the new Seals Stadium was expected to be ready in time for the 1931 season. As the Roaring Twenties ended, hopes were high for the Seals (who won at least 100 games in nine of the ten seasons), and the outlook for the Pacific Coast League was good.

By the end of the decade the Hollywood Stars had demonstrated the practicality and viability of air travel in professional baseball when they were the first team to fly. It was after a long doubleheader on Sunday, July 15, 1928, when part of the team had already boarded the train for Tuesday's series in Los Angeles and the owners chartered a plane to fly remaining players to Portland to catch the Cascade Limited for the rest of the journey. Though convenient, flying didn't become a standard mode of transportation in the league for several years.

All in all, Pacific Coast League baseball mirrored the "over the top" culture in America during the Jazz Age. It was exciting. It was raucous. The Deadball Era was gone and the era of power hitters had arrived.

1930–1939

Many described baseball during the Depression as the time the Pacific Coast League came of age. Key words for the era included survival, austerity, deals, gimmicks, excitement, and surprise. Just as all facets of American life adjusted under the cloud of the Great Depression, professional baseball dealt with pressures and challenges of its own. Major league attendance dropped from 10 million in 1930 to 8.3 million in 1931, and 6.3 million in 1933.[47] Without spare money for entertainment in family budgets, minor league attendance across the country declined and many leagues folded. In the first two years of the Depression, 1930–1931, the number of minor leagues dropped from 25 to 16. At the same time, youngsters seeing pro baseball as a way to earn a paycheck turned out in droves for tryout camps throughout the period. Former minor league player and longtime scout Jerry Gardner remembered being signed out of a three-day camp in Riverside, California, held by Branch Rickey and the Cardinals, saying, "I was a catcher, number 450-something."[48]

With its usual tenacity the PCL hunkered down and prepared for the long haul in its struggle to survive. Although it seemed that every year during the decade one team or another was in danger of financial collapse that threatened the entire league, but innovative thinking coupled with business acumen from different owners allowed them to carry on. They downsized both rosters and salaries as promotions-promotions-promotions became the standard — kids day, ladies night, doubleheaders, and special days honoring individual players on the various teams. Owners of all three Bay Area teams cut the price of admission in half. At different times during the decade most teams either continued or sought major league affiliations as a way of sustaining operations. Even the Seals organization that prided itself on its independence was affiliated with the New York Giants for the 1936 season.

On May 22, 1930, the first game under the lights was played in the Coast League at Sacramento, and six other teams either installed lights or were promised lights by club owners by the end of the decade. Ironically, while William Wrigley installed lights for his namesake field in the Coast League, he resisted the change as a threat to the ambiance of Chicago's Wrigley Field, which didn't host a night game until August 9, 1988.

While the league as a whole adapted to conditions of the time by keeping costs of operation low, the quality of baseball in the Pacific Coast League remained high. Players and fans alike considered it "our major league."

The Seals began the decade playing their last season at Old Rec Park in 1930 during the construction of Seals Stadium. Skipper Nick Williams led the team to fourth place, 17.5 games in back of winning Hollywood. Seals pitcher Jimmy Zinn, the workhorse of the squad, accrued a 26–12 record in 316 innings pitched.

In 1931, Friday the 13th of March was a lucky day in San Francisco when celebrities like Ty Cobb and other baseball notaries turned out for the ceremonies celebrating the first game in what was described as "finest baseball park in America," Seals Stadium. It was an exhibition game in which the Seals defeated the visiting Detroit Tigers. On Opening Day of the season fans packed the house that seated anywhere from 18,500 to 22,000 (depending on the source) and watched their hometown nine defeat Portland, 8–0. Everyone loved the wide open park with no upper deck so they could enjoy the warming sunshine. Seals Stadium featured all player and fan amenities of the day, including the first public address system in the league. It was praised for a layout that didn't allow space for the gamblers who were so prominent in old Rec Park. Since the park was also home to the Missions when the Seals were out of town, there was a third clubhouse just for their use which was later converted to meeting facilities after their departure.[49]

Shortly after the park opened, retired New York Giants manager John McGraw visited San Francisco to see owner Charlie Graham, his longtime friend, and the new ballpark. He praised the facility highly and firmly predicted, "You'll have major league baseball here someday, Charley."[50] How ironic that his New York Giants would be the "home" team when his prediction came true.

The Seals took two pennants in the decade: 1931 and 1935. Their first was in 1931 when all four teams in the first division finished just nine games apart. It was the last season before the San Francisco Seals would forever be associated with the name Joe DiMaggio. During 1932 outfielder Vince DiMaggio talked his 17-year-old brother Joe into a tryout with the Seals. The youngster made the team and the two were teammates in all three games in which Joe appeared at shortstop that year before he claimed the spotlight in 1933. Before the team took a second championship of the decade, DiMaggio had added his 61-game hitting streak to his resume. The Seals defeated Los Angeles for the pennant in 1935 under new skipper Lefty O'Doul, a San Francisco native and former major leaguer who remained at the helm for a 17-year tenure.

Following the 1934 season, O'Doul led a delegation of American all-star players including Babe Ruth, Lou Gehrig, and Jimmie Foxx on a barnstorming tour of Japan to introduce, promote, and teach the game there. The venture was so successful that it became an annual event for years before and after World War II. Baseball fans across the Pacific Ocean loved the man they called "O'Dou-San," and the press in both countries dubbed him "the ambassador of baseball." His accomplishments were his legacy to the game, and later the San Francisco Bay Area Chapter of SABR was named in his honor. He was posthumously inducted into the Pacific Coast League Hall of Fame in 1981, and into the Japanese Hall of Fame in 2002.[51]

The league continued its practice of selling players to major league teams as a major source of revenue for the minor league organizations, with one difference. Due to the belt-tightening that had occurred at all levels of the game, players were sold for a small amount of cash *plus* other players. Charlie Graham became a master of "the deal," as many of his transactions helped the organization remain financially solvent in tenuous times. One of the most notable in PCL history happened when Graham had his financial sights set high regarding Joe DiMaggio. After a 61-game hitting streak in his rookie season in 1933 that was eventually stopped by Oakland pitcher Big Ed Walsh, baseball scouts all wanted to sign him, and Graham intended to make a financial killing in whatever deal evolved.

But his hopes were dashed when scouts disappeared after DiMaggio injured his knee as he got out of his car and tripped on the curb. However, when Yankees scouts Bill Essick and Joe Devine talked with DiMaggio he assured them he'd be ready to play when the 1934 season started. It's said they took him to a New York doctor and then embellished the medical record "a bit" as they convinced tight-fisted Yankees general manager Edward Barrow to buy him from the San Francisco club for $25,000 in 1935. Though it was a great deal for New York, it was a disappointment for Graham, who had hoped to get $75,000 for his star. Later, after the 1939 season, Graham sold Dominic DiMaggio for $75,000.[52]

The league was realigned twice during these years. In 1936 "Hardrock"

Bill Lane, owner of the Hollywood Stars, grew tired of playing at Wrigley Field in Los Angeles when the Angels were out of town, and he resented what he called "high rent." Following the 1935 season he uprooted them for the last time. Although the league had twice nixed putting a team in San Diego due to a lack of population and an appropriate park, he dug in and built Lane Field near the waterfront and moved his team there as the San Diego Padres in 1936.[53]

Two years later, in 1938, after a dozen seasons in San Francisco without building the desired fan base to make the venture profitable, Missions owner Herbert Fleischaker moved his team back to the Los Angeles area, where they had originated in 1909 as the Vernon Tigers. Appropriately renamed Hollywood Stars, they would have such owners as Gene Autry, George Burns, Gary Cooper, and Bing Crosby among other Hollywood notables, and went on to play good baseball. They took up residence at Wrigley Field for that season while Gilmore Field was built, then began the 1939 season at their new ballpark.[54]

The decade was especially hard for baseball in Sacramento, as the unaffiliated team struggled through the perpetual lack of fan support and concomitant financial woes that had resulted in two moves earlier in their existence. After finishing sixth, third, fourth, and seventh (1931–1935), things came to a head in 1935. The bank foreclosed on team owner Lou Moreing and put former manager Earl McNeely in charge. In his attempt to regain a cash flow and regain financial solvency, he sold all but five of his players. By directive of Branch Rickey, who was building his farm system, the St. Louis Cardinals purchased the remnants of the team for $5,000. It was the first time the independent organization had a major league affiliation. Though the team was renamed Solons in 1936, the season was frustrating and dismal as they wound up solidly in the cellar because the Cardinals refused to send them good players. But 1937 was their best season in many years. Under manager Bill Killefer and with cooperation from St. Louis, which sent a steady flow of good players such as Cotton Pippen, Nick Cullop, Joe Orengo, and Tony Freitas, they won the pennant.[55]

Six different teams won pennants during the decade: Hollywood (1930), San Francisco (1931, 1935), Portland (1932, 1936), Los Angeles (1933, 1934, 1938), Sacramento (1937), and Seattle (1939). With the exception of 1934, when the Los Angeles Angels achieved 137 wins—the most in baseball history—and finished 35.5 games ahead of the second-place Mission Reds, a spread of six games or less separated the top two teams in the final standings every year.

In 1936 the league tried a new system for determining the league champions. They had played three playoff series against the top team in the American Association in 1919, 1924, and 1925 with the obvious problems of travel expenses and uncertain weather conditions. In 1928, 29, 30, 31, 34, and 35, they tried the split season approach unsuccessfully. Aware that something had to change to remain financially solvent during the depression, they tried a new plan officially called the Governor's Cup which lasted from 1936 to 1954. The complex new system immediately became controversial because it had the top four clubs at the end of the regular PCL season compete in a series of playoff games and the winner was awarded the Governor's Cup. Because a longtime minor league player by the name of Frank "Shag" Shaughnessy was credited with coming up with the idea it was often called "The Shughnessy System." Though intended to stimulate fan interest and raise postseason revenue for the clubs involved, the system was unpopular. Fans and clubs didn't like it because it meant the team with the best season record didn't always win. They fought to return to the system where the team that was in first place on the last day of the regular season won the championship. The league finally returned to that standard for the final three years on the Pacific Coast, 1955–1957.[56]

During those years the league produced its share of memorable characters. One of them was Seals light-hitting catcher Joe Sprinz, who in 23 seasons in the minor leagues became known as a guy always "up to something." In the spirit of wing-walkers in the previous decade, players competed to see who could catch a ball dropped from the highest height. According to *Sacramento Bee* columnist Stan Gilliam, Seals Publicity Director Walter Mails promoted and arranged for Sprinz to catch a baseball dropped from a blimp, which he did at the site of the 1939 World's Fair at Treasure Island in San Francisco. As 2,000 spectators watched in astonishment, he missed the first four balls, some of which dug deep holes in the ground as they landed, then "caught" the fifth. But it nearly killed him! It bounced from his mitt to his face at a speed later estimated by physicists at over 150 mph, shattered his jaw and knocked out eight teeth among other injuries that landed him in the hospital for over three months. He returned to the diamond and played 118 games in 1940, then added six more seasons before he hung it up. He frequently spoke of his stunt in press interviews and strongly advised others not to try it.[57]

The Depression years were a roller coaster ride up and down in the final standings more than any other time for the Seals: 1930, fourth; 1931, first; 1932, fourth; 1933, sixth; 1934, fourth; 1935, first; 1936, seventh; 1937, second; 1938, fourth; 1939, second. As the decade drew to a close, and the nation was pulling out of the doldrums of the 1930s, records indicated that 2.25 million fans had attended PCL games during the period. But other clouds loomed on the horizon as conditions in Europe were on the minds of players and fans alike.

1940–1949

This decade was like two separate eras for the nation as well as for professional baseball at all levels. World War II efforts impacted every element of the social fiber of the country, from Rosie the Riveter to the All-American Girls Professional Baseball League teams. The 1940s was the only period in league history when there were no franchise movements.

It's well known that future Hall of Fame pitcher Bob Feller enlisted in the U. S. Naval Reserve the day after the Pearl Harbor attack, and he was followed by numerous others who either enlisted or were drafted. Just as baseball had been a symbol of normalcy after the 1906 earthquake in San Francisco, President Roosevelt issued what came to be known as his "Green Light Letter" that served the same purpose, as he listed reasons why he wanted the 1942 baseball season to be played and even encouraged more night games so the working man could take his family to more games. Later, night games were banned on the West Coast in August 1942.[58]

Although play continued, the face of the game changed. The Pacific Coast League had wartime roster restrictions of 20 players, and umpiring staffs were reduced from three per game to two. Many players took war-related jobs that kept them out of the military but reduced them to part-time player status. For example, George Silvey, a longtime player-scout-scouting director with the Cardinals, recalled that minor league ball in his part of the country had stopped in 1943. He was in his 30s with a young family, undrafted, and went to work for Curtiss-Wright Aircraft in St. Louis where he used his prior drafting experience, and was a player-manager for the company team in a war plant league in the region.[59]

As more players were involved this way, the big leagues plucked more and more players from the minors to replace them. Soon the minors were forced to make adjustments of their own, and their new player pool consisted of those either too young or too old for military service. On one hand they recruited very young players like 15-year-old catcher Bill Sarni, who was signed by the Angels after his parents signed his work permit, and on the other, they lured back retired players like first baseman Gus Suhr and pitcher Herm Pillette (dubbed "Old Folks"), whose son Duane would later pitch for the 1957 Seals.[60]

Understandably, all these factors resulted in a reduced quality of play which often frustrated the players, but the fans remained loyal. During the war years, PCL teams periodically donated receipts of specified games to the military, as when the Sacramento Solons donated theirs to the army to build a swimming pool for airmen at nearby Mather Field.

Against the odds of difficult and expensive travel, nobody could deny the West was golden in terms of financial gains for a major league team. It seemed PCL owners looked at it in terms of reclassifying itself as the third major league. But another factor changed the playing field in 1941 when Don Barnes, owner of the St. Louis Browns in the American League, tried to purchase Wrigley Field in Los Angeles as a new home for his team, providing he could get approval from the American League owners as well as the necessary financing. Although it was on the agenda at the winter meetings that year, it was tabled during the war.[61] The Browns moved to Baltimore in 1954.

From 1940 to 1942 the Seals languished in the second division and Seattle finished first twice, in 1940–1941. The Solons won the last five games of the season to beat out Los Angeles for the pennant in 1942. It turned out to be their last year as a viable contender in the league. In 1943 Los Angeles took the title with the Seals 21 games back in second while the Solons plummeted to last place, a miserable 69 games back. At the end of the season St. Louis ended their affiliation. The Angels repeated in 1944. Second-place Portland was a dozen games behind and the Seals finished third, one game behind Portland. The 1945 season found the Beavers on top as the Seals limped into fourth place, 17.5 games behind. Through it all, San Francisco and Los Angeles remained the big market teams of the league.

The years 1946–1950 were called the postwar boom when as many as 50 minor leagues dotted the national map.[62] The Pacific Coast League was described as the league with the best players, several fine stadiums, and robust attendance, and the best travel conditions. Rumors about the possibility of the league being reclassified as the third major league flourished east and west of the Mississippi despite skepticism firmly expressed by the big leagues, fearing that the additional competition for players would drive prices up. "At the time there wasn't a great discrepancy between salaries in the Coast League and in the big leagues. In fact, some ball players were making more money in the Coast League than they did in the majors," veteran Portland first baseman Ed Mickelson remembered.[63]

When Paul Fagan, a colorful and persistent businessman who made his fortune from shipping-banking-Hawaiian pineapple investments, purchased controlling interest in the Seals in 1945, his longtime campaign for the change continued. Part of his strategy to force the issue encouraged all PCL owners to stop dealing their best players to major league clubs. But they could not operate without that income and declined. In the past, Commissioner Landis threatened to render the league "outlaw" if it attempted to push for major league ranking. But when Happy Chandler became Commissioner in April 1945, League president Clarence "Pants" Rowland, whom a *Time* magazine article (December 1944) described as "the cheerleader for the PCL cry for independence," decided it was time to take some serious steps in that direction. Rowland went to the 1945 Winter Meetings of the National Association of Professional Baseball Leagues (NABPL) with two proposals for consideration. He insisted the entire league be given major league status, which, in hindsight, did nothing more than complicate the situation.

Rowland's low expectations turned to cautious elation when he returned home with his proposals accepted, with stipulations that left players and fans alike with the hope that it was only a matter of time. After all, everyone believed the quality of baseball was as good as or better than big league play, and once the specs set forth by MLB were met things would move forward.[64]

The press across the country got on the bandwagon. Longtime *New York Daily News* journalist Bruce Chadwick described the Coast League as a league with its own unique baseball culture with more glitz and glamour than any other minor league in history, a league half a country away from the closest major league city, St. Louis.[65]

When the regular players returned for the 1946 season after the Seals enjoyed spring training in Hawaii, things improved. Coast League attendance passed the four-million mark which was an all-time high for minor league baseball. In the Bay Area the Seals-Oaks' heated rivalry picked up where it had left off. It lasted the entire season with the Seals finishing first and the Oaks just four games behind. The Seals and Angels took their battle down to the wire in 1947. They were tied after the last day of the season when Los Angeles won the championship in a one-game sudden death playoff game at Wrigley Field.

Brick Laws took control of the Oakland Oaks in mid-season 1943 and later hired Casey Stengel to manage his team. Longtime Yankees scout Joe Devine was often quoted as describing Stengel's managerial skills as "not fancy but solid." Baseball agreed. By 1948 the squad consisted primarily of older major league veterans, dubbed "the nine old men," whom he led to the pennant in one of the most exciting races of the decade, leaving the Seals in second place two games back. It was the first pennant for the Oaks since 1927 and the last in Oakland. The games and the rivalry were so intense that the Seals attracted 670,000 fans, establishing a PCL record that stood for almost 40 years.[66]

In 1949 it was a different story. Oakland ended the decade in another battle for the pennant but came in second, five games behind the Hollywood Stars, while the Seals hobbled to a dismal seventh, 25 games back, leaving Los Angeles in the cellar. The offseason was the high point for the Seals. At the request of General MacArthur, Lefty O'Doul took a team of 20 players, primarily Seals and a few major leaguers, on a 16-game goodwill baseball tour in Japan. O'Doul, already loved by Japanese baseball fans, was warmly received, and the press described it as the first peacetime cultural exchange of the post-war era between the two nations.[67] However, this was not the first baseball tour to Japan. As noted by Dennis Snelling (*The Greatest Minor League*, p. 317), in 1908, to reciprocate a visit from a Japanese team in 1905,

Mike Fisher introduced American professional baseball to Japan when he led a group of major and minor leaguers called the Reach All-Americans on a goodwill exhibition tour to China and Japan.

The 1940s was an ironic decade for the Pacific Coast League. After struggling through the uncertainties that occurred throughout the game in the first half because of the war, it then enjoyed a heyday from 1946 to 1949 with its greatest popularity and attendance ever.

1950–1956

But all the excitement and hopes of 1946–1949 were in jeopardy at the beginning of what turned out to be the final decade of the Golden Era of the Pacific Coast League.

Things began in a state of limbo. Fagan attempted to persuade PCL owners to drop out of organized baseball and operate as an independent league unless requests for major league recognition were discussed more seriously. While Fagan believed he and Los Angeles owner Phillip K. Wrigley, Jr., could afford that plan, owners of the other six clubs were intimidated by his bravado and voted it down.

When Ford Frick became Commissioner in 1951, he and the committee of major league owners and others weighed the pros and cons of the issue. In an attempt to placate fomenting frustrations, the Pacific Coast League was elevated to "Open Classification" in October. Not only was it the highest rating ever given to a minor league, but it also changed the way players could be drafted from it by the American and National Leagues. It gave players the right to sign a no-draft clause and raised the draft price from $10,000 to $15,000. But the classification was not a "gift," as it imposed numerous stipulations to be met by the league. Although originally reported by the press as the first Coast League victory, in reality it turned out to be the last.[68]

Like the flip of a light switch from on to off, things in general changed with the new decade. In response to attendance records set by the league the prior four seasons, the 1950 schedule was expanded to 200 games for the first time since 1930. When gate receipts dropped off by 15 percent, that experiment was scuttled after one season. But when the 1951 season returned to the 180-game schedule, attendance declined an additional 30 percent. One of the culprits was rumors and uncertainty regarding third major league status, and the other was television. Some games of the Los Angeles Angels and Hollywood Stars were televised as early as 1947, and by 1949 most of their home games were covered.

In 1950 the Hollywood Stars staged a unique publicity gimmick which not only reflected the tenacity of the league in general, but the character of that team in particular. A new team uniform was introduced which consisted of normal jerseys with Bermuda-type shorts. The weather was conducive to it, and some of the players even enjoyed the freedom of the cooler garb, while most said they were embarrassed. Despite fan approval, the idea was short-lived. But the Stars persevered and added a squad of cheerleaders. The press had a field day.

"Prince Fagan," as he was unflatteringly dubbed by the media, was confident his big market team could afford to ride out the storm and he stubbornly stuck to his guns, thinking he could afford it. He busily implemented some of the specified changes listed in the Open Classification declaration: took all the ads off the fences in Seals Stadium, added more outfield bleachers to increase seating capacity to the "suggested" 25,000, and gave the inside of the park its first paint job, a rich emerald green. To the delight of the players, he upgraded all salaries to the major league minimum of $5,000 and added more amenities to the clubhouses.[69]

Some additional stipulations to be met before the league could even submit its application for upgrade to major league classification were as follows: annual league attendance of 2.3 million plus average paid attendance of 3.5 million for three consecutive seasons, a combined park capacity of 120,000, and complete financial statements from all eight teams in the league, before the application preceding an application.[70]

Amid the confusion and uncertainties in the Coast League, things in New York were also on the brink of change. The Brooklyn Dodgers were nearing the end of their lease at Ebbets Field, a former state-of-the-art park built in 1913 in an area that had declined to ghetto status that deterred fans from attending night games.[71] And the New York Giants neared the end of their lease at the older Polo Grounds, built in 1891. Both parks were in a state of dilapidation and both teams faced building new parks or finding new homes.[72] Rumors of westward movement distracted attention from the PCL fan base.

But the games went on. While the Oaks edged out Padres for the pennant in 1950, the Seals rose to fifth place, which the fans wanted to believe was progress after the 1949 debacle. In 1951 San Francisco had a loose but disastrous affiliation with the New York Yankees that landed them deep in the cellar, 25 games behind. Seventeen-year skipper Lefty O'Doul, the highest paid manager in PCL history ($45–55,000 per season to keep him from being lured to the major leagues), also served as vice president of the Seals (1948–1951) until he was replaced by Tommy Heath for the 1952 season, when the Seals finished seventh.[73] He then managed in the Coast League six more seasons through 1957 with San Diego, Oakland, Vancouver, and Seattle as he logged a career managerial record of 2,094–1,970. He posted the most wins in league history.

Attendance continued to drop and, according to an article in *Baseball Magazine* (June 1951), the fans were becoming "indifferent to their teams because they had fallen under the spell of major league voodoo."[74] Pressure mounted in San Francisco until, in 1953, Fagan put a "for sale" sign on the Seals for $250,000 or $350,000, depending on the source, which included the team only as he would retain ownership of Seals Stadium and lease it to the new owners for $30,000 annually. Fagan's price, labeled as outrageous, coupled with his reputation, dissuaded all prospective buyers, even a loosely formed group that included Joe DiMaggio, Lefty O'Doul, and Bing Crosby, among others.[75]

In late September the league offered to buy the team and its players for $100,000, giving Fagan the option to buy it back at a later date. Under protest and with his back to the wall, Fagan agreed. The PCL took over operations and appointed his former secretary Damon Miller to take charge of the matter. He immediately formed The Little Corporation in an attempt to raise $100,000 to buy the team back from the league and operate independently. Under a deadline of December 11, he sold public stock for $10 a share, and took such other fundraising actions as selling television rights to the Golden Gate Broadcasting Company and selling books of ten tickets at reduced prices. After several owners meetings and with backing from the press, the community supported Miller's efforts. *Chronicle* sportswriter Will Connelly reported that $44,080 was raised from hundreds of individual investors, and said he couldn't remember a time when baseball was talked about more in San Francisco.[76]

The Seals began the 1954 season with cautious optimism. In a cost-effective move they reorganized the team and interwove longtime veterans with a youth movement that got them tagged "The Kiddie Car Express" by the media. The fans quickly accepted the new faces and loudly supported them: Mike Baxes, age 23, who manned shortstop and third base, appeared in 137 games in 1954 and 143 in 1955; outfielder Dave Melton, age 25, saw action in 82 games in 1954 and 162 in 1955; and Jim Westlake, age 23, manned first base in 142 games in 1954. San Francisco native Bob DiPietro played the outfield in 109 games in 1954 and his .371 batting average led the league in 1955 when his season ended after 64 games the day he broke his ankle stretching a long double into a triple. The Seals led the league in attendance as 298,908 fans passed through the turnstiles. Their 84–84 record landed them back in the first division in fourth place. But in spite of everything, the organization netted just $464 for the season.[77]

It became obvious that insolvency and bankruptcy loomed, which affected not only the Seals but the entire Pacific Coast League. San Francisco Mayor George Christopher put fact-finding and other committees in motion, seeking a solution. According to an article in the *San Francisco Chronicle* by

Darrell Wilson (February 10, 1957), in January 1955, Philip K. Wrigley presented a proposal to expand the National League to include Los Angeles and San Francisco. With a unanimous vote required by National League owners, it failed by a vote of 6–2 with the two dissenting votes coming from Ruley Carpenter (Philadelphia Phillies) and Horace Stoneham (New York Giants).

In July Cleveland GM Hank Greenberg offered to purchase the team and convert it to major league status as soon as possible. He offered to pay off all existing Little Corporation debts owed to the league. This offer was also rejected by the PCL owners, who feared the impact on the other teams.[78]

Meanwhile the season went forward as scheduled. It was Oakland's last hurrah before the team moved to Vancouver. The Seals plodded through it, ending with a record of 80–92 that put them in sixth place, three games ahead of the Oaks. Seattle took the championship, just three games ahead of the San Diego Padres. Because everyone knew the team was on the market and hoped big league baseball would come soon, attendance in San Francisco dropped by more than 140,000. Oakland had the lowest attendance in the league.[79] Final records show PCL attendance had declined at a greater rate than the major leagues, which meant the league's hopes for third major league classification continued to fade.[80] On the final day of the 1955 season, the *San Francisco Chronicle* headlines read, "Little Corp is now the Little Corpse."[81]

A major figure credited with keeping the Seals from going belly up financially was Seals business manager Bob Freitas, an astute and affable baseball man who served minor league baseball until his death in 1989 when he was President of the Northwest League. He was considered a brilliant innovator by his peers, who named the seminars at the annual winter meetings the Bob Freitas Seminars. In 1989 the minor leagues gave the first annual Bob Freitas Awards to the outstanding organization in each of the minor leagues.

A cloud on any possible "deal" for the Seals came from former owner Paul Fagan himself. He still owned Seals Stadium and announced that when his contract with the city expired in three years (after the 1958 season) he had plans to tear it down and use the property for more lucrative purposes. The team remained on the market with debts possibly as high as $285,000 (depending on the source). However, in November 1955, the purchase of the Seals for $150,000 by the Boston Red Sox was announced by Boston General Manager Joe Cronin.[82]

The Little Corporation was gone. In 1956–1957 the team was operated by Boston as their AAA farm club (although the league was still classified as Open) and restocked it with their own prospects. Smartly they kept the name Seals as well as three San Francisco fan favorites, outfielder Sal Taormina, first baseman Bob DiPietro, and catcher Nini Tornay. The new faces were warmly received and expectations were high for 1956 under new manager,

17-year major league shortstop Eddie Joost, a fiery player who turned out to
be a tough manager to play for because he was so demanding and volatile.
Former players said it was never a question of "*if* he would lose his temper
and rant, but *when.*"

According to Bob DiPietro,

> I remember when we had an exhibition game at the University of California
> [in Berkeley] in 1956, and they had a big black kid playing second base who
> was primarily a football star. Anyway, he just ran over Nini [Tornay] on a
> close play at the plate and really wracked him up. He didn't hurt Nini but he
> just leveled him. It was a clean play. So Joost, who only played in a handful of
> games before he got fired, put himself into the game, got on base, and tried to
> steal second. He didn't do it to help the team in any way. But he ran as hard as
> he could and slid into that kid spikes up and tore up his knee. It's hard to
> respect a guy who does things like that.

When his style of managing was not as successful for the team that was
hyped to take the PCL pennant easily, he was fired on July 9, 1956, and replaced
by future Hall of Famer Joe Gordon. In a later interview Joost defended himself as he explained, "the circumstances were such that the young players
didn't gel. There were many good prospects who will be heard from later."[83]
Under Gordon things improved in the clubhouse, but everyone involved was
disappointed with a 77–88 record that left them in lowly seventh place, a dismal 28.5 games behind the first-place Los Angeles Angels. Boston had seriously underestimated the prowess of its players and the overall level of
competition in the league in 1956, and that was a mistake they were determined to correct in 1957.

The winter passed and spring training began in preparation for the 1957
season without a decision or announcement about the potential move of the
New York Giants to San Francisco or the Brooklyn Dodgers to Los Angeles.
The fan bases and stadium improvements required to maintain Open Classification had not been maintained while things remained in limbo. One thing
seemed certain: the hopes of the Pacific Coast League becoming a third major
league were all but dashed. Most fans were aware of, if not yet excited about
the possibility of getting one or two National League teams as they kept up
with the latest developments in the press every day.

Notes

1. Dick Dobbins and Jon Twitchell, "Nuggets on the Diamond."
2. Paul J. Zingg and Mark D. Mederios, *Runs, Hits, and an Era: The Pacific Coast League,
1903–1958* (Urbana and Chicago: University of Illinois Press, 1994), 2.
3. Kevin Nelson, *The Golden Game: The Story of California Baseball* (San Francisco: California Historical Society Press, 2004), 4.
4. Dick Dobbins and Jon Twitchell, *Nuggets on the Diamond: Professional Baseball in the
Bay Area from the Gold Rush to the Present* (San Francisco: Woodford Press, 1944), 15.

5. Nelson, 9.

6. Zingg and Mederios, 16.

7. Dobbins, 20.

8. Bill O'Neal, *The Pacific Coast League 1903–1988* (Austin, TX: Eakin Press, 1990), 4.

9. Baseball Press Books, *The Early Coast League Statistical Record, 1903–1957* (2004), 19.

10. Tom Larwin, "The Pacific Coast League Championship Series," *The National Pastime*, 20 (SABR, 2000), 112.

11. Carlos Bauer, *Minor League Baseball Journal, 1* (SABR, 1996): 72–75.

12. Dobbins, 38.

13. http://www.baseball-reference.com/bullpen

14. http://www.baseballlibrary.com/ballplayers

15. Dobbins, 42.

16. Baseball Press Books, 36–39.

17. http://www.hawkeegn.com/Seals

18. Ralph Berger, *Ping Bodie*, http://www.sabr.org/bioproj.

19. F. C. Lane, *Batting* (Cleveland, SABR, 2001): 191.

20. Zingg and Mederios, 33.

21. http://www.baseball-reference.com/bullpen

22. Ibid.

23. Zingg and Maderios, 30–32.

24. O'Neal, 101–102.

25. http://www.minorleaguebaseball.com/team1

26. http://baseball-reference.com

27. James A. Riley, editor, *The Biographical Encyclopedia of the Negro Baseball Leagues* (New York: Carroll and Graf, 1944), 103.

28. Zingg and Mederios, 43.

29. O'Neal, 32.

30. Op. Cit, 39.

31. Zingg and Mederios, 46–47.

32. http://sportsillustrated.cnn.com/vault

33. Zingg and Maderios, 51.

34. Dennis Snelling, *The Pacific Coast League: A Statistical History 1903–1957* (Jefferson, NC: McFarland, 1995), 50.

35. Zingg and Mederios, 53–54.

36. O'Neal, 235.

37. Benjamin Rader, *Baseball: A History of America's Game* (Urbana: University of Illinois Press, 2000), 147.

38. http://www.baseballlibrary.com

39. Nelson, 126–132.

40. R. Scott McKay, *Barbary Baseball: The Pacific Coast League of the 1920s* (Jefferson, NC: McFarland, 1995), 104.

41. Nelson, 136–137.

42. McKay, 97.

43. Op. Cit., 101–103

44. Dobbins, 78–80.

45. Zingg and Mederios, 56–57.

46. McKay, 50.

47. Zingg and Mederios, 68.

48. P.J. Dragseth, *Eye for Talent* (Jefferson, NC: McFarland, 2010), 42.

49. Lowell Reidenbaugh, *Take Me Out to the Old Ball Park*, 2nd ed. (St. Louis, The Sporting News, 1987), 230.

50. Steve Treder, "Open Classification: The Pacific Coast League's Drive to Turn Major," *NINE: A Journal of Baseball History and Culture*, 15, no. 1 (University of Nebraska Press, Fall 2006), 88–109.

51. Dobbins, 146–147.

52. P.J. Dragseth, *Major League Baseball Scouts: A Biographical Dictionary* (Jefferson, NC: McFarland, 2011), 101.

53. O'Neal, 269.

54. Nelson, 185–186.

55. Lee Lowenfish, *Branch Rickey: Baseball's Ferocious Gentleman* (Lincoln: University of Nebraska, 2007), 182–183.

56. Donald R. Wells, *The Race for the Governor's Cup: The Pacific Coast League Playoffs, 1936–1954* (Jefferson, NC: McFarland, 2000), 1–3.

57. http://www.senior.spectrum.com./columnists

58. http://www.baseball-almanac.com

59. George Silvey, *Fifty Years in the Bushes, Baseball That Is* (Florissant, MO, 1999), 47.

60. Zingg and Mederios, 101–102.

61. Treder, 92.

62. Rebecca Kraus, *Minor League Baseball: Community Building Through Hometown Sports* (New York: Haworth Press, 2003), 91.

63. Ed Mickleson, *Out of the Park: Memoir of a Minor League Baseball All-Star* (Jefferson, NC: McFarland, 2007), 137.

64. Neil Sullivan, *The Minors* (New York: St. Martin's, 1990), 208–209.

65. Kraus, 17.

66. Dick Dobbins, The *Grand Minor League: An Oral History of the Old Pacific Coast League* (San Francisco: Woodford, 1999), 252.

67. Dobbins (Nuggets), 146–147.

68. Treder, 96–97.

69. Ibid.

70. Zingg and Mederios, 129–131.

71. Ron Smith, *The Ballpark Book*, revised edition (St. Louis: The Sporting News Books, 2003), 227.

72. Op. Cit., 288.

73. *Dobbins* (Nuggets), 247–248.

74. David Pietrusza, Mathew Silverman, and Michael Gershman, eds., *Baseball: The Biographical Encyclopedia* (Kingston, NY: Total Sports Illustrated, 2000), 841.

75. http://www.highbeam.com/doc/1G1-204205886.html.

76. Dobbins (Nuggets), 252.

77. Brent Kelley, *The San Francisco Seals, 1946–1957* (Jefferson, NC: McFarland, 2002), 182–183.

78. Darrell Wilson, "San Francisco Missed Franchise by Two Votes in 1955," *San Francisco Chronicle*, February 20, 1957, H1–H3.

79. Dobbins (Nuggets), 252.

80. Treder, 98.

81. http://www.timelinesdb.com/listevents.

82. Zingg and Mederios, 127.

83. "As Bill Leiser Sees It," *San Francisco Chronicle*, February 12, 1957, H1.

TWO

Spring Training

During the off-season between 1956 and 1957, as the San Francisco 49ers struggled to a fifth-place finish in the Western Football Conference under the leadership of such players as Hugh McElhenny, Bob St. Clair, and quarterback Yelberton Abraham "Y. A." Tittle, the Monday morning quarterbacks conducted business as usual in the coffee shops. Well, almost "as usual" as the passing weeks added to the speculation about how developments in New York would impact the fate of the Seals, the Angels, and the entire Pacific Coast League.

As had occurred for the past few years, talks of major league baseball coming to the west coast continued. Everyone assumed it would be resolved in one of two ways. One way would be an executive order from the major leagues elevating the PCL to the status of a third major league, an issue that had been on the table since 1945 at the request of league president Clarence Rowland. In 1946 the Coast League was elevated to "Open Classification" (a step above AAA, the only league in minor league history so designated) until that matter could be resolved. Or, as had been rumored for several years, there was the possible movement of a major league club to the west coast, but that was still considered wishing rather than reality at that time.

However, with the issue far from settled, teams throughout the Coast League readied for spring training. For them the expansion issue, which was far from new business in the PCL, was looked upon as a "behind the scenes" scenario. The Seals' training camp was in Fullerton, seven miles northeast of Anaheim. On March 4 the pitchers and catchers reported a few days before the rest of the team.

In 1956, the inaugural season as part of the Red Sox system, a great pressure was relieved as the team no longer faced bankruptcy. High expectations for a turn-around for the Seals prevailed thanks to the help of some of Boston's top prospects. Word was out that Boston was embarrassed about the poor showing and was even more intent on giving the fans a winner in 1957.

One of those prospects, speedy outfielder Tommy Umphlett, recalled,

Official Seals scorebook sold at every game. Note the autographs and the fifteen cents price on the cover (Doug McWilliams Collection).

"We had a poor season in '56 with two different managers, Eddie Joost and [then] Joe Gordon. The season seemed very long because we lost a hundred games, I think. [Actually the record was 77–88.] We ended up in sixth place almost 30 games back of Los Angeles, and everyone was disappointed. We all wanted 1957 to be better."

As the 1957 season rolled around, the players were aware of pending changes in the league. But it wasn't their concern. They described the chatter of the fans and media attention to the matter as "background noise." As baseball players still do today, they read the sports pages in the papers with an eye to articles written about their own performances and the progress of other teams in the league. Everything else was essentially superfluous to them. When interviewed, most said, "Our job was playing baseball and winning as many games as possible, and we did them. Everything else was out of our hands."

The usual pre-season attitude of high hopes for a good season on the personal level that would also convert to a winner for the team permeated daily activities. There was reason for optimism. Prior to spring training, Boston acquired power-hitting first baseman Frank Kellert and designated him for assignment to the Seals. It was a trade that sent pitcher Bill Henry and cash to the Cubs.

They were happy with their lodging arrangements at the Disneyland Hotel that were set up by trainer Leo "Doc" Hughes and equipment manager Joe Mooney. They knew that once manager Joe "Flash" Gordon, former Yankees second baseman (and future Hall of Famer), and coach Glenn "Cap" Wright," also a longtime major leaguer, established the camp rules and schedules, they were expected to tow the line and work hard to win spots on the roster. They jumped right into a rigorous schedule of workouts and the usual intra-squad games in preparation for the upcoming exhibition game schedule slated from March 15–April 10.

Boston put ticket books for the new season on sale: box seats ($2.00), reserved seats ($1.65), kids under 18 ($.90), general admission ($1.25), or five general admission tickets for $5.00. In addition they announced that the big club planned a spring training exhibition schedule that included three games against the Seals in Seals Stadium on the weekend of March 22–24, a Friday night game followed by afternoon contests on Saturday and Sunday. Baseball fever was alive and well in the Bay Area.

There were six familiar faces among the 16 at the start of camp: Albie Pearson, Joe Tanner, Gordy Windhorn, Eli Grba, Bob DiPietro, and Sal Taormina. The group of new faces was a mixture of well-known veterans and youngsters from Boston's minor league system: Harry Dorish, Duane Pillette, Roy Tinney, Jack Thomas, Jerry Zimmerman, Augie Amorena, Pumpsie

Green, Dick Hargenrader, Don Martin, and Earl Wilson. From that point there was a steady flow of players, and by the start of the season many in this original group would be gone due to trades, releases, or injuries.

The first to fall victim to injury was a likeable 22-year-old RHP Earl Wilson, dubbed the hardest thrower in camp, who was lost for a few days when he severely twisted his back during sliding practice. When he got back on his feet he was having a successful spring when he left the team and enlisted for a two-year stint in the U.S. Marine Corps. Upon his return he became the first black pitcher in Boston Red Sox history in 1959, and the first black pitcher in the major leagues to throw a no-hitter in 1962 when he overwhelmed the Los Angeles Angels.

As the days passed, Frank Kellert took over first base duties with young Larry DiPippo as his temporary backup, which pushed Bob DiPietro back to right field where his career had started. Returning catcher Eddie Sadowski and pitcher Bill Abernathie signed following brief holdouts for higher pay. When shortstop Jim Mahoney was drafted into the army, longtime minor league shortstop Harry Malmberg was brought into the fold. Soon another Boston prospect, outfielder Hal Grote, and former major league pitcher Walt Masterson, easily recognized by his trademark sunglasses, were added to the roster.

Masterson graduated from high school at 17 and signed with the Washington Senators. After pitching just 7⅔ minor league innings he was summoned by Senators owner Clark Griffith, broke into the major leagues on May 8, 1939, and didn't look back for 14 seasons. By the time he got to the Seals for the 1957 season he had completed a big league career with three American League organizations: Washington Senators (11 years), Boston Red Sox (four years), and Detroit Tigers (one year). He posted a deceptive 78–100 record with a 4.15 ERA in 399 games and 1,649⅔ innings pitched. One of his favorite memories was the first game he played after returning to the Senators in September 1945, when he defeated Bob Feller, 1–0.

Although the camp had the usual daily routines as players honed their skills amid competition for specified positions, the atmosphere was relaxed. Humor and even some pranks prevailed. The news regarding pending westward movement of two National League teams was getting around, but they had more important things to occupy their time and their thoughts.

The journey to the PCL pennant began in their first spring training game. Popular sportswriter Bob Stevens accurately summed up events when he wrote, "The San Francisco Seals made their first bid for an undefeated season today by climbing on the shoulders of shortstop Joe Tanner to a 5–2 victory over the Sacramento Solons" (*San Francisco Chronicle*, March 15, 1957).

Their 11-hit onslaught was highlighted by two humongous round-trippers by Tanner, who earned four RBI for his efforts. Three Seals pitchers, "can't miss" Ted Bowsfield in the starting role followed by a recovered Earl Wilson and Jim Konstanty, held the Sacs to five hits. It would be one of the few games in which the hard-luck and injury-prone Bowsfield appeared.

Konstanty was 40 years old when he signed to play the final year of his long baseball career with the 1957 Seals. His athletic resume began at Arcade Central High School in Strykersville, New York, where he earned multiple letters in football, baseball, basketball, and soccer before graduating from Syracuse University with a degree in physical education. The 1950 season, as a member of the Philadelphia Phillies Whiz Kids, was the highlight of his career: a 16–7 record, saved 22 games, and a 2.66 ERA in a league-leading 74 appearances, all in relief. In addition, he was on the National League All-Star team and was voted the National League's Most Valuable Player. Ironically, he was given the honor of pitching Game One of the World Series, the only game he started that year, as the Phillies were shut out, 1–0.

Two days later the Seals struck again, this time with an eight-run eighth inning rally to beat the Seattle Rainiers, 12–5, with San Francisco legend Lefty O'Doul at the helm. After his late arrival to camp put him in poor stead with Joe Gordon, young shortstop Pumpsie Green redeemed himself somewhat as he sparkled defensively, went 3-for-4 at the plate, stole a base, and collected four RBI for his day's work.

The next day Boston farm director Johnny Murphy announced that Boston had optioned three more players to the Seals, two pitchers and an outfielder: RHP Al Schroll, aptly nicknamed "Bull," who was plagued with arm problems during his brief stint with the Seals in 1956 and was not even around long enough for a spring training cup of coffee in 1957; blond 5'9" Tommy Hurd, a RHP dubbed "Whitey," who spent 1954–1956 in the American League with Boston, who was sent to shore up the bullpen in middle relief; and Tommy Umphlett, described by many as the best defensive center fielder in a Seals uniform since Joe DiMaggio, who had appeared in 120 games in 1956 until his season was cut short by injury. There had been a lot of attention given to the lengthy list of players sent to the Seals. The early results of all this "help" from the parent club was a lot more work for Gordon, who had just a few weeks to trim the squad down to the 21 permitted by the league.

By mid–March veteran Grady Hatton, described by legendary Red Sox scout Joe Stephenson as "a guy who has played everything but the piano in the major leagues," joined the fray (Bob Stevens, "Hatton Is One Man Team," *San Francisco Chronicle*, March 28, 1957). Hatton had never played as much as an inning of minor league baseball before his long and successful major league career. At age 34, with 11 major league seasons under his belt, the agile and capable athlete appeared in 117 games and batted .317 during the 1957 season. His other duties included hitting coach, fielding coach, and personal discipline advisor as necessary.

Aware that nothing had been settled but that the idea of big league baseball in the city was everywhere, Hatton recalled,

> The Red Sox wanted to win the pennant and leave a good taste in the mouths of the people in San Francisco. And part of my job was to be vigilant and help make that happen. We had a great ballclub with a crazy manager, Joe Gordon. He was a wonderful guy who had been a great player. He and Glenn "Cap" Wright loosely ran the team and I helped with some of the younger players. Joe didn't show up a lot of the time until game time and Glenn, a great player in his time, was way up in years by then, so I helped as player-coach. The team had a lot of established players who didn't need much help with their personal tools or anything like that, but in spring training we made them work hard and put them through their paces.

But the big news in baseball that day was in the huge article on the same page that reported Cleveland general manager, future Hall of Famer Hank Greenberg, had walked away from a million dollar cash offer from Boston's Joe Cronin and Tom Yawkey to buy the contract of the Indians 23-year-old strikeout pitcher, Herb Score. It was the largest amount offered for a player in baseball history, and there was no doubt that Score was "the phenom" of the era. He had struck out 245 batters in his rookie season in 1955, and another 263 in 1956. The generally tight-fisted Red Sox officials explained their generosity, saying he was on his way to becoming the best pitcher in the game. But Greenberg declined, gambling that Score could achieve that mark in a Cleveland uniform. The players made prickly jokes about keeping some of that money to pay their salaries.

That night the Bay Area boys topped the Rainiers, 7–6, as young third baseman Doug Hubacek walloped a long homer and Jim Konstanty held the lead for the victory. With a 4–1 record in the books, the team headed home to San Francisco to host the big event of their spring schedule, a three-game weekend series against the parent Red Sox in Seals Stadium.

Once the dates for that series were decided before the beginning of spring training, it was the job of the Seals publicity department to "spread the word." Actually, the entire department consisted of one man, former major league pitcher Walter Mails who, during his playing days, was often described as one of the most disliked men in the game because of his pomposity, brazen manner, and abrasive behavior toward teammates and others. Born in San Quentin, "outside the walls," he was always quick to emphasize, he broke into the majors in 1915 for a brief stint with the Brooklyn Dodgers, where his hard-throwing pitching style and deliberately knocking down batters earned him the nickname "Duster." He unabashedly called himself "The Great Imperial Duster," which was too much for the press and fans alike, so he shortened it to "Walter The Great Mails." It stuck.

His big league career was interrupted when he was sent back to the PCL in 1917, and he returned to the majors for the final weeks of the 1920 season to help Cleveland in a tough down-to-the-wire pennant race. He went 7–0 and helped the Indians to their World Series win over the Brooklyn Robins. He loved to talk about it. By the end of his career he had pitched 14 seasons in the PCL, including 1926–1929 with the Seals, and had three 20-win seasons. When he hung it up as a player Mails remained in the game as a successful baseball promoter in the Bay Area until 1972.

The press, coupled with radio appearances by Walter Mails, spread the word to greet the visitors at the airport and make them welcome with the hope of attracting capacity crowds at the games. Fourteen brand-new Mercury convertibles and two Lincolns donated by local dealerships for the occasion were scheduled to caravan the Bostonians and local civic officials from the airport to their hotel, and fans were encouraged to join in the festivities. With his usual flair, Mails led the parade wearing his long black cape and a top hat, and carried a gold-knobbed walking cane.

Red Sox manager Mike "Pinky" Higgins announced his plans to bring his big timbers with every intention of winning: infielders Dick Gernert (first base), Gene Mauch (second base), Billy Klaus (third base), and Ted Lepcio (shortstop), and outfielders Jackie Jensen, Jimmy Piersall and Ted Williams, with Sammy White behind the plate. But Joe Gordon was ambitious. He wanted to fight the good fight with his A team and possibly pull off a sweep. The press and fans alike thought it could never happen ... but ... on the other hand ... maybe the Seals could do it. It seemed the biggest problem was not the Seals' success, but the weather.

As usual, it had been a cold and wet spring in the Bay Area. Columnist Art Rosenbaum reflected the concerns about the weather for the set in his "Overheard" column in the *Chronicle*: "Rain or cloudy Friday morning but clearing Friday night in time for Bosox-Seals game; clear Saturday and Sunday" (March 17, 1957, 2H).

There was no rain. But it was San Francisco after all, and there were minor earthquakes throughout the day Friday. The first reaction to the quakes came in the form of a teletype message from the front office in Boston. It read: "Can you say if Red Sox to play tonight in view of quake?" The reply, with usual San Francisco tenacity, read, "The Seals and San Francisco do not quake before temblors. GAME ON."

Once that was established, everyone who worried that rain would deter attendance at the game also gave thought to the quakes. Initially their worst fears were realized when only 400 fans graced the stands an hour before game time. They began the planned hitting competition which was won by Dick Gernert, with Ted Williams second and Bill Renna third. By the first pitch the crowd had swelled to over 20,000 in a stadium with a capacity of 22,900. Although the stands roared with excitement and support for the Seals, everyone realized the big attraction was the "Splendid Splinter" as they waited to see him bang a long one over the fence. One box office employee later reported that only 15 calls canceling tickets were received, all from policemen and firemen.

Sports pages in the morning papers continued the word play about the quake as they discussed how the Seals "shocked" the Red Sox in front of 20,023 fans who enjoyed the 5–2 victory. They out-hit the visitors 11–5, and were never behind in the game. Beloved favorite Bob DiPietro made his spring debut in right field and got two of those hits to the loud pleasure of the crowd. One of them came after Red Sox pitcher Tom Brewer threw the ball into center field in an attempt to pick off Grady Hatton at second, allowing the Seals to tie the score at two in the fourth. DiPietro, the next batter, hit the deck to avoid a high-inside pitch from the frustrated twirler before getting his second hit. The Seals took the lead in the sixth and never looked back. A 1956 favorite, Frank Malzone, who was then fighting for third base duties with the Bosox, received a boisterous "welcome back" when he got a single in a pinch-hitting role.

Afterward, as the crowd exited the stands and walked across the field to the opened doors in the center field wall, they were noisy as they celebrated a long day. In a relaxed interview the following day, Ted Williams jokingly denied that he had done or said anything that had caused the earthquakes.

Though the joy of victory didn't turn into the agony of defeat, it was short-lived as Boston won Saturday's game easily, 9–3, while the Seals managed to eke out just a handful of hits. The clincher on Sunday was played in front of the first overflow crowd at the Stadium since the New York Yankees had appeared in a 1951 exhibition. The Red Sox led, 3–0, into the bottom of the ninth inning, when the Seals surged with a three-run rally to tie the game, only to lose in the tenth, 5–4, off the bat of another 1956 Seals player, powerful catcher Haywood Sullivan, who put one in the seats with a runner on base. Though San Francisco lost the series two games to one, Gordon considered them winners because they fought valiantly and had many individual stars. Bill Renna batted .600 in front of the 57,000 fans who attended the three-game set.

With good attendance in the Red Sox series, rumors of a different nature popped up in the papers. According to *San Francisco Chronicle* columnist Bill Leiser, Boston general manager Joe Cronin was preparing to raise money to finance a big league club in San Francisco, and the co-owner of the Yankees,

Del Webb, would liquidate his interests there and establish a team in Los Angeles, thus making it an American League expansion. Paul Fagan, owner of the Seals and Seals Stadium, was outraged, saying this was nothing more than a smoke screen to confuse the issue. After that he adamantly insisted Seals Stadium be made into a major league park. As it turned out, although Leiser got a few more columns on the subject, he was not taken seriously.

After a day off Monday, they returned to Fullerton to begin the final 16 days of the pre-season schedule. Gordon was aware of the deep talent pool in his camp and felt pressured by the need to make deep cuts which he had already announced wouldn't happen until after the last game at Fullerton on April 6 when they would break camp and play their way back to San Francisco for Opening Day. He used those games to experiment with lineups and worked with new arrivals. They got back in the saddle when they hosted Portland on Tuesday.

That game was a surprise wake-up call! The Beavers garnered eight hits that turned into eight runs in the first inning off Walt Masterson. Despite a determined Seals lineup, they were unable to intimidate Portland's young LHP, Marty Garber, who held on for the victory to become the first pitcher in the league that spring to go a full nine innings. The loss brought their record to 4–2 against PCL competitors.

The team pushed forward in spite of a tragic distraction when pitcher Bob "Riverboat" Smith left the team for a few days to be with his family after his third son, Roger, a year old, had been taken to the Orange City Hospital in Fullerton in critical condition, severely burned when he pulled a pot of steaming coffee on himself. Because prolonged hospitalization that included multiple plastic surgeries was necessary, Seals president Jerry Donovan arranged to have the little one transferred to a hospital in San Francisco.

The squad then headed to San Bernardino to face Seattle for the third time. Gordon used a lineup that had some positions solidified. Outfielder Albie Pearson, described throughout the league as the "most spectacular little man in the game," owned the leadoff spot. Big Bill Renna had cleanup duties sewed up. Nini Tornay, teased as the big basher of the team as he enjoyed the best spring training of his career with many hits of all sizes that left him carrying a batting average over .500, vied with Eddie Sadowski for catching duties, with all odds favoring the younger Sadowski with Tornay in the backup role. In addition, Joe Tanner's hot bat and sparkling defense guaranteed him a place on the roster, but the question for Gordon to resolve was Tanner's position. His good feet and good hands helped the team at both shortstop and third base.

While Gordon dealt with lineups, roster cuts and the like, the Seals destroyed Seattle, 10–3, in the first game of a nine-game winning streak that lasted through April 5. It seemed the team could do no wrong on the field. The press tagged them with such colorful nicknames as "the swashbuckling Seals," "the terrors of the orange blossom circuit," and "the Gordons."

Meanwhile Gordon dealt with his managerial tasks and the tough job of paring down the squad to 21 players. Pumpsie Green, Larry DiPippo, Don Martini, Augie Amorena, and Bob Thollander were optioned to AA Oklahoma. On March 30, Bill Renna, Jim Konstanty, and Grady Hatton were away from the team and participated in the annual Pacific Coast League All-Stars versus the Hollywood Stars, an exhibition game to benefit the Kiwanis Crippled Children Foundation.

On April 1, in the midst of the streak, Joe Gordon had "had it" with the no-show status of Umphlett and Kiely, who had been optioned to the Seals on March 18, then disappeared off the radar. He loudly exploded when he made it clear their jobs were not guaranteed and they'd have to earn spots on the team just like everybody else. In fact, he was quite impressed with big outfielder Hal Grote and had been working with him personally on ways to improve his hitting. In a final fit of rage, Gordon yelled for all to hear, "Let it be known for now and forever more that I want guys on my club who come to play!" (*San Francisco Chronicle*, April 1, 1957).

April 2 was a better day. Gordon announced he'd learned that two stars from the 1956 Seals, outfielder Marty Keough and second baseman Ken Aspromonte, were optioned back and would arrive in a few days. Keough, touted as one of the greatest athletes ever produced in Southern California, had suffered a broken ankle chasing a fly ball after 79 games that ended his 1956 season. Aspromonte played in 141 games and batted .281 despite missing action while recovering from an emergency appendectomy. Everybody agreed that their return confirmed that Boston was building a pennant-winning team for the Bay Area fans. Aspromonte recalled:

> In 1957 I started with the Red Sox big league club in Sarasota and, although I thought I had a good spring, they decided I wasn't good enough so they optioned me to the Seals. Of course it was a disappointment but, honestly, I thought I needed another year before going up. I had just gotten out of the service in time for the 1956 season, and felt it would do me good to get more seasoning because when I went to the big leagues I wanted to be able to play well enough to stay there. Once I got to San Francisco I felt comfortable. I knew most of the guys who were optioned out with me like Marty Keough and a few others. Joe Gordon was our manager and he was an easy guy to work with. He molded the team into what he wanted and we had a good ballclub.

They kept winning through April 6, when the streak was stopped by the Sacramento Solons, 5–3, in Bakersfield. Undaunted, especially with Fritz Dorish on the mound, they went after their 15th win and began a new streak the following day when they squashed the Solons, 9–0, in spite of falling victim to a triple play in the second inning. Bill Renna's single off Cloyd Boyer extended his hitting streak to 16 games. After the game Gordon announced that Dorish had earned Opening Day starting honors.

Things lightened up for the players when they read the Las Vegas odds for the PCL in the sports pages and had a good laugh for themselves. The 1956 league champs, Los Angeles, stood at 2–1, Sacramento at 30–1, 50–1 for the Seals, and the Mounties out of sight at 150–1. Grady Hatton said, "Fifty to one! Now just where can a man make a little bet on that deal? I haven't seen a club yet we can't lick, and we're getting better. Keough and Aspromonte's a comin' down, y'know." It was the topic of laughter throughout the season as the Seals and Mounties turned those odds upside-down and inside-out.

Things were not quite as jovial in Seattle. The *Seattle Times* reported a financial statement from the owners of the Seattle Rainiers, the Sicks Brewing and Malting Company, which reported a loss of $41,597 in 1956 when they finished in second place. That was an improvement over the $45,809 loss for the 1955 season when they won the pennant in a down-to-the-wire race. There was fear in the region that any changes in the Coast League in 1957 or the near future could force them to exit the league.

Shortly thereafter Seals president Jerry Donovan, called a wise old sage of the game at age 51, commented on Seattle's situation and offered advice for their dilemma: "If you buy a ball club, buy it for personal health and amusement, not for profit."

After the Seals broke camp in Fullerton on April 6, they played their way home with games against other PCL contenders in Bakersfield, Fresno, and Atwater. By the time they played their final exhibition game on April 9, a laugher which the Seals won, 14–0, against the Fresno State College Bulldogs, these athletes had gelled into a team to be reckoned with. During their stellar spring they played 22 games in 34 days in which they set and broke Pacific Coast League Spring Training records for wins, consecutive wins, hits, and extra-base hits, not to mention strong performances from starting pitchers and those in the bullpen. They developed a winning attitude that carried through the entire season. They were confident but never cocky as they knew the task they faced required hard work every day (*San Francisco Chronicle*, "PCL Baseball Shorts," April 8, 1957).

According to what had become an expected PCL Opening Day match-up, they headed to Seals Stadium to host the Portland Beavers. That day was the first of a vagary of Pacific Coast League traditions and idiosyncrasies that ended one by one during the 1957 season. Tommy Umphlett remembered:

> It couldn't have been a better spring for us. We started winning from the get-go and that gave us a lot of confidence in the beginning of the season. Every-

body likes winning! It put a different attitude on the club, I mean a better feeling on the whole ballclub, a feeling that we couldn't lose. Of course the sports writers worried that we'd played so well and won so many there we didn't have enough wins left in us to accomplish much in the season. But we knew better.

Meanwhile, away from the diamond, the press kept a sharp eye on events as they unfolded during the off-season and kept fans abreast of the goings-on facing the league in 1957. An article in the *San Francisco Chronicle* (February 10, 1957) reminded readers that the City had been given three opportunities to get a major league baseball team in the past but nothing came of them.

One was in 1955 when Chicago Cubs owner Philip K. Wrigley proposed that the National League expand to ten teams, adding Los Angeles and San Francisco. A unanimous vote of all National League owners was required for it to pass. It failed by a 6–2 margin, the two dissenting votes were cast by Ruley Carpenter (Philadelphia Phillies) and Horace Stoneham (New York Giants).

The second came from Cleveland Indians General Manager Hank Greenberg, who submitted a proposal to purchase the Seals "with the view of converting the franchise to big league baseball as soon as possible." Cleveland offered to pay off all debts against the Little Corporation. In prolonged talks, all agreed that San Francisco was in a pickle over one certainty: the lease on Seals Stadium would lapse in 1958 with no plan by the city to build a park for a future major league team. The press reported that many elements of Greenberg's elaborate plan slapped San Francisco's immediate hopes for a major league baseball franchise in the face with a wet towel. In addition, other PCL owners found his plan and his attitude threatening to the future of the league and rejected it outright.

Apparently another offer came to the fore briefly during the 1956 World Series. Clark Griffith, owner of the Washington Senators, had threatened to move his team the previous season without results, and was rumored to be testing the waters in San Francisco. However, after brief discussions meetings were halted and never renewed.

The histories of both New York clubs were written about on sports pages of all papers up and down the Pacific Coast League. It was no secret that the New York Giants and Brooklyn Dodgers were having troubles of their own. Since the first game was played in the rebuilt Polo Grounds on June 28, 1911, the park had slipped into a state of disrepair, and the Giants' lease was about to expire. In Flatbush the Dodgers were described as "a victim of the times." Sociological and economic factors resulted in a population flux since the first exhibition game in Ebbets Field on April 5, 1913, at the park built on the former site of the Pigtown garbage dump, and the area had become a ghetto.

Attendance regularly declined as fans, fearing for their safety, avoided night games. Both teams were beloved by their fans, and their historic rivalry was one of the best in the game. The issues facing both franchises were obvious: both facilities needed costly but necessary repairs, and there was resistance to using public funds to build new parks.

Throughout spring training, headlines in the sports pages and talk on the radio about the many cross-country flights of San Francisco Mayor George Christopher kept his push to bring major league baseball to San Francisco on the minds of the fans. Their attitude was to worry about the on-field play and let the politicians worry about the rest, because this topic was nothing new, and in the past things were stalled short of commitments from any of those involved. For the moment, at least, it was nothing to get excited about.

On March 2, PCL owners met at the Hamilton Hotel in Bowling Green, NY, for what they called "an emergency meeting" to discuss the pros and cons of a possible move of the Brooklyn Dodgers from Flatbush to California, specifically Los Angeles. Walter O'Malley was quoted as saying he bought the team for the express purpose of someday moving west, explaining that he would operate the team as a minor league club in the PCL. But Coast League owners expressed mixed feelings about it, fearing the impact on the existing teams in the league. In a preliminary vote, San Francisco, Los Angeles, Portland, San Diego, and Hollywood approved while Sacramento and Seattle were holdouts, and Vancouver (because it was a new city in the league) abstained.

But by the end of the meeting it was unanimously decided to transfer the PCL Angels from being a farm club of the Chicago Cubs to the Brooklyn Dodgers, who could then purchase Wrigley Field in Los Angeles as part of the deal. Another element of the deal included plans for a ten-year Pacific World Series between the PCL champions and the professional champs of Japan. Approval was given for the Dodgers to move west, but as a minor league team.

The following day, writer Joe King revealed that Horace Stoneham said he didn't want to leave New York and the fans, but felt business factors were "squeezing sentiment out of it" and forcing a move (*San Francisco Chronicle*, March 3, 1957). He added that as attendance declined, the organization had essentially survived on revenues generated by television. But things had reached a point where the best hope was to explore cities seeking a major league team. He had four cities on his short list: San Francisco, Toronto, Dallas, and Minneapolis as the front runner because of the newly built Minneapolis Stadium.

Simultaneously the press began reporting that the best-case scenario for all concerned would be a double move with the Dodgers in Los Angeles and the Giants in San Francisco, where the two teams could continue what was always described as their historic feud. For example, front page news in the *San Francisco Chronicle* (March 6) said Los Angeles Mayor Norris Poulson was optimistic about the Dodgers' move to his fair city and O'Malley had said the trial balloons were in the air. With that announcement he committed to build a new $9 million baseball stadium in a then-unknown place called Chavez Ravine. Throughout those weeks the public became familiar with the two owners. Stoneham's more reflective and contemplative demeanor was described as a polar opposite to the "put the peoples' feet to the fire" attitude of O'Malley (*San Francisco Chronicle*, March 3, 1957).

Both teams were beloved by their fans, and their historic rivalry was one of the best in the game. Both organizations had their backs against the wall and eminent action was imperative if they were to survive. The parks were in a serious state of disrepair and the cities were unwilling to raise money to build new ones for their beloved teams. The fans considered themselves not only powerless but the biggest losers if their teams moved 3,000 miles away.

It was common knowledge that in 1954 San Francisco had passed a bond issue by a three-to-one margin to allocate $5 million to either upgrade Seals Stadium or build a new stadium in hopes of attracting major league baseball to the area. It turned out to be a significant bargaining chip in future negotiations.

As Opening Day approached and briefly thereafter, "baseball business" was relegated to the sidelines as the "game" of baseball moved to the forefront in the Pacific Coast League. Speculation about new players for the Seals and an improved season had been growing as reports of their successful spring training ventures reached the hometown fans.

THREE

April

April 11–14 (Thursday–Sunday) home vs. Portland
April 16–21 (Tuesday–Sunday) home vs. Seattle
April 23–28 (Tuesday–Sunday) home vs. Vancouver
April 30 (Tuesday) at Seattle

The first month of 1957, as with all seasons, was a time of adjustment for all eight clubs. Fans came to see what the new version of last year's Seals was all about. Though there were changes on the field, one thing remained constant: Bay Area weather. The day games were sunny and comfortable, though sometimes cool, while night games were cold-cold-cold. A handful of unpredictable rainouts were seen as business as usual by the locals.

Another thing that was business as usual was a unique element of the ambiance of Seals Stadium. There was a shiny bell from a World War II naval vessel that was donated to the team and hung from the roof of the broadcast booth. It was in the custody of a nattily dressed older gentleman named Jack Rice, whose job was to ring it at the bottom of every inning that the Seals scored, one ring for each run. Those melodious dings were always received with cheers.

There was also the Hamm's Brewery across the street that not only sent alluring smells wafting across the stadium, but also entertained the fans with its giant beer mug that looked like an oversized brandy snifter of yellow lights. It was located on the top of their tall office building for all to see as it slowly filled up to a frothy white foam that overflowed and ran down the side, then drained only to repeat the process over and over. It was especially effective during night games. It was said to have helped beer sales in the park even though a different brand was sold there.

More often than not San Francisco faced Portland in the initial series of the season. This time the festivities were in San Francisco on Thursday night, April 11. Though the first encounter between the two squads was expected to be interesting, everyone, including the press, said the Seals were overmatched. With Bill Sweeney at the helm, Portland had finished third in 1956 and was predicted to be one of the powerhouse clubs in the PCL in 1957 by the wise prognosticators of the day.

It had been a warm but windy day in the City and everyone was excited. Seals players arrived at the park early, joked and listened to music on the radio in the clubhouse as they put the finishing touches on their bats and gloves; trucks unloaded supplies as vendors stocked their wares in preparation for a big night; batboy Mike Murphy helped equipment man Joe Mooney put necessary paraphernalia in the proper places in the home dugout; the longtime scorekeeper climbed into the scoreboard loft to organize the numbers to be hung inning by inning during the game. Portland's players arrived and proceeded to their assigned clubhouse which had been prepared by regular clubhouse man Bill Soto. And the groundskeeper waited for the completion of batting practice to apply the white lines, insert game bases, and otherwise ready the diamond for action. At last the turnstile attendants and ushers took their posts, ticket offices opened, and fans started flowing into the emerald cathedral.

Opening ceremonies included a mock one-pitch game in which San Francisco Mayor George Christopher took the mound, threw the first pitch to catcher Frank Ahern (S.F. Police Chief), while Fire Chief Bill Murray stood in the batter's box and faced an infield manned by Chamber of Commerce dignitaries. The festivities officially began when the Queen of Chinatown, Ruby Kwon, in the role of umpire, cried, "Play Ball!"

Joe Gordon had not yet decided on the makeup of his squad and continued his spring training pattern of juggling the lineup. He penned the following on the lineup card for game one: Albie Pearson RF, Harry Malmberg 2B, Grady Hatton 3B, Bill Renna LF, Frank Kellert 1B, Nini Tornay C, Hal Grote CF, and Joe Tanner SS. Veteran pitcher Harry Dorish, in his first start since 1955 when he became a successful member of the bullpen, took the mound against Portland hurler Dick Fiedler.

After Dorish yielded two walks in the top of the first inning, then escaped without yielding a run, the Seals came to bat for the first time and quickly took command of the game with two unearned runs. Speedy Albie Pearson reached first on an error before he scored their first run of the season on a hit-and-run play by Malmberg that was good for a double down the right field line. A sacrifice by Hatton and a long fly out by Renna got Malmberg around one base at a time for their second run. The Seals scored the final run of the night in the fifth.

In the sixth Portland had the bases loaded with one out when Hatton caught a scorching line drive and threw to second to double off the returning runner. The team started to exit the field when colorful umpire John Nenezich loudly yelled, "Safe!" Gordon flew out of the dugout at top speed and got into the ump's face. In their usual style, Seals fans deluged the field with the striped cushions they had rented for 15 cents. After the dust settled, the call stood and the runner remained at second. But just two pitches later Joe Tanner made a spectacular catch of what turned out to be a foul ball down the third base line and saved the shutout. Final score: San Francisco 3, Portland 0.

After Dorish's first outing and first win in a Seals uniform the press jokingly reported, "Dorish is mean, so mean that Ted Williams refused to hit against him when both were with the Red Sox."

Portland, touted by pre-season writers as one of the hardest hitting teams in the league, was held at bay by Dorish, who earned a complete-game, four-hit shutout. He later said it was the first game he'd completed since 1954 and it felt good. The small but happy crowd of only 6,412 excited fans left the park in the usual fashion as they were admitted onto the infield, walked across the grass, and exited through the open double doors in the center field wall. It was settled. The San Francisco Seals were open for business and ready to take on the PCL for the 1957 season.

Former manager Eddie Joost, who had been replaced by Joe Gordon on May 9, 1956, after a few weeks' tenure, was among the first into the clubhouse at the end of the game to shake Gordon's hand and congratulate the team. The press had a field day. One Friday morning paper quoted Gordon as laughingly saying, "We are undefeated, untied, and un-scored on. We may make the Rose Bowl." In another he repeated something he'd said during spring training: "I should have my head examined if we don't finish in the first division" (Art Rosenbaum, *San Francisco Chronicle*, April 12, 1957). Everyone hoped that was a gross understatement because the Seals and their fans had their eye on the championship!

Sportswriters also reported that San Franciscans agreed they had shared in a perfect evening of baseball, except for one disappointment. Since the Seals had drawn over 57,000 in their recent three-game exhibition with the Red Sox, a capacity crowd was predicted for Opening Day. When bewildered club president Jerry Donovan and others sought explanations for the low turnout, they concluded the culprit was a Thursday night game and remained optimistic for a better weekend.

The 1957 season was in full swing around the league. Seattle defeated Sacramento, Los Angeles beat Vancouver, and Hollywood topped San Diego. The first casualties occurred in San Diego when Hollywood shortstop Dick Smith and second baseman Spook Jacobs collided while chasing a pop fly which dropped between them. Both Twinks ended up in the hospital for the night. While Jacobs was merely shaken up, Smith suffered a broken jaw.

By the time players reported for game two on Friday, Gordon had spent the day in his office making phone calls and plans. He expected the Red Sox to option a few more players to shore up his roster. That was the good news. The bad news, as he had summed up in an earlier press conference, was the tough decision he faced in order to reduce the list of pitchers to nine and trim his roster to the 21-man PCL player limit by the May 11 deadline.

But one victory does not a season make. In Friday night's game Seals LHP Bob Smith faced Beavers sidearm RHP Bill Werle, a former major leaguer with the Pirates, Cardinals, and Red Sox. The tight game was a nail-biter as the two teams fought toe-to-toe in front of another disappointing crowd. A native of Clarence, Missouri, Smith, dubbed "Riverboat" because he had the poise, bearing, and confidence of a riverboat gambler, held his own as he was backed up by his defense. Bill Werle, an Oakland native, held San Francisco to four hits as Portland came out on top in the struggle. For those who missed the game, sportswriter Bob Stevens summed it up in one sentence: "Smith, who failed to finish his last 23 starts with the Seals in 1956, and Jim Konstanty, the Flower of the Fire Department, combine to choke off the Bevos with six hits, [but] barely lose 1–2."

After the game the team learned that Boston optioned 30-year-old RHP Bert Thiel to the Seals. Thiel remembered:

> The Red Sox drafted me from Dallas in 1956 after I had an 18–6 record and was Texas League Pitcher of the Year. All of it was as a starter. So when Boston brought me to spring training in preparation for the '57 season I knew I wasn't going to be a starter for them at the major league level. And I also knew I wasn't going to stay with the Red Sox. Grady Hatton, Harry Dorish, Tommy Hurd, and I knew they were stacking the Seals ballclub with veteran ballplayers, and the rumor around camp was that we were headed to San Francisco. I was excited to get out there and play with these fellas. They told me my place would be in the bullpen. Though initially disappointed and not especially happy about that, I understood and did my job there.

Game three on Saturday was Shriners' Day at Seals Stadium. From the first pitch both ends of the baseball spectrum were apparent. Portland's 21-year-old Darrell Martin faced veteran Duane Pillette, who had appeared in 188 big league games with the Yankees (1949–50); St. Louis Browns/Baltimore Orioles (1950–55), where he pitched the first win for the new Orioles in 1954; and Philadelphia Phillies in 1956 before he returned to the Pacific Coast League to finish his career there. He was the son of major leaguer pitcher Herman "Old Folks" Pillette who had played one game with Cincinnati in 1917 followed by three seasons with Detroit (1922–24), then over 20 more seasons in the minors until he retired at age 49. Due to his unique pitching motion, Duane was plagued by arm problems throughout his career. But the tall, lanky pitcher still had a lot to offer and quickly proved himself a valued asset to the club.

In addition to Pillette's prowess, the team was strengthened by the return of second baseman Ken Aspromonte, a top prospect with Boston who had played the final 18 games of the 1956 season in San Francisco after returning from a tour of duty in the U.S. Army. He explained:

> In 1957 I started with the Red Sox in Sarasota and, although I thought I had a good spring, they decided I wasn't good enough so they optioned me to the Seals. It was a disappointment, but honestly, I thought another year of seasoning before going up would do me good because when I went to the big leagues I wanted to be able to play well enough to stay there.

Saturday afternoon "the Gordons," as they were tagged by the media during spring training, took the field in the top of the first with Renna in left, Keough in center, and Pearson in right. Around the horn Tanner was at third, Aspromonte at short, Malmberg at second and Kellert at first, with the battery of Pillette and Tornay. For six innings Pillette shut out the Beavers lineup of Solly Drake (CF), Jack Littrell (SS), Luis Marquez (LF), Joe Macko (1B), Eddie Basinski (2B), George Freese (3B), Frank Ernaga (RF), and catcher Sam Calderon.

Meanwhile the Seals came out swinging in the first inning for what could have been a big inning, but their own overzealous baserunning tripped them up. Pearson, who had singled, went all the way to third when Malmberg executed a hit-and-run. At that point things seemed out of control. With Keough at the plate Pearson gestured as if to steal home. Everyone was on alert. Keough hit the next pitch to Macko at first base. Portland yielded second to Malmberg, and executed a perfect, though unusual, double play by throwing Pearson out at the plate and getting Keough by a step at first. When the dust settled, Malmberg was the only Seals player left standing when Frank Kellert stepped into the box, took two pitches, then slammed a long single that allowed Malmberg to score the first run of the game.

The second and what turned out to be the winning run was scored by Pillette himself in the third. After he reached first as a hit batsman and was advanced to second on a Pearson sacrifice, he sped home when Malmberg hit a tremendous fly that dropped between outfielders Drake and Marquez. The Beavers finally broke up Pillette's shutout in the seventh when Joe Macko, hit by a pitch, scored after Frank Ernaga hit a line drive to left that a hustling Bill Renna "snow-coned" and dropped in what would have been the best play of the game.

The 4,125 fans were kept on the edge of their seats until the game ended as a 2–1 victory for the Seals. Young Darrell Martin, who pitched eight innings of seven-hit baseball and made a good showing, took a tough loss. Pillette earned his first complete game victory in a long time as he allowed one run on six hits with five strikeouts. Ironically, the hit batsmen for both teams scored. But, for the sportswriters, Pillette's command was the name of the game. In addition to the five whiffs, only two outs were recorded in the outfield. With that outstanding performance, he also made Joe Gordon's "pitching dilemma" more complicated.

Umpires Emmett Ashford, John Nenezich, and Al Mutart had their hands full as they attempted to maintain order during the first Sunday doubleheader, which began under the warm afternoon sun and concluded under the lights. The 11,014 fans in attendance got their money's worth. It was described by sportswriter Bob Stevens as a day when "San Franciscans proved again they can win 'em easy and they can win 'em tough" (Bob Stevens, *San Francisco Chronicle*, April 15, 1957).

In the first game, the Seals, behind Walt Masterson on the mound, exploded with a 16-hit attack against three Beavers hurlers, each of whom trudged off the field unable to contain the onslaught. While Masterson limited the visitors to just three singles, one double, and one run in his first complete game since 1953 with the Washington Senators, the man behind the sunglasses was the only member in the Seals lineup to go hitless. But nobody cared. Most memorable Seals swats were triples off the bats of Keough and Pearson, and two doubles from Aspromonte, as 16 baserunners were stranded while nine put tallies on the board.

Between games the clubhouse was alive with laughter thanks to a group of veterans led by jokester Bob DiPietro, a San Francisco native who always enjoyed what he called "those little Sunday get-togethers" at Seals Stadium. He was a man who never met a stranger and was always there for his friends, and his endless supply of baseball memories and stories kept the team loose. One of his favorite topics was Sacramento skipper Tommy Heath, his friend and the Seals manager from 1952 to 1955. Out of the blue DiPietro would say,

> Did I ever tell you guys about the time I went to a Chamber of Commerce luncheon a couple of years ago when Heath was the guest speaker? I was sitting close to the speakers' table listening intently, as I'm known to do, and Tommy stopped in the middle of a story and looked over at me and acted surprised to see me there. He exclaimed, "Well, look, here's Bob Di Pi ... DiPi ... what the hell's the guy's name? I can't remember him too well because I coached at third base and I didn't see a lot of him."

The nightcap began as a deceptively calm contrast until the Seals came to bat in the bottom of the fourth inning, trailing 1–0. They scored two runs in the frame thanks to a Renna home run followed by a walk to Tornay, who was driven home by a thundering double by Joe Tanner. In the fifth, with Malmberg on first, Frank Kellert bashed his first four-bagger of the season. LHP Roy Tinney entered in the top of the sixth with a 4–1 lead and some breathing room, or so he thought. But the Beavers had other ideas as they had a breakout inning that yielded four runs that gave them a 5–4 lead. The Seals immediately tied it up in the bottom of the inning, and the game remained tied through nine thanks to the relief work of Bill Abernathie and Jim Konstanty.

The Beavers faced reliever Leo "Black Cat" Kiely in their scoreless top of the tenth. The sixth Portland pitcher, veteran Ray "Snacks" Shore, who would go on to a long career in scouting, had the job of containing the Seals and getting the game to the 11th. But it wasn't his day. After he walked "Mighty Mite" Albie Pearson, who got to second on a Malmberg bunt, Keough was given an intentional pass that brought Kellert to the plate, and brought the fans to their feet clapping and cheering. When he hit a routine grounder to short, Pearson took off for third, which momentarily blocked the view of shortstop Jack Littrell, who lost sight of the ball as it rolled into left field. With that Pearson ran home and scored the winning run. Game over.

That's when the fireworks came! Shore blew his top as he screamed, "Interference!" The entire infield, with arms flailing in anger, shouted in the face of infield umpire Al Mutart that the ball hit Pearson's hip, rendering him out, the ball dead, and the play nullified. But Mutart didn't see it that way, called Pearson safe and said the run counted. Some fans ran onto the infield and joined the players pushing Mutart around until security police charged onto the field and frantically escorted Mutart off the field and down the runway that led to the umpires' room behind the clubhouse. At the same time, fans in the stands charged the field and took swipes at any players who were not Seals. The first rhubarb of the season started and ended in a matter of minutes. The game was over, the doubleheader was captured. But the discussions had just begun.

In a post-game interview Pearson told the press that though the ball took an awkward bounce, it did not hit him. Ray Shore told the press, "Plate umpire Emmett Ashford told me, 'Yes the ball hit him, but it's not my call.'" Portland catcher Danny Baich said he heard Ashford's comment. Ashford told the press, "I never said it." The players called the team of umpires the worst in the Pacific Coast League, accused Pearson and the Seals of cheating, and were eventually calmed down by skipper Bill Sweeney, who agreed the ball hit Pearson but there was nothing they could do about it. That's baseball.

Years later Marty Keough laughed when talking about Ashford. He remembered, "Emmett Ashford umpired in the PCL the entire time I was there and he was a terrible umpire! I mean he was always a little erratic, and if a play was close a guy had to be safe by a mile to get the call, or out by a mile for the defense to get it. Everything close seemed like guesswork possibly done with his eyes closed, ha-ha-ha. But he was always smiling and very good-natured. He just miscalled plays all over the place."

Di Pietro agreed, saying, "He may have been the loudest umpire in the league. When he was behind the plate his gyrations when calling balls and strikes were pure showboating and we wondered if people all over the City could hear him call 'ballllllll" or 'steee-riiiiiiike.' We always counted on him for entertainment but his calls were not always dependable. He was a real character."

After spring training observations, the press agreed that the team was strong in power but weak in pitching. However, when the Seals took four of five games in the abbreviated series, they felt they had proved them all wrong and intended to make headlines that would set them on their ears as the season progressed. In addition, to the delight of business manager Bob Freitas, the series gate of 25,910 was up 1,500 from 1956. Despite the cloud of uncertainty about the future the Pacific Coast League itself, the future of the 1957 Seals looked bright. After the first week, Hollywood led in the standings with a 5–1 record, with San Francisco and Vancouver tied for second at 4–1, half a game back.

While the Seattle Rainiers traveled to San Francisco on Monday and readied for the start of the new series, the Seals were not idle. The top of their priority list was finding local lodging. Returning players and veterans helped the new guys with the task, and longtime baseball man Evo Pusich helped Tom Umphlett find a little house to rent so he could bring his wife and young son to town. Some found apartments. Sal Taormina and Bill Renna, both from San Jose, remained home with their families and took turns driving to games. Other Bay Area locals like Bob DiPietro and Nini Tornay did likewise. Three pitchers who had left their wives and school-age children home for the season got rooms at the Spaulding Hotel in Union Square. According to Thiel, "That's how Tommy Hurd and Harry Dorish and I got to be such good friends. They were in the same boat I was in and we all had rooms in the same hotel, I think it was called the Spaulding, in the downtown area. We spent a lot of free hours talking together about our families and baseball and so on. We took the streetcars to the park and had fun with that."

Confidence was high as they readied for a series against the team they had defeated in all four encounters during spring training. The Seals carried a 4–1 record, had a team built to win, and were ready to continue on the path to the PCL pennant. However, first-year skipper Lefty O'Doul, beloved baseball figure in the Bay Area who had managed the Seals for 17 years (1935–1951), brought his Seattle Rainiers to town with other ideas on his mind. But the Tuesday and Wednesday night games were rained out.

With no Seals baseball to fill the sports pages, Bill Leiser attempted to fill in the gap as he wrote in his column "As Bill Leiser Sees It" (*SF Chronicle*, April 19, 1957), that "rains dampen things, including enthusiasm." His column suggested that when there are no games to attend or read about, fans lose interest and stop talking about their team and baseball in general. He even went so far as to conclude that the Little Corporation might have been more successful were it not for the number of rainouts early in the season. For his efforts he received a lot of reader backlash.

Although dry weather permitted game one of the series to get into the record books, news of the sudden death of popular Portland manager Bill Sweeney permeated the Pacific Coast League and all of baseball with a sense of sadness and loss. During the wee hours of Thursday morning, 53-year-old Sweeney passed away following emergency surgery for a perforated ulcer. He had become ill during Tuesday's opener in San Diego, but insisted he was able to complete the game and remained at his post in the third base box where all managers stood in those days. After the final out, he was rushed to the hospital where he had emergency surgery, but died a few minutes after midnight on Thursday morning.

The powers that be agreed Sweeney would not want the league disrupted, and all scheduled games went on as planned that night. So many PCL players knew him well and shared remembrances of him. Sweeney was a baseball man. The first baseman played in the PCL from 1925 to 1942 with time out from 1928 to 1931 to play major league ball with the Detroit Tigers and Boston Red Sox. He managed in the Coast League from 1936 to 1957 with Hollywood, Los Angeles, Seattle, and Portland, with time out in 1947–1948 when he was a coach at Detroit. During that tenure he led his squads to three championships, one with Portland in his premier season and two others with Los Angeles. Former major league RHP "Barnacle Bill" Posedel and minor league infielder Frank Carswell, who had played 16 games with Detroit in 1953, shared managerial duties for the remainder of the season.

Out of respect and to honor his long career, flags in all PCL cities were flown at half-mast for 30 days at the request of league president Leslie O'Connor.

Thursday night both teams sent their opening day winning pitchers back to the mound. Harry Dorish faced George "Red" Munger, former three-time National League All-Star (1944, 1947, 1949) with the St. Louis Cardinals. Rumors abounded that the Suds "didn't have a chance" against Dorish, who had kept sharp during the rainy days by actually suiting up and pitching to DiPietro in one of the stadium's inner sanctum halls. The problem was that DiPietro was the known source of the rumors, which he considered part of his "scare tactics" to help his team win.

The festivities started with a somber moment of silence for Sweeney before the big bats of the Seals continued their bombardment of the team from the north that was unable to stop the bleeding as the Bay Nine defeated them 6–1 in a 15-hit onslaught. After a scoreless tie through four innings, the Seals came to bat in the bottom of the fifth trailing 1–0 thanks to back-to-back hits, a single from Ray Orteig followed by a resounding double by young Maury Wills. But the San Franciscans retaliated with a rally of their own. Renna led off with a single, Aspromonte beat out a scratch bunt for a single, and catcher Eddie Sadowski cleared the bases with a searing line drive over the left field fence, giving the Seals a 3–1 advantage. With two outs and the bases loaded in the sixth, Aspromonte hit a smoking line drive single that scored Keough, on base with his fourth hit of the night, and Kellert. Seattle reliever Glenn Isringhaus yielded the final run of the game in the eighth. Final score: Seals 6, Rainiers 1.

The morning papers lauded the Seals' prowess at the plate, but paid special attention to Harry Dorish as they praised him for his second complete-game victory, spotlighting that he had allowed just one earned run in those 18 innings. Dorish, a plumber by trade in the off-season, was establishing himself as a fan favorite in San Francisco and a hurler to be respected throughout the league.

Friday was a long night for both clubs. The scheduled game was changed to a twin bill to pick up one of the two lost to rain. The action began at 6 P.M. and by the time the dust settled a few minutes before the date changed, both teams had played hard only to finish with a split. The Seals took the opener, 2–1, then trailed all the way until they lost the closer, 6–4.

Game one began as a pitching duel between Seattle veteran Clarence "Bud" Podbielan and Duane Pillette in his second start. Podbielan was well known to Coast League batters after 11 seasons of minor league ball with periods when he moved between major and minor league play from 1949 through 1955.

After three scoreless innings, the Suds drew first blood in the fourth when they put one unearned run on the board. Former Seals shortstop Leo Righetti, safe at first on an overthrow by Aspromonte, made it around to score via sacrifices from his teammates. That short-lived lead ended when the Seals returned the favor and restored the deadlock. Kellert reached on a single, followed by a walk to Aspromonte and a long, two-out single to left by Eddie Sadowski.

Things looked precarious for the Seals as tension heightened in the seventh inning when Pillette loaded the bases with one out. But Kellert saved the day when an attempted squeeze bunt turned into a weak pop fly down the first base line. He made a spectacular diving catch, then beat the runner back to first for the inning-ending double play.

It was all decided in the bottom of the eighth when Aspromonte smashed a scorching double up the middle, Sadowski received an intentional walk, and both advanced one base when Seattle reliever Howard Judson threw the ball into center field on an attempted pick-off play at second. Joe Tanner walked to load the bags. Pillette batted for himself and took a called third strike. After Pearson attempted a squeeze bunt that went foul, he worked the count to 3–2 before he slapped a single to right that plated Aspromonte. The Seals edged the Rainiers, 2–1.

Both starting pitchers hit the showers early in the second game. Seals LHP Riverboat Smith left in the second inning after the Suds got to him for four runs. Charlie Rabe lasted into the fifth, when the Seals got three of them back. They were never able catch O'Doul's crew and lost the capper, 6–4.

It was a costly night for both teams, as Bud Podbielan left game one with a wrenched knee that kept him out of action for five weeks, and Seals catcher Nini Tornay suffered a split thumb in the nightcap.

Saturday was one of the fans' favorite promotions at the stadium. Before the game they were allowed to enter the field and take pictures of or with the players. As expected, Albie Pearson got the most attention as he patiently posed and visited with them.

The Seals took the diamond Saturday in first place with a 6–2 record and with every intention of increasing that lead. Joe Gordon rested Bill Renna and Joe Tanner and rearranged his lineup by moving Aspromonte to the cleanup spot, Sal Taormina to left, and Grady Hatton to third. But with longtime veteran

SAL TAORMINA

THE SAN JOSE LAD HITS LEFT AND RIGHT HANDED PITCHING EQUALLY WELL. HOW MGR. O'DOUL TO KEEP THIS YOUTHFUL SENSATION OF THE SEALS' CAMP OUT OF THE STARTING OUTFIELD? SAL'S MUSCULAR SHOULDERS GIVE HIM A HOME-RUN PUNCH BUT HE CLOUTS SHARP LINE DRIVES TOO.

Hal Bruntsch ——96

Sal Taormina at spring training in Hawaii, 1946 (sketch by Hal Bruntsch. Source: Sal Taormina family albums, donated by Sal Taormina, Jr.).

Larry Jansen on the mound for Seattle, it wasn't in the cards. Jansen, age 37, was another beloved player in San Francisco since he won 30 games on the Seals' 1946 pennant-winning squad. He spent eight seasons as the darling of the New York Giants before returning to the PCL with Seattle.

Without run support, starter Walt Masterson, who yielded a run in the first, was unable to match Jansen's mound skills and was replaced by Jim Konstanty before he could log five innings in the books. By the time things were said and done, Jansen not only pitched a sparkling five-hit shutout, but helped his own cause with a solo homer in the eighth, just the second in his long professional baseball career. The Seals were limited to singles by Malmberg, Keough, Hatton, and two from Jansen's teammate in 1946, Sal Taormina, who jokingly insisted he was robbed of another one by the fancy footwork and quick hands of Leo Righetti at short. With that game, the Mounties took first place from the Seals and left them in second, a half-game behind.

On Easter Sunday, Bay Area fans and the team itself laughed at Art Rosenbaum's *San Francisco Chronicle* column which said Las Vegas odds on the Seals winning the pennant in the Pacific Coast League had steadily dropped from 50–1, to 15–1, to 8–1, while Portland and Seattle stood at 6–1, Sacramento at 30–1, and Vancouver at 50–1. At the same time, the Santa Anita Turf and Sports Club showed a 5–1 spread for the Seals. "How about that?" they laughed, and they went on with the business of winning ballgames.

Bill Renna was sidelined with a slight muscle pull, and Gordon gave DiPietro his first start of the season as his replacement in left field in the opener. Southpaw Roy Tinney learned the meaning of frustration as he suffered the consequences of a lazy defense, what was later described as one of the weirdest plays ever seen at the stadium. After the Seals plated the game's first run in the first inning, the Suds got two in the third, another in the sixth, and took a 3–1 lead into the seventh when the bottom fell out for the home nine. With Juan DeLis on third and veteran pitcher Marion Fricano at the plate to execute a squeeze bunt, the tap he delivered traveled less than three feet, stopping inside the batter's box and thus a foul ball. However, none of the three umpires (Mutart, Ashford, or Ninezich) called it foul. DeLis scored, and while an irate Gordon and Seals infielders argued at the plate, leaving the infield unmanned, Fricano kept running and ended up on second with an RBI double.

Things didn't improve when play resumed as Seattle ended up with seven runs in the inning, making the score 10–1. San Francisco knew they faced a tough hill to climb, but went down battling as they staged a mini-rally in the bottom of the ninth. A Frank Kellert homerun drove in one, and with two on base Albie Pearson's long double drove them home. The excited 8,220

Easter Sunday fans in attendance clapped, whistled, and shouted for their team to pull it out. Alas, it didn't happen, and the locals suffered their third consecutive loss, 10 to 4.

Another new face took to the mound for the Seals in game two, stocky Bob Thollander, a converted outfielder from Texas and son of Ernest Thollander, who had a brief pitching career of his own with Calgary in the Western Canadian League in 1920–1921. Thollander won a dozen athletic letters in high school and was voted all-league in football and baseball, before he decided to pursue a career in baseball. He made his way to St. Mary's College in Moraga, California, in order to play under coach Bill Cunningham, former New York Giants outfielder. He excelled and was named to the All-Pacific Coast Intercollegiate team in 1952, and then signed with the Boston Red Sox. Following an outstanding rookie season in San Jose in the California League, he was drafted into the military. Back in San Jose in 1954 after two years in the army, he pitched for the Montgomery Rebels of the South Atlantic League in 1955 where he compiled a 12–8 record. In 1956 he appeared in three games with the Seals before he was optioned to Louisville. He rejoined the Seals after the 1957 season began.

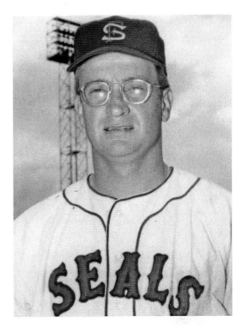

Bob Thollander (Dave Eskenazi Collection).

In game two he didn't start with a bang when he took the hill and quickly gave up a first inning run when Bobby Balcena bashed a fence-rattling double, then ran home on a long single by Juan DeLis. But he settled down after that and allowed the visitors only two more scattered hits as he garnered a complete game victory. Ironically, the young pitcher was the impetus for both run-producing rallies by his team.

In the second inning, with Harry Malmberg on second, the slugging pitcher hit a long double to right that scored Malmberg. With the game tied so quickly, pitcher Joe Black, a former Brooklyn Dodger, seemed agitated as he walked Pearson before Grady Hatton doubled both runners across, making the score 3–1. The third proved to be the final inning for Black as the Seals' bats got to him for three more runs aided by sloppy Seattle defense. Frank

Kellert reached on a single, was forced at second by Bob DiPietro, Malmberg walked, and a line drive single by Eddie Sadowski scored DiPietro. Thollander approached the plate with Malmberg on third and Sadowski on first. He hit a fly ball to right that fielder Joe Taylor was slow to return to the infield, allowing Sadowski reach the plate all the way from first, making the score 6–1, where it remained.

San Francisco and Seattle split what turned out to be a six-game series with one make-up game to be announced later. At this early stage of the season, the Seals were a game and a half behind front-running Vancouver, the team coming to town for the next series at Seals Stadium.

Meanwhile, Joe Gordon had made some announcements about his team. In the hitting department, though not written in stone, Albie Pearson remained in the leadoff spot, with Bill Renna batting cleanup followed by Frank Kellert. Defensively, the infield was solid with Kellert at first, Malmberg at second, Aspromonte at short, Hatton and Tanner platooned at third, and Renna, Keough, and Pearson left to right in the outfield. Eddie Sadowski was the better hitting catcher with Nini Tornay as a strong backup man.

According to Marty Keough,

> At that time the Red Sox weren't big on stealing bases and all that. They never were. But Joe liked that kind of thing. He would walk up to you at third base from the coaching box and say, "Go on the next pitch" and walk away. It used to scare me to death because he never gave a sign to the others or anything like that. You were always afraid that one of the big hitters would hit a ball at your head on the way in because he didn't know you were coming down the line. He was like Billy Martin that way, did anything to score a run.

The Vancouver Mounties, an affiliate of the Baltimore Orioles, managed by colorful and feisty Charlie Metro in his rookie season at the helm, had finished in the cellar, 38.5 games out of first, under manager Lefty O'Doul in 1956. And their losing record in spring training didn't bring any glowing reviews from the experts who predicted the team would finish at the bottom of the second division in 1957.

Far from satisfied with that, General Manager Cedric Tallis fortified the team with help from the parent club. In addition to having big plans for the new season, Metro, known for never concealing an opinion, called the experts "yo-yos" as he vowed to make them eat their words. Gordon agreed with Metro, adding that the latest efforts improved the team and its chances for success, and said, "they had the tools to fix any club's clock on any given night."

Joe Gordon was well aware that the 52-year rivalry between his club and the Mounties when they were the Oakland Oaks, 1903–1955, was one of the most written about aspects of Pacific Coast League history. Competition was historically intense laced with grudge matches that often resulted in fights among the fans in the stands. It's been said by some that the intensity between the teams was at its peak between 1946–1948 when Lefty O'Doul skippered the Seals and Casey Stengel managed the Oaks. The Seals took the pennant in 1946 and Stengel's so-called "nine old men" won it in 1948.

As a matter of fact, one example of each club's drive to defeat the other has evolved into a common element in the game we watch today. While coaching in the third base box, O'Doul regularly pulled a bandana from his back pocket and waved it at the opposing pitcher to distract him and incite fans. Once fans got the idea, they waved bandanas of their own.

In 1957 the Mounties fielded a strong team that included veteran pitchers George Bamberger (34), Morrie Martin (34), and Charlie Beamon (22), who were well fortified by outfielders Tito Francona (.298) and Lenny Green (.311), shortstop Buddy Peterson (.298), and third baseman Kal Segrist, both backed up by Spider Jorgensen (37), and first baseman Jim Marshall, who appeared in all 168 games that season and drove in 102 runs. Their success that year was a happy surprise for their fans and was respected by all clubs they faced for the duration of the season. Early predictions by sportswriters picked the Seals, the Mounties, and the Padres to "fight it out to the wire."

In their first confrontation the series got off to a flying start for the hosts, as Harry Dorish pocketed his third consecutive win against veteran George Bamberger in a game that saw a total of 13 hits and a final score of Seals 3, Mounties 2. The Seals were up and running in the first frame. Albie Pearson reached on surprise bunt single. When Keough singled through the hole Pearson ended up on third, and was driven home by a Bill Renna sacrifice fly.

Both pitchers held the opposition in tow until the top of the sixth, when Jim Marshall hit a routine grounder to short and was safe at first thanks to a wide throw by Ken Aspromonte. He advanced to third on a Kal Segrist double and scored on a sac fly by outfielder Joe Frazier. Game tied at one.

The game remained deadlocked until the Seals had a small explosion in the home half of the eighth that drove Bamberger from the hill. On a two-strike count Pearson got his second single. Hatton, batting second, hit a grounder to Marshall at first. But he never got a handle on the ball and when the dust settled Pearson was on third and Hatton on first. A second single by Keough sent Pearson to the plate for run number two, Hatton to second, and Bamberger to the showers. Reliever Dick Marlowe came in, got Renna, walked Kellert, and should have had an inning-ending double play on an Aspromonte grounder, but it was muffed and Hatton scored the Seals' third and final run.

In an interview following Tuesday's game, Charlie Metro predicted that the Seals were the team to beat in the Pacific Coast League and that his team was the one most likely to do it.

In the six face-offs left in the series, the Seals closed the gap with the Mounties to just one game. Activity off the field was busy for both clubs. Injury-prone pitcher Ted Bowsfield, born in British Columbia, Canada, was optioned to AA Oklahoma City from San Francisco, and the Mounties were bolstered when Baltimore optioned slugger Tito Francona (father of future Red Sox manager Terry) to them. Though the loss of Bowsfield was insignificant, the addition of Francona made Vancouver a stronger and more threatening force in the league.

After two hours and nine minutes of baseball on Wednesday, the Seals had played themselves into 5–3 victory and a tie for the PCL lead with Vancouver with matching 9–4 records. It was an action-filled two hours! After Vancouver drew first blood with a run in the first inning and the Seals matched it in the second, the contest took on all characteristics of a pitching duel between Duane Pillette and Babe Birrer, with umpire Chris Pelekoudas calling balls and strikes, though not very well ... at least according to Joe Gordon.

Tension heightened in the fifth inning when the Seals put another run on the board, and then turned to fireworks in the seventh when Marty Keough bunted but was hit by the ball and called out when Pelekoudas ruled the ball fair. Gordon charged him in loud protest, declaring it foul. The "discussion" was brief, the call remained unchanged, and Gordon got the heave-ho, his first of the season. Thanks to doubles off the bats of Aspromonte and Malmberg with runners on, the Seals collected two more runs in the inning. With the score 5–1 the Mounties tried to come back late, but fell short. It was Pillette's third consecutive win.

When teammates kidded Pillette about his pitching "not giving the other team a chance," it's said that he explained that he owed it all to his Dad, Herman "Old Folks" Pillette, who retired after 25 minor league seasons at age 49 with a 264–264 record. Duane didn't get to watch him pitch very much as a child because the family didn't live in the same city as his team. But when he was a teenager he used to sneak away from home and watch him pitch with the Padres at old Lane Field, where he also sold peanuts. His father discouraged him from making baseball his career, but Duane's love of the game was the deciding factor.

Riverboat Smith pitched a three-hit shutout on Thursday, his first complete game since May 19, 1956, 26 starts ago, to give the Seals a full game edge over the Mounties on top of the league. The Seals smacked nine runs on 11 hits as Bill Renna led the pack with three including a massive homer over the left field fence, while Aspromonte and Kellert each had two. While Nini Tornay nursed his split thumb and was limited to warm-up duties in the bullpen, Eddie Sadowski took over behind the plate and added hits to the box score.

Things were different on Friday. The Mounties came out swinging from the words "Play ball!" Their 16-hit onslaught humiliated starter Walt Masterson and three relievers (Bert Thiel, Tommy Hurd, and Bill Abernathie) as they inflicted the worst beating of the season on the Seals. The 12–3 score was only part of the story. The Seals lost the services of Grady Hatton for at least a week when he suffered a groin pull in the fourth inning while running on a fly ball to right dropped by Tito Francona.

Veteran pitcher Mel Held scattered eight Seals hits that produced two tallies in the first and one more in the second, then nothing more. The men from British Columbia sent ten batters to the plate and drove five of them home in the second inning and again in the ninth.

Around the horn in the league, the Angels defeated the Solons, 3–2, for the second game in a row in Sacramento; after a dense fog rolled in at Gilmore Field the Portland-Hollywood game was called in the top of the fourth inning due to the "fog out"; and Seattle one-upped San Diego. All that resulted in a three-way tie for first between Seattle, Vancouver, and San Francisco as the Seals went from a game out to sole possession of first to this tie in a matter of a few days.

But they bounced back Saturday in front of 6,011 excited fans when they sent a dozen men to the plate in the fifth inning. They all used their best bats, and by the time the third out was made Marty Keough, Bob DiPietro, Frank Kellert, Eddie Sadowski, and Joe Tanner all singled, and Tommy Umphlett, Kellert, and Tanner also doubled.

Leo Kiely was in charge all the way for the Seals for his second win against no defeats. It was his first complete game since he twirled for the Army in Japan in 1953. Bill Renna's name was added to those in sick bay when he left the game in the fourth inning with a severe muscle pull in his leg. At the end of the day the Seals reclaimed sole possession of first place with two games left in the series, the Sunday doubleheader. Although the Seals won the series four games to three, they were obviously not satisfied.

Monday morning sports pages summed up Sunday's activities in front of the largest crowd of the season, 12,940, as "from first to fourth." The score of 5–4 appeared twice in the twin bill with the Seals on the short end both times. Actually, they were tied for fourth with Lefty O'Doul's Seattle club, one and a half games behind the new league leader, Los Angeles. Over the course of the afternoon Dorish logged his first loss against three wins, Marty Keough walloped his first homer of the season, and pinch-hitter Bill Renna hobbled to the plate with the bases loaded in the seventh of the nightcap and struck out. Grady Hatton appeared in the same capacity and managed a single but it was obvious he was not ready to return to the lineup as he literally hobbled to first base. At the same time, Tito Francona put the Seals on notice that he had found his power at the plate. Seals fans hated to see him come to bat because it always meant one thing for them: danger.

Monday the team boarded the plane and left for its first road trip in the nick of time to avoid what was described as a "serious heat wave" in the Bay Area that included record high temperatures of 85 degrees in San Francisco. Ken Aspromonte remembered, "Travel in the PCL was as good if not better than the major leagues at that time. We traveled by commercial prop jet."

With the May 11 deadline less than three weeks away, Joe Gordon made announcements regarding some roster moves: pitcher Al Schroll was optioned to AA Oklahoma City, while pitcher Roy Tinney would stay behind awaiting future assignment (optioned to AAA Indianapolis); Nini Tornay didn't make the trip due to his split thumb; Bill Renna went despite medical advice to remain behind; and with Grady Hatton down with a groin pull, leaving third base vulnerable, pitcher and former infielder Bob Thollander, who carried a dependable bat, remained behind to work on third base drills "just in case." Others attempting to play through injury included Ken Aspromonte (groin), Joe Tanner (sore throwing arm), and Marty Keough (slight leg pull). Though Gordon was naturally concerned with so many injuries, he decided not to ask for some new recruits from Boston.

The team traveled north for two rematches, first against Seattle, then Vancouver. As it had been since the first experiment in 1946 with broadcasts of Saturday games, die-hard Bay Area fans now kept up with all home and road games on radio station KSFO, with skilled and beloved broadcaster Don Klein. He did not travel with the team and did his play-by-play recreations roughly 15 minutes behind the action. It was just like being there for his listeners. Because he took on additional broadcasting tasks in the Bay Area, his duties with the 1957 Seals were shared with Bob Fouts. Both were inducted into the Bay Area Radio Hall of Fame, Class of 2008.

On Monday, April 29, a travel day, the club headed for Seattle where they played the role of the gray-clad visitors in the Rainiers' home opener in Sick's Stadium, built in 1938 and named for Emil Sick, who owned the team and the local Rainier Brewing Company. While people in San Francisco and throughout the Bay Area endured what the papers called "a dangerous heat wave," the Seals endured a dilemma of their own in the day-night doubleheader.

Before game time a surprised Gordon learned of a complicated trade involving Washington, Boston, and Detroit which would send 35-year-old versatile infielder Jack Phillips to meet the club in Vancouver for the next series. Unfortunately, that was the best news the Bay Nine got that day, as they dropped both games to the Suds, the second twin bill they'd lost in three days, four losses in a row which pushed them into the second division in fifth place.

In the afternoon game Duane Pillette had a rematch with Red Munger. On an abnormally warm 80-degree, sunny day in Seattle, the Seals trailed 2–0 through six innings. Seattle put up four more runs in the bottom of the seventh, three of those on a huge Joe Taylor home run hit off reliever Jim Konstanty. But the fight wasn't over, as the Seals avoided the shutout and put up four runs of their own in the top of the eighth, making the score 6–4. But they couldn't catch up in the ninth, thwarting Pillette's effort to collect his fourth win in four attempts.

Bert Thiel, in his first start, fared no better when he faced Larry Jansen under the lights in game two. Seattle drove eight runners across the dish, six of them attributed to two more homers off the bat of Joe Taylor, giving him nine RBI for the day, and was described in the morning papers as "the greatest thing to hit Seattle since the pontoon bridge." Jansen had a whitewash going with two outs in the ninth, when the Seals saved face as Marty Keough walked and was driven in by a Sal Taormina double, his second hit of the day. But they still came up seven runs short.

Meanwhile, Bill Renna had been put on notice by his personal physician, the team doctor, and trainer Leo "Doc" Hughes that his leg injury was worsening and required complete rest.

As the May 11 deadline to reduce the club to 21 players approached, everyone speculated about who would be cut and who would remain to complete the season. Most of the chatter that "analyzed" the situation under the "guidance" of the media concluded that outfielder Hal Grote, pitchers Al Schroll, Jim Konstanty and Walt Masterson, plus old favorites Bob DiPietro and possibly Sal Taormina, might find themselves on the trading list, or worse. The thought of losing Taormina and DiPietro evoked mixed emotions on all fronts and weighed heavily on Gordon.

But that didn't put a damper on DiPietro's stories. After "some" encouragement, he told the one about how Lefty O'Doul was responsible for his career.

> When I was in high school former Seals outfielder Neill Sheridan was one of our coaches, and I knew he was good friends with Lefty O'Doul. So I asked Sheridan if he could get permission for me to work out with the Seals at Seals Stadium sometime. O'Doul was the manager and said, "Sure, let the kid come out and we'll take a look at what he's got." O'Doul liked me and said, "Kid,

come out any time you want." To cut to the chase, at that time *Esquire* magazine used to sponsor a game pitting teams east and west of the Mississippi
River against each other, all high school players. They scouted probably hundreds of games and eliminated players until they had enough for two teams
left. I had one of those lucky days when they watched my team and got
selected. Under the auspices of the magazine they sent us all to New York for
the "big final game." I represented the west. When I got back there the manager of the eastern team was Babe Ruth, and our manager was Ty Cobb. Can
you imagine? "Oh my gosh, I thought, here are two of baseball's icons and I'm
preparing to play in front of both of them!" It was really something. But they
were not the heroes I had expected because they used a lot of foul language
and weren't too friendly.

When the month ended the Seals had put together a 12–9 record that
landed them in fifth place, two games behind first-place Los Angeles, with
Hollywood, Vancouver, and Seattle tied for second at one game back. San
Diego, Sacramento, and Portland filled the sixth, seventh and eighth slots.
The gap between first and last place had already stretched to ten games.

Renna remembered being disappointed with his April performance.

Before the season started in 1957 there was a lot of stuff in the papers about
my joining the team because a lot of people in the Bay Area remembered when
I played football with the [University of Santa Clara] Broncos, and they knew
I had spent time in the big leagues. As for the season, well, I remember how I
didn't have a good start and the fans didn't like me and called me all sorts of
names. I was in one of those slumps for almost the entire month of April and
just wasn't getting it done at the plate. I had a couple of good hits but no con-
sistency. When that happens the dugout seems a long, long way from the bat
rack when you had to walk up to get your bat. Because of all the preseason
press and then starting in a slump, the fans yelled, "Take your press clippings
and see how much they help you hit," and things like that. But that happens
on occasion and the swing was out of sync. Everybody on the team told me to
stick with it and use the swing that earned all the press in the first place. Eventually things returned to normal and the team and I both had a good year. In
fact, after that early slump I had some hot streaks, and I don't know why, but
they were timely.

Joe Gordon was a very good manager who helped everybody out and
didn't force you to do things you weren't accustomed to doing. He told
me, he said, "Go up to that plate, button your top button or whatever makes
you comfortable up there, and swing that bat!" I remember one time when
we were playing against the Angels and I'd hit a homerun and we were ahead.
I was up for my last at bat in the game and decided I would really swing. I
was going for it. So they threw me a high fastball and I hit that thing solid. I
don't think I'd ever hit one that hard because I was swinging with everything
I had. And the ball was a huge shot that went straight ahead and bounced
off the scoreboard in center field. I couldn't believe it! So when I went back to
the dugout I told him, "Well, I did what you asked me to do," and he just
smiled.

Meanwhile, away from the diamond, news about the pending move of major league baseball was relegated to the back burner while fans and teams throughout the league settled down for the new season. In San Francisco the small crowd of 6,421 on opening day fell far short of the 12,000 to 15,000 anticipated, and since the franchise knew the size of its fan base would be an important element in the effort to lure major league baseball, concern about attendance became the focus.

FOUR

May

May 1–May 5 (Wednesday–Sunday) at Seattle
May 7–May 12 (Tuesday–Sunday) at Vancouver
May 14–May 19 (Tuesday–Sunday) home vs. Los Angeles
May 21–May 26 (Tuesday–Sunday) at San Diego
May 28–June 2 (Tuesday–Friday) home vs. Sacramento

To date they had only seen Portland, Seattle, and Vancouver in April, and half the league remained untested. They entered May facing a heavy schedule: on the road at Seattle and Vancouver, home against Los Angeles, at San Diego, then back home facing Sacramento.

Lefty O'Doul's Rainiers had already proved themselves tough opponents in the opener, and the San Francisco squad knew they had their work cut out for them. Because of the scheduling in the final days of April, the series opener in Seattle was Wednesday, rather than the usual Tuesday. The Seals approached the challenge determined to break through the blockade of the trio tied for second. Riverboat Smith got the task of containing pitcher Lou Kretlow when they faced the Suds. Earlier that day it was announced that young outfielder Hal Grote, who batted .271 in nine games, was optioned to AA Oklahoma City with the knowledge that his potential had been recognized and expectations for his future were good. Veteran Jim Konstanty was given his outright release. Gordon was unsuccessful in his efforts to find a new home for him.

Determined to return to their winning ways, the team hit the diamond running. By the end of the second inning they owned a 3–1 lead thanks to an excuse-me single by Smith himself with the bases loaded that scored two. The third tally was driven home by an Albie Pearson sac fly. Seattle's second and final run came in the fifth when switch-hitting Maury Wills hit a single with two aboard. But the boys from the California weren't finished, as they pushed across another duo in the eighth when Pearson hit his third single of the night to score Tanner and Sadowski.

In addition to Smith's win, other Seals highlights included a booming triple by Marty Keough, two singles by Ken Aspromonte, and a single and double by Joe Tanner in his first game back in the lineup. Thursday morning sports pages cleverly said, "The Seals floated out of the wilderness of defeat aboard the Riverboat."

The 4–1 victory was tempered by other news of the day. San Francisco fans were heart-broken to learn that Boston had sold popular Bob DiPietro to the San Diego Padres for an undisclosed amount of money in order to make room for LHP Jack Spring. It was reported that Boston took a loss in the deal in order to honor DiPietro's request to remain in the Pacific Coast League. At the time of the sale he toted a .364 batting average in six games and looked forward to being a right-handed bat on the predominately left-handed hitting Padres squad.

The Seals struggled through another disappointing game on Thursday in which they carried a 4–0 lead into the bottom of the fifth inning when things got out of hand. The Rainiers, led by former S.F. catcher Ray Orteig, exploded against Leo Kiely for four runs to tie the score, then clinched it with a two-run seventh followed by two more in the eighth. This 8–4 loss gave Kiely his first loss as a starter and the team a 12–10 record, still two games behind the top four clubs. Around the league, the Padres occupied sixth (4.5 back), the Solons fell to seventh (8 back), and the Beavers brought up the rear in eighth (9.5 back).

While standing around the batting cage during pregame workouts, the players expressed concern about the condition of Cleveland's hot young pitcher Herb Score, who was hit in the face by a line drive off the bat of Yankees batter Gil McDougald on May 7. Years later McDougald told me that event was the worst of his baseball life. He was so shaken he decided to retire from the game if Score were left unable to pitch, and he was timid at the plate for a long time afterward. Score did return to the mound but was never the same and eventually became a broadcaster for the Indians.

Friday night, Harry Dorish pitched a four-hit shutout, his second of the season, that included eight strikeouts and allowed the Seals to post a 9–0 win, with five of those tallies driven in by Frank Kellert. It was a night for overcoats for the 4,550 fans in the seats. One of them was one of the best outfielders in PCL history, Earl Averill, part of the famed 1920s Seals outfield of Averill, Roy Johnson, and Smead Jolley.

There were colorful events in the game. When Tom Umphlett hit a long double to right, the runner on base, Aspromonte, charged for the plate but tripped rounding third, fell flat on his face, and was thrown out. He got up with a sheepish grin on his face and hustled into the visitors' dugout. With the writing on the wall in the eighth inning, O'Doul sent infielder Jack Lohrke to the mound to get the final six outs and save his pitching staff for another day. All the fans knew his dramatic story.

Jack Lohrke was mustered out of the military in 1946 and returned to San Diego but was soon optioned to the Spokane Indians in the Northwest League, where he remained until late June when he was called back to San Diego. After a night game the team left by bus for a series in Bremerton and Lohrke caught a plane to San Diego. It was a rainy night and the roads were slick. On the way, one of baseball's worst tragedies occurred when the bus swerved to avoid an oncoming car in the wrong lane, went over a 300-foot cliff, and burst into flames. Eight players were killed instantly and a ninth died a few days later. Many others were seriously injured. Because fate put him in a different place a few hours earlier, he was forever after dubbed "Lucky" Lohrke.

On Saturday, Seattle played a bunting game that took the Seals by surprise. Bob Thollander, who did not remain behind in San Francisco to learn third base when it was learned that Jack Phillips was on his way, took the mound against Red Munger in what was an eye-opening defeat for the Seals to say the least.

Seattle baffled their opponents with nine hits, four of them bunts that didn't travel as far as 25 feet. The strategy to confuse and agitate the non-third baseman, Ken Aspromonte, and other infielders worked to a tee as the Rainiers put two runs on the board in the first, two more in the fifth, and one more in the eighth while the befuddled Seals defense was little better than a comedy of errors with overthrown balls, missed balls, and dropped flies. They did manage a couple of mini-rallies but were stifled for the most part until they got their only run, unearned, in the seventh.

Things got hot in the fifth. Thollander purposely walked Jim Dyck to load the bases and face Bobby Balcena. However, like most best-laid plans, it didn't work out that way. Tempers flared when the umpire ruled that Balcena was hit by a pitch which sent him to first base and pushed across a run. Gordon sprang out of the dugout shouting that the ball hit the bat and veered into Balcena's arm, making it a foul ball, and all runners should return to their bases. However, Gordon overstayed his welcome in that argument and got the boot for the second time that year.

The small crowd of 5,000-plus at the Sunday doubleheader was understandable because of the well-hyped and very popular Apple Cup Hydroplane Races, Seattle's answer to the Indianapolis 500, at the end of the month. Nini Tornay rejoined the team late Saturday, taped thumb and all, ready to give Eddie Sadowski a breather behind the plate in the second game while Gordon waited impatiently for the arrival of his two Jacks, Phillips and Spring. Still adjusting before the deadline, Gordon evaluated Leo Kiely's strengths and strongly considered moving him to the bullpen as the number one reliever if Spring could successfully assume a starting role.

Rumors were floating that Joe Gordon and Lefty O'Doul actually agreed on something: that young shortstop Maury Wills had the best throwing arm in the minors with above-average speed, but would have to hit more than bunts to make it in the majors.

San Francisco faced Sunday's encounter knowing they needed to take both ends if they wanted to split the series at four games apiece. Pillette easily earned win number four by a margin of 8–3 when his teammates supported him with a 15-hit, eight-run barrage that included a homer that Marty Keough hit out of town. On the other hand, the defeat in game two was the kind that left everyone shaking his head in disbelief. Bert Thiel gave up two homers before he exited in favor of Leo Kiely in the second inning. With seven innings to close the gap, they were unable to deliver and took the 3–2 loss. Not only did the Suds hang on to take the closer, they handed the Seals their first lost series of the season.

Seattle had climbed over them and reached second place in the league standings, which was not good since all the experts rated San Francisco as the better team. Even worse, the three-way tie for second was broken and the Seals were left at the bottom of that group, three games behind league-leading Los Angeles followed by Seattle, Vancouver, and Hollywood. But that turned out to be temporary.

After the game a tired Seals team eagerly boarded the bus for what turned out to be a relaxed, quiet, 140-mile drive to Vancouver to face the Mounties Tuesday night in Capilano Stadium. However, as was pointed out by the morning press, although Seattle won the series, Lefty O'Doul and others were amazed at the similarity of marks stacked up by the two foes: San Francisco out-hit Seattle 73–64, but were outscored 35–34; Albie Pearson intimidated Rainiers pitchers as he posted a .367 average; the Seals logged a .269 team batting average to .262 for the Suds; and Seattle noted a formidable Seals pitching staff, especially southpaws Riverboat Smith and Leo Kiely. Different newspaper articles concluded, in essence, that, "all things considered, the Seals came out of last week's fuss with the Rainiers in pretty good shape ... lost the series but began to resemble the team experts and fans thought they would be."

Capilano Stadium in Vancouver, rebuilt in 1951 after a devastating fire had reduced it to rubble, was a popular destination for all the teams in the league. But it had a serious problem: Canadian Blue Laws which originally prohibited baseball on Sunday but were later revised to permit play within specified hours only.

After the off-day Monday, May 6, both teams came to the park refreshed and eager to win on Tuesday. The opener turned out to be a 31-hit slugfest in which neither Riverboat Smith nor undefeated Mel Held could contain

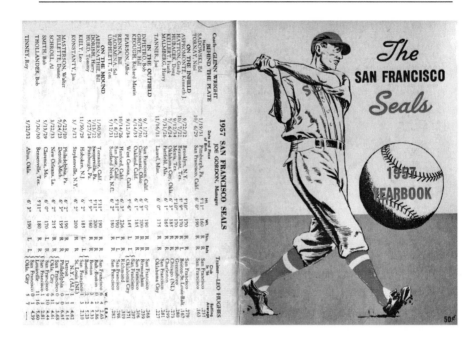

1957 Seals Yearbook cover (Doug McWilliams Collection).

the batters. Although every position player on both teams got at least one hit, the game turned out to be a nail-biter. The Seals were out-hit 17–14, but they managed to outlast their hosts. The scoring started in the third inning when the Seals drove three runs across. They added three more in the fourth, then one each in the fifth and sixth, which left them ahead by one, 8–7, approaching the eighth. At that time Gordon allegedly detected lackadaisical defense by the Mounties and took full advantage of the situation. After Kellert (competent, but no speedster on the base paths) walked, Aspromonte pumped a double to right. Gordon waved Kellert home. Kellert later joked that he was out of breath for a week after that dash around the bases. The Mounties managed to get one more run on the board in the bottom of that inning which left them behind, 9–8, and that's how the action ended.

The Seals had many highlights: a first-inning single by Marty Keough kept his hitting streak alive; Grady Hatton played his first game at shortstop in ten years and, though a little stiff at the end, he was an obvious catalyst that solidified the entire infield, not to mention going 2-for-4 for the day; Tom Umphlett, in one of his rare starts, went 3-for-5 including a double; Ken Aspromonte got a single and double in three official trips; and Harry Malmberg, Nini Tornay, and Riverboat Smith each tapped Vancouver hurlers for singles.

The press gave Tornay credit for the "most spectacular" play of the game in one filled with exciting activity. It was a "wham-bam" play in the sixth when Mounties catcher Lenny Neal tried to stretch a single into a double but tripped as he rounded first. Tornay ran up the line to cover the bag after Kellert lunged for the ball and missed. Pearson fielded it down the line in right and threw a bullet to Tornay, who let Neal tag himself out on his return to first.

Infielder Jack Phillips arrived that afternoon, worked out with the team during batting practice, and was ready for action whenever called. Young Jack Spring was still in transit.

The game on Thursday went into the books as a 3–2 comeback victory for Vancouver as they handed the second loss to an unhappy Pennsylvania plumber, Harry Dorish. In Jack Phillips' debut at third, which sent Aspromonte back to shortstop, he batted in the second slot and started the scoring when he doubled and was driven home by a Kellert line drive single in the first inning. The Seals put the Mounties on notice in every inning but were only able to score twice thanks to frustrating double plays. A unique play put the Seals ahead in the sixth when Marty Keough struck out swinging but the ball got by the catcher and he got to first ahead of the throw. That not only gave the Seals a fourth out in the frame, but gave them their second run when he eventually scored.

With the game tied at two apiece, outfielder Jake Crawford crushed a homer into the stratosphere in the seventh that put the home boys ahead by one. In a desperate attempt to get more tallies, with two down in the top of the ninth and Kellert on first thanks to a long single, pinch-hitter Sal Taormina slammed a double, sending him to third. But it was his final stop as Nini Tornay's infield grounder ended the game.

Despite taking ten innings to do it on Friday, the Seals walked away with a 5–4 victory and a tie for third place with Seattle. They logged a dozen hits, led by Ken Aspromonte who got his third in the top of the tenth with two outs, driving Keough home to take the lead. Leo Kiely, on the mound in relief of a sore-armed Pillette, got the win. The Mounties could have used the services of Tito Francona's big bat but he had been recalled to Baltimore.

Saturday, May 11, was the big day for Gordon and the Seals, deadline day when all team rosters had to be reduced to 21 players by midnight. But for the players it was first-things-first. They had a game to win.

For Riverboat Smith, things struck closer to home when he learned mid-afternoon that his little son Roger, who was badly burned by a spilled pot of coffee during spring training, was scheduled for emergency surgery the next morning. In response, he requested and was granted permission to pitch out of order and start the game so he could fly home to be with his family. But he wasn't his usual self on the hill, got into trouble early and left the game in the second inning behind, 3–0. Relievers Bob Thollander, Bill Abernathie, and Bert Thiel were unable to corral the Mounties.

The Seals were flat the entire game, which temporarily dashed their hopes of climbing closer to the top of the PCL pack. If it weren't for a single by Frank Kellert in the fifth inning and another by Nini Tornay in the sixth that resulted in the Seals' only run, Mounties hurler Charlie Beamon could have added a no-hitter to his resume.

The press had a field day colorfully describing the 12–1, 13-hit onslaught as a game in which "the Seals succumbed to a brutal lacing," as the "marauding Mounties" got their second win of the series. While the Seals pitchers "suffered statistical mutilation" Beamon struck out eight and enjoyed "a riotous night at the plate" as he went 3-for-3 plus a walk. The hosts now led the series three games to two against the struggling visitors.

In another call that afternoon, Joe Gordon finally heard from Jack Spring, already missing for ten days in Gordon's mind, saying he was home in Spokane, Washington, and would report to San Francisco in time for Tuesday's game. A cold, authoritative, and annoyed Gordon told him he had better be ready to go, and brusquely hung up.

Spring remembered:

> By then I was married and had two little girls aged one and three. It was a little difficult, but I drove cross country to Spokane and left my family back home. It took several days and made Joe mad because he thought I had dilly-dallied. When I went to San Francisco I was a starter. Kind of the way it worked in those days was that younger pitchers were usually starters. I was 24 and the Red Sox wanted me to be a starter at that time. Relieving was not that big of a deal then like it is now. Back then the prospects were the starters, and the 'other guys' would be worked into the pen as relievers.

In order to escape back to the United States with a series win, the Seals faced two must-win games on Sunday. They were on their way to that achievement with a 5–2 victory in game one. But things were different in the nightcap. The game was close until Bert Thiel started a four-run rally when he hit a low line drive that hit pitcher Mel Held squarely in the knee and literally knocked him off the mound. By the end of that inning the Seals were in the lead, 4–2, with one out in the sixth inning of the seven-inning contest when the game was suspended due to the six o'clock curfew, for the second Sunday in a row, and was slated for completion on August 10 before the regularly scheduled ballgame.

Bert Thiel got his first win of the season in game one when he relieved starter Walt Masterson in what turned out to be his last hurrah with the Seals. On a more positive note, Seals power at the plate was emerging: Albie Pearson, commonly dubbed "Mighty Mite" or "Mighty Mouse," hit a healthy home run and Tommy Umphlett collected a triple.

Whew! It was a hard-fought road trip in which they broke even in 14 games. Players were tired. Though Joe Gordon had met the 21-man player limit, his dilemma wasn't resolved. He had many good players and now had to figure out how to get maximum production from them. Eventually he decided to leave Renna in left and Keough in center, but would try a platoon system with Pearson and Umphlett in right (even though both batted left-handed) and possibly Hatton and Aspromonte at third, a move designed to use the right-left-handed batters against the pitchers faced; Phillips, Malmberg, and Tanner would cover short or second with Kellert at first. One aspect of his plan was met with immediate protest by the press and fans, who complained that Aspromonte, although insecure at third, was "much too good a hitter to bench for even five minutes."

Gordon knew paring down a team with too many talented players was a problem any manager would envy, but with an eye on the PCL pennant he intended to "get it right."

The team returned to San Francisco to host what was called a "crucial seven-game set," May 14–19, with the Los Angeles Angels, current occupants of first place, just a half-game ahead of the Hollywood Stars.

The Angels were the 1956 Pacific Coast League champions with a 107–61 record under skipper Bob Scheffing, who was named manager of the Chicago Cubs in 1957. Longtime minor league manager Clay Bryant took the helm of the team, and there was a little surprise that they had a slim lead they were not predicted to hold one month into the 1957 campaign because players like Gene Mauch and Jim Bolger, who had helped them win last year, were gone. In their stead new faces appeared: future Hall of Fame manager George "Sparky" Anderson at second base, veteran outfielders Bert Hamric and Tom Saffell, third baseman Jim Baxes from Portland, and shortstop Wally Lammers.

From their fans' perspective, the best news was that big number 30, Steve Bilko, returned at first base. In 1956 he was named Most Valuable Player in the Pacific Coast League for the second consecutive year, and he won the Triple Crown (162 games, .360 average, 55 homers, 164 RBI). The career of this likeable and popular slugger was an enigma. He played 13 minor league seasons interlaced with 600 major league games with six different teams, but the three seasons with Los Angeles, 1955–1957, went uninterrupted. In the minors he logged a career batting average of .312 with 313 homers, 56 of those in 1957 when his batting average "slumped" to .300. But he was never able to master major league pitching and posted a .249 career average at that level. Anyone who saw Pacific Coast League baseball games, regardless of the team they followed, knew of him and respected his talent. Today, almost 60 years later, when asked for memories of that era, everyone mentions Steve Bilko.

As the Gordons began this series, San Francisco fans hoped their heroes would upset league standings as other teams faced each other as follows: first-place Vancouver hosted weak San Diego, seventh-place Portland faced the cellar-dwelling Solons in Sac town, and Seattle challenged Hollywood at Gilmore Field. The Seals started three games behind with an eye to gaining ground with the help of the other teams. The series, filled with exciting moments, was no disappointment.

In the first game Gordon gave the ball to Harry Dorish to face San Francisco's Mission High School graduate Dickie Hanlon. Thanks to a two-run homer from Jim Baxes, older brother of one-time Seals third baseman Mike Baxes, the Pennsylvania plumber looked at a two-run deficit in the first inning, then was driven from the hill before he could get the third out in the second after yielding two more runs. Riverboat Smith and relievers Kiely and Thiel all pitched respectably, giving up just one more run in the fifth, but the game was already out of the reach. Both teams were limited to just five hits but Los Angeles made each one count. The Seals scored their only run in the bottom of the third when Eddie Sadowski tripled and was driven home by a Harry Malmberg single. It was a well-played game on both sides, with the outcome decided in the first inning by the Baxes homer. Final score: Angels 5, Seals 1. Harry Dorish took his third loss against four wins. The small crowd of 2,758 went home disappointed but not disillusioned.

The Seals claimed a much-needed 8–5 victory on Wednesday. In the home half of the third inning, with the Seals behind 3–1, starter Duane Pillette was replaced by pinch-hitter Ken Aspromonte, who sent a long single to left. By the time the third out was made the game was tied at three and Thollander made his way to the hill. The game was settled by an eighth-inning blitz by San Francisco that started when Frank Kellert doubled, then scored on a Bill Renna single, and continued with a Jack Phillips double that brought L.A. pitcher Jim Hughes to the mound in relief. Things didn't improve much for the L.A. crew as Hughes promptly walked Nini Tornay, who ran home on a double by Joe Tanner. After a one-two-three ninth, Thollander collected his second win that brought his record to 2–2 with a 3.52 ERA. Shortly thereafter he was sent to the Oklahoma City Indians in the AA Texas League. At the same time Hollywood beat Seattle and the Angels found themselves in second place, a half-game behind the Twinks, and the Seals moved to fourth, two and a half back.

According to Bill Renna,

One thing that always kept us focused was Joe Gordon. He was a very good manager who helped everybody out and didn't force you to do things you weren't accustomed to doing. He told me and other hitters he thought may be struggling a little bit from time to time, "Go up to that plate, button your top button or whatever makes you comfortable up there, and swing that bat!" I remember one time when we were playing against the Angels and I'd hit a home run and we were ahead. I was up for my last at-bat in the game and decided I would really swing. I was going for it. So they threw me a high fastball and I hit that thing solid. I don't think I'd ever hit one that hard because I was swinging with everything I had. And the ball was a huge shot that went straight ahead and bounced off the scoreboard in center field. I couldn't believe it! So when I went back to the dugout I told him, "Well, I did what you asked me to do," and he just smiled.

Simultaneously things were busy behind the scenes. Pitcher John "Windy" McCall, acquired from the New York Giants after he pitched just three innings in 1957, arrived, and veteran Walt Masterson (1–2, 4.95 ERA) was given his unconditional release. Marty Keough, who had been hospitalized briefly with a curious stomach ailment, was expected to return to the lineup in a day or two. Also, Steve Bilko, the 1956 PCL Triple Crown winner, a perennial home run basher with the Angels who had been sidelined with a shoulder injury attributed to his numerous hard swings for the fences, was expected back in time to torment the Seals. Fortunately the big man was seen only once in a pinch-hit role and he went 0-for-1. Sometimes it really is better to be lucky than good!

San Diego general manager Ralph Kiner announced that the Padres had fired manager Bob Elliott and replaced him with former longtime minor leaguer George Metkovich to help with the club's morale. Despite the Pads' recent 9–7 record, Kiner said the team was far better than the record indicated and he owed the change to his players to enable them to realize their potential.

In a complete-game effort on Thursday, Dorish got his fifth win and third shutout of the season as the Seals got to Ben Flowers for three runs in the first inning. Though that was all they needed, they added three more for good measure and nailed down a 6–0 win. Ken Aspromonte got a night of rest as the infield was manned by Phillips (3B), Malmberg (SS), Tanner (2B), and ever-reliable Frank Kellert at first.

While Gordon and the team focused on the series at hand, Walter Mails and his assistants prepared for the Seals Old Timers' Game scheduled for Saturday. Although Joe DiMaggio sent his regrets saying he was unable to attend the festivities, the game was to feature the famed 1928 outfield of Earl Averill, Roy Johnson, and Smead Jolley. California governor Goodwin J. Knight would be on hand to present a congratulatory scroll to former Angels outfielder Sam Crawford, the newest member of the Baseball Hall of Fame.

Friday was one of those games that some would refer to later as "one of those typical minor league games." It had showered on and off all day and Angels manager Clay Bryant wanted a postponement, saying the field was too wet and unsafe for the players. Chief umpire Mel Steiner, known as a rather hard-nosed fellow, disagreed and the game started on time. With fewer than 2,500 fans in the stands, Steiner called "play ball" and the competition began, that is, until Bryant demonstrated his dissatisfaction by going out to the mound to talk to his pitcher in the bottom of the first inning wearing a shiny McIntosh raincoat and matching hat! The Seals gave starter Tommy Hurd a quick 2–0 lead. The players endured the rain and wind until 9:11 p.m. when Steiner finally called the game. It washed away all stats, and the entire game would be replayed on August 5 or 6 when the L.A. crew returned.

Ironically, this was the second time that week that Hurd was the pitcher of record and had the lead in an incomplete game. He was on the mound five days earlier when the game against the Mounties was suspended. Meanwhile everyone's fingers were crossed that the rain would not put the skids on Saturday's Old Timers' Game.

To the disappointment of everyone, there was no Saturday baseball in Seals Stadium thanks to a mid-morning cloudburst. But Sunday was a different story. The sky was clear and the sun was shining as 7,687 noisy fans witnessed the home team eke out two come-from-behind victories. Bill Abernathie, in relief of Pillette, collected his first win of the year in game one. Highlights of game two included McCall's complete-game victory in his San Francisco debut. After a seventh-inning pinch-hit single, Ken Aspromonte experienced a career-changing moment when Joe Gordon had him remain in the game in his first appearance at second base. The Seals took the series four games to three and flew to San Diego a game and a half behind first-place Hollywood.

In between games on Sunday the canceled Old Timers' Game was celebrated without their anticipated ballgame when 77-year-old "Wahoo" Sam Crawford tearfully accepted a scroll honoring his induction into the Baseball Hall of Fame, and several Seals old timers still in the area were met with applause as they were introduced at home plate: Earl Averill, Ping Bodie, Del Young, Pard Ballou, Bill Steen, Gus Suhr, Joe Sprinz, Al Wright and two DiMaggio brothers, Vince and Dominic.

The scheduled eight-game set with the Padres in what the press described as "termite-tormented" Lane Field, the old wooden ballpark built by team owner William "Hardrock" Lane and completed in time for opening day of the 1936 season, was exciting. Since these two teams never faced each other in spring training, their inaugural encounter was the series opener on Tuesday night.

Looking back on the season, it seems odd now that the Portland Beavers were predicted by pre-season writers to be the best hitting team in the league and one of the hardest to beat. Perhaps it was because San Diego had a poor 1956 season in which they finished seventh with a 72–96 record, 35 games behind the pack. But the Padres were always a challenge in the hitting and pitching departments, and by mid-season they had become somewhat of a "force to be reckoned with," as the saying goes, thanks to the managerial change from Bill Posedel to George Metkovich.

The team was a balanced blend of youngsters on their way up the ladder and typical PCL veterans with varied amounts of major league experience under their belts. Probably the most noted in 1957 were 21-year-old RHP Jim "Mudcat" Grant, whose ultimate 18–7 record led the staff at the beginning of a long career, and RHPs Dick Brodowski and Vic Lombardi. Outfielders Rudy Regalado, Earl Averill, Jr., and Earl Rapp and infielder Al Federoff all intimidated opposing pitchers at home and on the road.

In his regular column "As Bill Leiser Sees It," the writer mentioned what he considered necessary strengths required to lead the PCL and eventually win the pennant. Based on prior seasons, teams that ended with a winning percentage of .600 usually walked away with the flag, and the Seals flew south at .595. To continue his point, he mentioned that recent batting statistics for the league showed that the five top spots were occupied by Seals: Grady Hatton, Sal Taormina, Frank Kellert, Joe Tanner, and Marty Keough. He concluded that the Seals had established themselves as the team to beat when they took the series with the Angels, dumping them to fourth place.

While the manager contemplated possible strategies against this foe from San Diego who had already improved with George Metkovich at the helm, the Seals players enjoyed a brief reunion with their old friend Bob DiPietro. Gordon was glad it was Harry Dorish's turn in the rotation, as he pitted his 5–3 record and 1.57 ERA (thanks to three shutouts) against RHP Pete Mesa. Gordon reasoned that San Diego was predominantly a right-handed pitching but left-handed batting club, which played right into the hands of the out-of-towners. He planned to use the left-handed bats of Sal Taormina and Grady Hatton which enhanced rather than diminished the club's threat.

When Gordon told Ken Aspromonte he was slated to own second base for the rest of the season and bat cleanup, it was a game changer for the team as well as a career-maker for the young infielder from Brooklyn. No more worries about defensive errors at short or third base, and time to focus on helping the team with his bat. Knowing cleanup batters hit with power, which Aspromonte did with extra-base hits though slugging home runs was not his forte, Gordon told him he was expected to put the ball in play, spray hits to all parts of the ball yard, and drive in as many runs as possible. Aspromonte never let him down. It was as if someone had waved a magic wand over his head once that issue was resolved. From that game forward he received recognition for his hard work and potential, and was more relaxed on the field, which rendered his defense almost flawless. As the season progressed there was no doubt that he was one of the 1957 stars of the Pacific Coast League.

With his back against the wall, and against his better judgment, a frustrated Gordon made another change that day when he explained to veteran Duane Pillette who had a 4–1 record and a 2.91 ERA, that the Seals had to let him go to make room for younger Red Sox prospects. Everyone was surprised by that one. Out of respect, Boston told Gordon to give him the opportunity, if he wanted it, to make his own deal with another team. He went to Seattle.

Bill Renna remembered,

> I hated to see Pillette go. He was quite a guy and a lot of fun to be around. He was my roomie on the road. I used to tell everybody that I didn't room with Pillette, I roomed with his bags! He was quite a pitcher, had good breaking stuff and everything. But they traded him when Boston said he had to go to make room on the roster for some of their pitchers who were almost major-league-ready. Duane was older [34] at that time and his big league days were behind him. So he went to Seattle and we faced him a couple of times after that.
>
> I especially remember way back when we faced each other in the major leagues. I'd get a base hit off him, break the bat, and the ball went dribbling through the infield, or I'd hit a pop-up that nobody could catch. I was always getting base hits off him without hitting him that well. And he still kids and says, "Hell, Bill, I kept you in the major leagues!"

Tommy Umphlett recalled, "I really missed the guy when he left. We got to know each other fairly well and we always joked around and kept things loose."

The Seals took the field anticipating their fifth consecutive win. However, the Padres had other ideas, handcuffed the team as they held them to just two hits, and won, 3–2. Harry. Dorish's penchant to toss the home run pitch was his downfall and cost him defeat number four.

The Seals turned things back in their favor by winning the next three games in the series. In an unusual game, to say the least, on Wednesday, they struggled past 11 strikeouts, took advantage of eight walks, and prevailed despite being out-hit, 11–5, to take the game, 3–2.

It took ten innings to do it, but Eddie Sadowski got the final RBI when he drew a walk with the bases loaded in the tenth. It was their fifth extra-inning victory. Ken Aspromonte manned second base flawlessly and contributed one hit as he was more comfortable now that he had found his permanent niche in that spot. The other four hits were by Harry Malmberg, Marty Keough, Frank Kellert, and Grady Hatton.

The newspapers laughingly reported that somebody plotted to keep the baseball fans up all night when the Thursday night double dip was scheduled. It turned out to be much more fun for the San Francisco nine than for their hosts as they clinched two victories, 5–3 behind Riverboat Smith, and 7–3 with Tommy Hurd on the hill. Leo Kiely relieved in the late frames in both games. During that effort he gave up a walk to Eddie Kazak, his first in 36⅓ innings pitched. And Aspromonte demonstrated how the lack of pressure in the field affected his hitting, as he collected five hits for the night.

League president Leslie O'Connor announced a substantial increase in the number of complaints filed from fans as well as visiting managers, including Joe Gordon, against the organist at Lane Field. He was requested to cease and desist from playing a funeral dirge as visiting players returned to their dugouts after striking out. Priceless. Only in the minor leagues! It was also announced that Sal Taormina was fined an undisclosed amount by the league for not wearing the required helmet liner while batting.

The Seals' little winning streak met its untimely end on Friday when Hank Aguirre out-pitched McCall for a 2–1 win, but both veterans did themselves proud that night. Jack Phillips got three of the Seals' five hits, one of which was a screaming home run and another a line drive that hit the outfield fence so hard fans jokingly said it rattled and started to fall down.

The Padres bested the Seals with homers Saturday, 7–6. In a nutshell, the Seals tied the game at six in the eighth thanks to a timely double by pinch-hitter Sal Taormina that brought his record in that role to 6-for-12, a .500 average. But the Padres put together the winning run in the bottom of the ninth with no outs. Riverboat Smith, the second reliever for Harry Dorish behind Bert Thiel, took the loss which moved his season record to the losing column at 3–4.

The two teams exchanged shutouts Sunday in games as different as night and day. The visitors from San Francisco managed one run in the first inning thanks to a Ken Aspromonte double, then Jack Spring held the hosts to five scattered hits for the victory. Albie Pearson, back in action in the leadoff spot, went 2-for-3.

By contrast, game two saw a difference of 13 runs between the winner and loser as the Padres managed to score 13 when only one was needed. There were no Seals footprints on the plate in that one! To make things worse, veteran pitcher Vic Lombardi coasted to his victory as he limited his foes to just one hit, an Aspromonte double, before the team was excused to return to the Bay Area with a disappointing 4–4 split. Gordon said he wasn't worried: "If we can break even on the road and win at home we'll do all right."

They were eager to get back to the emerald confines of Seals Stadium to face the lackluster Sacramento Solons, who limped into town with a 12–29 record and had occupied the basement for most of the season. Former Seals manager Tommy Heath, in his second season at the helm of the Solons, had led his team to a fifth-place finish (84–84) ahead of the sixth-place Seals (77–88) in 1956, and was well-liked by his players at every stop in his career.

But he was not given a strong team in 1957 and struggled all season to find some kind of winning combination. His most successful players were first baseman Nippy Jones, versatile infielder-outfielder Harry Bright, and outfielders Jim Greengrass, Al Heist, and former Seals first baseman Jimmy Westlake. In addition, despite having a pitching staff that included veterans Gene Bearden, Milo Candini, and Earl Harrist plus Marshall Bridges, Joe Stanka, and Roger Bowman, their collective record for the entire season was 63–105.

The Seals, on the other hand, brought a 26–19 record home with them, 11–11 on the road and 15–8 at home. Because the press laughingly referred to the Solons as a team that "couldn't beat the Molly Putts Bloomer Girls," Gordon called a quick clubhouse meeting after batting practice and gave his "play hard and stay on guard" speech in which he firmly warned his players not to underestimate that team and reminded them that Heath had been named co-manager of the year with Bob Scheffing (Angels) in 1956. He told them to remember the Sacs were coming off a 4–3 series win against Hollywood that knocked the Twinks out of first place.

In retrospect, what was initially predicted to be a "clash" between the two clubs turned out to be more like a "blitzkrieg," as the Seals rather easily took six of seven from the visitors.

Game one was the match-up of 6'6" Oklahoma youngster Joe Stanka, who would go on to play a few major league games in 1959, and 5'7" Tommy Hurd, with 99 big league appearances with Boston under his belt before 1957. That was the night Hurd got his revenge for the possible wins taken from him by curfew and rain. He blanked the Solons, 6–0, to make his season record 2–0. He was focused on the job at hand as he yielded just four hits, two of those by Jimmy Westlake, and didn't allow a runner past second base. The Seals put together six tallies with two walks and only seven hits: four singles divided among Keough, Malmberg, and Kellert (two), with a triple by Renna and a double and single by Aspromonte. Despite it being Family Night at the Stadium, only 1,857 showed up for the contest.

Still, it was an all-round good day for San Francisco. In addition to their own success, San Diego defeated Los Angeles, Vancouver aced Hollywood, and Portland topped Seattle.

It took ten innings and some fireworks to win Wednesday night. After the lead switched back and forth one run at a time and was tied at three apiece after nine, the Seals took charge in the home half of the tenth. It started when

Frank Kellert hit what should have been a routine grounder to short, but scooted through Leo Righetti's legs. He stole second on the next pitch to batter Jack Phillips. "Lanky Leo" took the throw to the bag and went ballistic when the runner was called safe. As he loudly stormed the umpire in protest, he threw his glove in the air, an offense for which PCL rules required automatic ejection from the game. When Righetti got tossed, Tommy Heath angrily joined the fray but was quickly ordered back to the dugout, and action continued. Phillips received an intentional walk and with two on base, Nini Tornay was pulled with a 1–2 count for pinch-hitter Sal Taormina, who walked to load the bases. Kellert was forced at home on a weak hit by Tommy Umphlett (in for the pitcher). Bases still loaded with Phillips on third, Taormina on second, and Umphlett on first, and Phillips scored the winning run when Albie Pearson got his second hit of the night, a zinging line drive that careened off the shin of first baseman Nippy Jones, and that was that. It was the sixth extra-inning win against no losses and the tenth game the Seals took by one run.

Before Thursday's two-game, 16-inning event, fans learned in the morning papers that infielder Joe Tanner, never able to play regularly due to painful back issues, had been optioned to Oklahoma City in the AA Texas League, where it was hoped the warmer climate would help him regain his form. Harry Malmberg owned shortstop, which added strength and dependability both offensively and defensively. To placate the left-right-handed batting zealots, Gordon decided to platoon Grady Hatton (batted left) and Jack Phillips (batted right) at third base.

That week the Malmberg family announced the birth of their first child, a baby daughter named Karen. Also, the publicity department put out the word that 3" × 3" stamp photos of each player would be given to each ticket-holder through September 15. The fans loved it.

Harry Dorish triumphed as he scattered nine hits in a complete-game shutout, his fourth, in game one. Jack Spring and Bert Thiel combined to take the nightcap, 4–2, but not without some excitement. In the third inning, when a balk was called on Spring and both Jack Phillips and Gordon charged umpire Chris Pelekoudas in a rowdy argument, they were both ejected. Then 10,807 irritated Seals fans on the premises kept up a high noise level in support of Spring and littered the field with their rented seat cushions.

However, Spring, obviously unnerved, proceeded to load the bases on walks before Jim Mangan belted a searing line drive to right. Thanks to the efforts of what was described as a theatrical event, speedy Albie Pearson ran down the ball and caught it just short of the wall, but his own momentum sent him crashing into it. With the wind knocked out of him, he fell over in a crumpled heap for a second, then pushed himself up against the wall and held up his glove to show the ball in it for the out before running forward hard to return the ball to the infield to stop advancing runners. It only cost Spring one run. The Seals retained the lead, 3–2, and no more Solons crossed the plate.

Friday, the last day of May, with three games left in the series over the weekend, it looked like lefty Marshall Bridges, who held the Seals to three hits and carried a 2–1 lead into the ninth, would collect a well-deserved win. But things changed on a play Kevin Costner might have staged in one of his movies about the game. Both managers got the boot for separate incidents in the bottom of the ninth, Gordon for a dirt-kicking dance at the plate while losing an argument about whether or not a pitch hit Marty Keough in the hand or hit the knob of his bat.

With the game deadlocked at two, it was Heath's turn. He exited angrily a few plays later after Aspromonte walked and the Sacs muffed a double play on a Bill Renna grounder to third. Frank Kellert was walked to load the bases when, with one out, lumbering Jack Phillips approached the plate and bashed a walk-off grand slam to take the game, 6–2. Riverboat Smith started the game, gave up an unearned run in the first and another in the third, then held the line through eight innings when he was lifted for pinch-hitter Nini Tornay. Bill Abernathie pitched the ninth and was credited with the comeback victory.

May ended with a bang for the team, especially since Vancouver was again defeated by Portland. The Seals were on a roll and approached June in a virtual tie with the Mounties atop the league, .005 percentage points behind, a mere technicality.

With Harry Malmberg Day scheduled for Sunday, he displayed his wares in Saturday's game by getting two hits in three at bats as the Seals thumped the Solons, 9–3. "Magnificent Marty" Keough, as he was branded by the local press, led the attack with two long hits. One was a triple in the sixth with Malmberg on first. After sliding into third, Keough quickly jumped up and scored when the throw back to the infield was off-target. Scheduled starter Windy McCall was scratched earlier in the day with a sore back and Jack Spring filled the spot, earning his second win against two 8losses.

Joe Gordon, in a jovial mood, was overheard laughing with friends after the game as he explained his curiosity about the fans. He said he'd never understand fans who sit in the farthest extremities of the parks and boo themselves buggy-eyed at ball and strike calls. How can they tell a ball from a strike from their location when the batters in the box, and some umpires, can't tell half the time?

The activities on Sunday in front of the third-largest crowd of the season,

11,124, began with the pregame celebration of Harry Malmberg Day. The non-flashy player contributed a quiet stability, first at second base and then at shortstop, that won him a special place in the hearts of the San Francisco fans. In addition to accolades from appreciative fans and gifts from local businessmen, he was honored by a variety of teen youth groups and youth teams he had coached and mentored over the years in nearby Antioch and Pittsburg.

The fans witnessed an interesting afternoon of baseball and saw things they may never have seen again, at least not all in the same day. Sportswriter Bob Stevens described this as "an unforgettable doubleheader punctuated by the skulling of an umpire, a strip-tease done by a catcher, and the establishing of an Olympic and American record for one manager getting tossed off the court." Between the first pitch of the afternoon and the last out, fans observed a colorful gamut of baseball moments.

When catcher Eddie Sadowski was given the day off to rest his aching back, Nini Tornay caught both games, got five hits for his trouble, and boosted his batting average from .189 to .250. It was a rewarding outing for the veteran catcher whom everyone knew was an excellent defensive player and hoped the hot bat he displayed in spring training had returned.

Despite a gallant effort, the sizzling Seals lost the opener by margin of one run, 5–4. Starter Tommy Hurd, in his best outing of the season, saw his complete-game effort collapse in the ninth inning when the Sacs rallied for three runs. It seemed that if Hurd didn't have bad luck, he'd have no luck at all.

Between games there was a brief ceremony when a surprised Harry Dorish was called to the plate and presented with a new suit by a local clothier in appreciation for his contribution to the team, especially his four shutouts.

Then the Seals bounced back in a big way in the second contest and collected a 13–0 shutout pitched by Bill Abernathie, who ran his record to 3–0 as he came "that close" to pitching the season's first no-hitter in the PCL. It was broken up in the seventh inning by a weak line drive off the bat of Leo Righetti that landed inches inside the right field foul line, just inches out of reach of a diving Albie Pearson.

Earlier, infield umpire Chris Pelekoudas got an early exit when he was hit in the temple by a hard throw from shortstop to second base as he leaned in to call a close play at the bag. It knocked him unconscious, and an ambulance took him to the hospital for observation. He returned to action the following day.

It was another rough day at the office for a disgruntled Tommy Heath, as he broke his own record by being evicted from both games. In game one he argued too loudly and too long after Seals base runner Jack Phillips, rounding third and headed for home, was sent sprawling after an accidental collision with the Solons pitcher as he got into position to back up a throw to the plate. The umpire called interference, granted Phillips the next base (home), and credited the Seals with the run.

The second heave-ho, in game two, was somewhat controversial. Renna was called safe at second when fielder Artie Wilson dropped the ball while transferring it from his glove hand to his throwing hand, attempting to complete a double play. All hands were safe. While the fans screamed with delight at that turn of events, Heath ran out shouting at the umpire and pointing his finger at second base. At the same time catcher Jim Mangan went ballistic. He threw his glove high into the air, threw his helmet, pulled off his chest protector and threw it to the ground, and was loudly ejected. But he wasn't finished yet. He dramatically pulled off his shin guards one at a time and carried them to the dugout, then threw them back onto the field. The next day the press corps reported the umpire got the call wrong, but may have gotten it right if he had looked at the play.

With the final series in May in the record books, the Pacific Coast League standings had a 17-game spread between first and last place. Things were tight in the first division. Vancouver and San Francisco were tied for first, Hollywood two games behind, and Los Angeles was in fourth, back by four and a half. The second division was another story. While a half-game separated San Diego and Seattle, Portland was 11 games back and Sacramento lingered in the basement, 17 behind.

After an easy flight to Hollywood, the Seals were eager to test the waters in the Southland in a seven-game face-off with the Hollywood Stars.

Meanwhile, away from the diamond talks about the westward expansion continued. Articles in the papers concerning progress in that direction, or lack of it, were to be found up and down the league. Possibly the least informed of those current events were the players themselves. And they seemed to like it like that.

According to Bill Renna,

> It was an odd time. The Pacific Coast League was classified as "Open," which was a step above AAA, but we players considered it the third major league. It was much better than the other two AAA leagues, believe me. We all knew that sooner or later major league ball would arrive in the City, but when it became official that the Giants were coming we read it in the paper just like everybody else. There was never any conversation about it or anything like that among the players. To tell you the truth, I don't think any of us took it very seriously because it had been rumored for quite some time without anything happening.

Early in the month, on Sunday, May 5, the pot was stirred when the media revealed undercurrents in the plans to get a major league club to San

Francisco. Mayor Christopher said he expected an announcement within two weeks regarding a move by the New York Giants to San Francisco. Many details were put on the table in a Friday night meeting with Los Angeles Mayor Poulson and Walter O'Malley, and it was becoming clear that the deal hinged on the move of the Dodgers to Los Angeles. The best way was to move both teams west and continue their traditional rivalry.

Christopher cautiously projected a good outcome for San Francisco before he flew to New York to continue business. He left the locals with his belief that there was a 75 percent chance that the major league expansion would happen in time for the 1958 season. As usual, San Francisco Supervisor Francis McCarty, head of the San Francisco Committee for Big League Baseball, accompanied him.

In a speech in Houston, Commissioner Frick criticized baseball for "sitting tight" for more than 50 years and said the major leagues must be extended from "coast to coast and from north to south" for the game itself to survive and grow. He even mentioned that, because the center of the American population had shifted westward during those years, a third major league might be the answer. He added that National rather than American League expansion was more likely. He concluded by invoking baseball's rule prohibiting public discussions about progress on the issue during the season.

Finally, in what made it appear that decisions had been made and contracts had been signed, front page headlines in the *San Francisco Chronicle*, in two rows of inch-high letters above the name of the paper that nobody could miss, said, "N. Y. GIANTS: SURE for S. F. in 1958." The article explained that despite a variety of unresolved issues connected with the move, it would happen, and 1957 would be the last hurrah for the Seals.

But the following day, in a clumsy attempt to clarify things, Christopher backtracked somewhat as he affirmed big league baseball would move to the West Coast but muddied the waters locally by adding that specific teams had not been selected, and concluded he was "far more than 75 percent optimistic about San Francisco's chances" to get a team.

It was expected, though not absolutely decided, that the Giants would occupy Seals Stadium until a park of their own with a seating capacity of 70,000 could be built in the South Basin, which involved more bond issues and other legalities that rested with the federal government's condemnation practices at that site. The following day the press continued the story, saying the Brooklyn Dodgers were slated to play in the Los Angeles Coliseum.

Pasadena Star News sports editor Rube Samuelson wrote that in a short press conference on May 6, O'Malley, who "didn't put on much of a poker face," made it clear that he was either unable or unwilling to make comments or decisions about any proposed move of his club to Los Angeles until studies about relevant costs were complete. He was especially concerned about the travel expenses for cross-country road trips of the team during the season.

Starting Saturday, May 11, and for the ensuing couple of weeks, an angry Mayor Christopher held heated press conferences complaining that he wasn't sure the talks were serious or done in good faith. On May 18, the sports headline in one paper was "Baseball Here 'Almost Killed,'" and Christopher attacked the New York baseball teams as not being serious about the move and instead using San Francisco as bait to see how much they could "bleed" interested cities financially. He went so far as to accuse some of the San Francisco supervisors on the committees of attempts to sabotage things, and authorized a study by the finance committee to analyze the facts accurately and submit a report in two weeks.

On May 24 National League president Warren Giles called an emergency meeting of National League directors for the following Tuesday, May 28, in Chicago to sort out the pros and cons that had been decided to date. It was a surprise that invited a guessing game for all since the topic was allegedly kept "top secret." Furthermore, since a regular meeting of the group was already on the calendar for the mid–July All-Star break, having it this early created an aura of urgency. Under those circumstances, many predicted the issue could be resolved very soon.

Rumors flew in all directions. One suggested that Boston owner Tom Yawkey said he wouldn't stand in the way of a major league move to San Francisco and would sell his rights to the territory. General Manager Joe Cronin made it known that he supported a move because of the success of the Seals–Red Sox weekend exhibition series that drew 57,000 fans. Another said Yankees co-owner Del Webb was interested in selling his New York interests and establishing a team of his own in Los Angeles which would force the American League to expand to ten teams. According to San Francisco columnist Bill Leiser, Los Angeles was considering building a new stadium "in some ravine" (Chavez Ravine) to make themselves more attractive for major league baseball. Although the pressure was on to find ways to upgrade Seals Stadium into a major league facility, Seals Stadium owner Paul Fagan resisted and Christopher didn't feel the expense was worth it since the lease was scheduled to expire in September, 1958.

As it turned out, some agreements were reached but mostly future talking points were decided upon and meeting dates for those discussions were set. A big concession came from Fagan when he agreed to extend the lease on the stadium for "a couple of years" to accommodate a major league team until its own stadium was built. The battle over pay-television rights needed further clarification from all sides on both coasts. The growing fears of the remaining six PCL franchises needed to be addressed.

On the same date, after a bond issue to assist Los Angeles with the construction of a major league ballpark passed by a hefty three-to-one margin, Los Angeles Mayor Poulson held a press conference and said, "The action taken by the National League has practically ruined the Pacific Coast League." Though he didn't predict any violent reaction from members of the PCL, he continued, "As far as Los Angeles is concerned, the PCL has folded."

FIVE

June

June 1–2 (Saturday–Sunday) home vs. Sacramento
June 4–9 (Tuesday–Sunday) at Hollywood
June 11–16 (Tuesday–Sunday) at Sacramento
June 18–23 (Tuesday–Sunday) home vs. San Diego
June 25–30 (Tuesday–Sunday) at Los Angeles

The squad left San Francisco on a positive note after they humiliated the Solons by taking all but one game of their series. Before going to Sacramento for a rematch, their first destination on this road trip was Gilmore Field in Hollywood, home of the fading but still dangerous Stars, who were coming off what the press deemed a "5–2 splattering" at the hands of Los Angeles. It was the first head-butting between the two clubs since the Seals took two out of three from them in spring training.

In Hollywood the Seals approached their 54th game of the 168-game season with a 33–20 record. Their fans had started paying attention to the scoreboards during games, keeping track of the opposition. Wins/losses by other PCL teams had already helped San Francisco in the standings, and the general opinion was that if they held it together and did their part, the Seals could return from this two-series roadie firmly atop the league.

Meanwhile, background rumbles about the ins and outs of the so-called major league invasion had fans buzzing while players up and down the league treated it all as white noise and went forward one game at a time. To a man the Bay Area nine seconded Seals President Jerry Donovan's evaluation of the situation: "There's nothing we can do about it from here. We'll just keep trying to win the PCL pennant." The team didn't disappoint.

With Harry Dorish facing Bob Garber, the two teams put on quite a contest. After the Seals got three singles that put one run across in the first inning, things calmed down until the top of the fourth when they added a deuce. Jack Phillips, named the league's Most Valuable Player when he played with Hollywood in 1954, slammed a homer with one on that brought the score to 3–0. After Aspromonte hit a single to start the sixth, Renna knocked his team-leading sixth round-tripper of the season, which put the Seals ahead, 5–0.

The fireworks started when the Stars plated two runs in the sixth, then pushed three more across in the seventh to tie the score at five. Gordon gave Dorish an early exit and sent Leo Kiely to the rescue. He held the Stars in check, keeping the game tied at five. In the top of the ninth, with one out, Nini Tornay singled and Hatton, brought in to hit for Kiely, also singled. Pearson muffed his chance to be a hero when he was out on a weak can of corn fly just beyond the infield. With two on and two out, Sal Taormina was called on to bat for Malmberg. He worked the count to 2–2, then singled to left, scoring Tornay and putting the Seals ahead, 6–5.

But Hollywood had three outs coming to them in the bottom of the ninth with Bert Thiel on the mound, and they put them to good use. It was a valiant effort that kept the 2,161 in attendance on the edge of their seats. With two out and nobody on, Bill Causion singled, followed by a searing double off the bat of R.S. Stevens right past the outreached glove of Frank Kellert. Because he didn't touch it, it reached a charging Pearson sooner, and he threw a bull's eye shot to the plate which held the tying run at third. Even the game-ending third out was an exciting play. With the runner headed home on contact, Grady Hatton briefly bobbled a hot grounder, then made an off-balance throw to Kellert to end it, giving Leo Kiely the victory.

Wednesday was another close game which found the visitors on top 3–2 in what one sportswriter called "a marriage of brilliant relief pitching of bulky Bill Abernathie, married to the clutch clouting of Aspromonte and Phillips." McCall lasted into the fourth inning when he was felled by back pain, and Bill Abernathie made his entrance. Aspromonte single-handedly contributed to the run total when he slammed a long homer, his first of the season. The magnificent running catch by center fielder Marty Keough on a line drive hit by Spook Jacobs in the ninth was described by film actor and avid Stars fan George Raft as the finest catch he had ever seen. The Seals were on a roll with 17 victories in their last 22 games, and their total of one-run victories in their pockets had risen to an even dozen.

On the same page as the PCL box scores there was a brief article reporting the death of famed Yankees scout Paul Krichell, who had signed Lou Gehrig and Seals legend Tony Lazzeri, among numerous others since 1920.

The next day when a reporter told Taormina his pinch-hitting .538 batting average made him the best in that capacity in the PCL, he laughingly explained his success by saying, "I just start swinging as soon as I leave the dugout, that's all." At the same time the stocky, hustling, and hard-working left fielder was gaining league-wide recognition for his excellent defense. His teammates appreciated the level of play he brought to the yard every day as well as his humor in the clubhouse.

Albie Pearson personified their thoughts:

> The team played well together and we had a good time that season. The younger guys like myself were allowed to play and develop confidence and the veterans were always available to help us out with tips if we asked them. They were never pushy about it. And it was good watching them play to see the things that kept them in pro baseball for so long. One of them I particularly remember is Sal Taormina. He was a tremendous pinch-hitter. If we were tied or behind late in the game, Joe put him in and he waited for a ball to drive, then made good contact to beat somebody. He was amazing. He couldn't run that well but he always hit it hard enough to get the job done. And he always made a special effort to be available if some of the younger guys like myself wanted some tips and the like.

Thursday, Friday, and Saturday were frustrating. The team found itself mired in a three-game losing streak. Thursday they were blanked, 2–0. They were unable to put their eight hits together to create a rally. In a rare event, Aspromonte took the collar, 0-for-4. Tommy Umphlett, batting for Spring in the seventh, struck out. Both Hollywood runs came off two swings of the bat by outfielder Bill Causion, and went into the books as two of the longest home runs ever recorded in the 18-year history of Gilmore Field. Both were measured at over 500 feet as they soared over the center field fence.

Although they faced the next game as they did every game, determined to end on the winning side of the ledger, they lost 6–5 despite an exciting five-run rally in the ninth inning that ruined the shutout in progress. After surviving 20 consecutive scoreless innings, they came back to life in the ninth, batted around, and pushed five runs across the dish, one short of a tie to extend the game. Tommy Hurd went all the way but wild-pitched in what became the winning run and took the loss thanks to three Seals errors, making his record 2–2. It was a tough night in other ways as Vancouver beat Portland and bumped San Francisco to second place by half a game.

For the Saturday game, Gordon tweaked his lineup in a sort of experiment. He bumped Keough to the leadoff spot and moved Pearson down to the second slot. He knew they could both get on base, but hoped this would increase their opportunities to run the bases more successfully and produce more runs.

According to Keough,

> At that time the Red Sox weren't big on stealing bases and all that. They never were. But Joe liked that kind of thing. He would walk up to you at third base from the coaching box and say, "Go on the next pitch" and walk away. It used to scare me to death because he never gave a sign to the others or anything like that. You were always afraid that one of the big hitters would hit a ball at

your head on the way in because he didn't know you were coming down the line. He was like Billy Martin that way, did anything to score a run.

Saturday, June 8, was summed up in one paragraph by *Chronicle* sportswriter Bob Stevens:

> In spite of a brilliant job of relief pitching by Leo Kiely the ambulant skeleton of the bullpen, the Seals took another stabbing by the Stars today, 2–0, as Hollywood nailed down its third consecutive win over the slump-plagued ex–league leaders. It was a pitiful event in the life of Kiely [who] worked 6⅓ innings completely blacking out the Stars, and ran to 15⅔ consecutive rounds of scoreless baseball he has pitched in relief. All he got out of it was exercise."

In that fourth whitewash of the season, they were limited to just five hits, one each by Hatton, Umphlett, and Aspromonte, and two by Kiely. Though the Seals didn't gain ground on Vancouver, they didn't lose any either thanks to Portland's 8–4 defeat of the Mounties. They remained a half-game behind in second place.

Sports pages all over the country published articles that were almost unnoticed by the public. A three-day feature series in the *Chronicle* presented a study by the AMA into the "shocking" reports of widespread use of pep pills by athletes, identified as an amphetamine known as Benzedrine and its derivatives. It said the AMA made a resolution that called for a study by AMA Trustees, plus forceful action to halt any abuses of drugs to make players "super athletes." It seems laughable today based on what has transpired since 1957, but at the time it was kept hush-hush and very little attention was paid to the issue.

But that was the last thing on the minds of Seals regulars as they snagged both ends of the doubleheader on Sunday. By this time it seemed the entire lineup was composed of star players, some of whom stood out on a daily basis while the others took turns in the spotlight.

The opener should have been played in Seals Stadium because the home fans would have loved it. With Dorish on the mound they hammered the Twinks in a 16-hit barrage that gave them a 7–3 victory. In addition to ending the losing streak, the team found their batting eyes in a big way. Umphlett almost hit for the cycle with a homer, double, single and a walk for three RBI; Aspromonte went 3-for-4 with a homer and 3 RBI; Hatton went 4-for-5 with two driven in; Marty Keough got a double and a single; catcher Nini Tornay got two singles; and Harry Malmberg and Frank Kellert each singled. The only player who went hitless was the power man, Bill Renna.

The seven-inning finale, the rubber game of the series, got off on a good footing. Keough, on first after a single, was driven home by Umphlett, giving the Seals a 1–0 lead. The Stars tied in their half, and the Seals got one more tally in the top of the second and could have headed for the airport right then with the victory because the Stars never caught up. After San Francisco brought the score to 4–1 in the top of the sixth, starter Abernathie ran out of gas. Leo Kiely took over and that was that.

The press pointed out and put a stamp of approval on the way Gordon juggled his outfield in both games Sunday. The object of his actions was Tommy Umphlett, who didn't waste the opportunity. He replaced slumping Pearson in right, and went 3-for-4 in the cleanup spot with Aspromonte batting fifth. Game two found him in left, and he went 2-for-3 batting third with Aspromonte back in his cleanup slot.

With this series win in the books, four games to three, the team had won six series out of the seven played thus far and was confident it would win the upcoming challenge in Sacramento. The team was healthy except for two members: Windy McCall still struggled with back problems and Eddie Sadowski, though still unable to swing the bat due to a slow-healing muscle sprain, still ran the bases efficiently. But there was another perceived weakness by the name of Bill Renna, who was not hitting as advertised.

They went to Edmonds Field with the intent of upsetting Tommy Heath yet again. But the first meeting turned out to be more challenging than anticipated. It took four S.F. twirlers, a pinch-hit home run by Renna, and 11 innings to nab the 5–4 win. But this seventh extra-inning victory was costly. With the Seals on top 3–0 in the third, starter Jack Spring yielded a triple to Ed White that made the score 3–2. As soon as the play was completed, he limped from the mound in obvious agony with a hamstring muscle pull in his left leg that left his thigh black and blue.

Bert Thiel, Bill Abernathie (who got the win) and Leo Kiely contained the Solons as the lead changed hands a couple of times until the regular nine innings saw the teams tied at four. But the issue was resolved in the top of the 11th by a man name Renna.

Game two on Wednesday was one of the toughest losses of the season leaving the Seals scratching their heads. Despite several opportunities, the scoreboard showed nothing scored by either team going to the ninth inning. Starter Tommy Hurd had allowed just four hits as he stacked eight zeroes on the scoreboard, while Joe Stanka had equal success. After Frank Kellert doubled and was sacrificed to third, the Seals got a break when Nini Tornay hit a grounder that was too hot for shortstop Leo Righetti to handle. Kellert scored, Tornay was safe at first, and Righetti collected an error. (After the game it was learned that Tornay suffered an ankle injury that would keep him out of action for a few games.)

The Solons went into the home half of the ninth down by a run. Gordon watched intently as Hurd returned to the hill to register the final three outs and his third win. But you know what they say about best laid plans. With

Chico Heron brought in to run for Nippy Jones after his second single of the night, Al Heist hit an easy pop fly to right center that was called for by both Albie Pearson and Marty Keough, but caught by neither while Heron circled the bases and tied the game.

After Jim Westlake flew out to right, Gordon could no longer stand the pressure, and instructed Hurd to intentionally walk the next batter, Cuno Barragan. But on the first pitch Barragan reached well out of the zone and made contact for a single that scored Heist and won the game, resulting in another loss that made unlucky Tommy Hurd's record 2–3. It's a good thing the 1,326 fans clapped and yelled loudly, otherwise they would have heard a barrage of X-rated language out of the mouth of the Seals manager.

The team was able to relax Thursday morning when they saw the headlines of other games around the circuit: "Stars Whip Mounties on 3-Hitter," "Grant Fans 13 as Pads Beat Angels," and "Suds Edge Beavos in Tight 2–1 Tilt." They went to the ball yard Thursday knowing they were still a half-game ahead of the pack with Vancouver second, Hollywood third, and the other contenders slipping behind.

It was the start of a mini-streak where three more games were entered in the win column for San Francisco. Riverboat Smith squared off against Don Fracchia, who limited the Seals to just five hits. The scoring started and ended early for the Seals. In the first inning, after Pearson and Hatton grounded out, Keough slammed a huge home run. Smith held the fort in the home half, then the Seals' rally continued as they drove Fracchia to the showers while adding three more tallies in the second thanks to sloppy defense supplemented by hits by Harry Malmberg, Smith, and one of three in the game by Grady Hatton, who was dealing with a severe cold of his own. Sac reliever Mike Coen contained the opponents until the eighth when Chico Heron homered to become the only Solon to cross the plate. Their 4–1 victory lifted Smith's record to 4–5.

On Friday, with the Plumber, Fritz Dorish, on the hill, a suited-up and fit-looking Joe Gordon remained in the dugout but relinquished his managerial chores to coach Glenn Wright, who manned the third base box, while Sal Taormina took over the first base line while the boss attempted to recover from a severe cold. Late in the game Taormina successfully appeared in a pinch-hit role. It was an exciting victory for the Seals, the tenth win in the dozen confrontations between the two squads.

After scoring a single run in the second, third, and fourth frames, the Seals found themselves behind 4–3 in the eighth. Grady Hatton led off with his third single of the night and Sadowski was sent in to run for him. Keough sacrificed the catcher to second. After taking two pitches, Aspromonte smashed his second two-bagger and fourth hit of the night, and Sadowski put his wheels in high gear and scored to tie the game. Renna fooled everyone including himself when he beat out an "excuse-me" infield roller, moving Aspromonte to third. Frank Kellert was whiffed for the second out, which brought Sal Taormina to the plate, hitting for Nini Tornay. He hit a weak liner to second base which was caught but dropped by Artie Wilson. Running on the pitch with two outs, Aspromonte scored, giving the Seals a 5–4 win. Leo Kiely, sometimes called "Mr. Bones" by admiring sports writers, entered the game in the seventh and got the win, number seven against two losses, which added a total of 23⅔ consecutive scoreless frames to his accomplishments.

Bob Stevens wrote, "A semi-line drive by pinch hitter Sal Taormina with two outs in the eighth inning that turned into one of the freakiest plays of this or any other year, shoved the Seals into a 5–4 victory over Sacramento as the Bay boys held their PCL lead."

But the news wasn't all good for the Seals. In the first inning, when Marty Keough was caught stealing on a close play at second, umpire Chris Pelekoudas accidentally spiked his hand when leaning in to get a better view of the play. After a brief delay while the injury was evaluated in the dugout and the trainer bandaged his hand, Keough remained in the contest.

During that week a Sacramento sports writer reported that Tommy Umphlett, in protest at not seeing enough game time, conducted his own private sit-down strike by not participating in pregame workouts in Sacramento. When questioned about it, Gordon said Umphlett would get plenty of playing time later, but he needed right-handed pinch-hitters against the Solons pitching staff, and he had assured left-handed batting Umphlett there wasn't anything more to it than that. The problem was that the Seals were so heavily stocked with excellent players, every day was a big decision for Gordon when he prepared the lineup.

Saturday afternoon in Sacramento was a hot day made hotter by the flaming bats of both teams, as the hits total was 27, 14 for the visitors and 13 for the home team. Starters Windy McCall and Rocky Bridges learned early that everyone ate his Wheaties for breakfast. After the Sacs drove McCall out of service when they put two on the board in the second inning, making the score 2–1, Bert Thiel came in and coasted for six innings until Leo Kiely closed things down for the Solons as he tossed 13 pitches and got out the only five batters he faced. Malmberg bashed a two-run homer, his second of the season. Pearson hit a solo four-bagger, and Frank Kellert's seventh of the season was dubbed "a moon-denter." In addition to spectacular defensive plays that saved some runs, Aspromonte slammed a line drive triple down the right field line.

Sunday was a different story. They split the twin bill in which, despite their best efforts at the plate, they beat themselves with sloppy defense that cost them the first game, 8–7, before they bounced back and beat the Solons 3–2 in the nightcap.

Once again starter Tommy Hurd's luck held true, as he was the victim of three errors and three unearned runs in the first inning of the opener. Once the squad fell behind 4–0 in the fourth, Riverboat Smith and Windy McCall tried to stop the bleeding. After disappointing errors by Hatton, Aspromonte, Kellert, Tornay, and Malmberg throughout the contest that left them in the hole 7–3 in the ninth, it seemed the writing was on the wall. But they fought back with a vigor that included a couple of two-run homers, one by Renna and one by Sadowski, making the score 7–7 with plans to take it into extra innings. But their hopes were dashed when a final error by Jack Spring allowed the winning run to cross the plate. Spring took the loss.

One memory shared by several players was of batboy Mike Murphy, who was generally at the plate to welcome batters at home with a handshake after they hit home runs. Grady Hatton elaborated,

> Our batboy before and during the 1957 season, a tall kid named Mike Murphy, loved the players and always did special things for us. He kept our clothes clean, shined our shoes, and sometimes ran errands if asked. He was hired by the Giants right away for 1958 and is still with them after all these years. In fact, hanging in my closet is a sweat suit he sent me when the Giants came in. He was always thoughtful and we all appreciated it.

The scheduled seven-inning closer went into the ninth tied at two until an Eddie Sadowski solo homer gave the Seals their eighth consecutive extra-inning victory, 3–2. Leo Kiely, who had relieved Abernathie with two out in the seventh, got the win, bringing his record to 8–2. By taking that series, 5–2, San Francisco fortified their place atop the Pacific Coast League, 2.5 games ahead of waffling Vancouver.

They relaxed on the flight back to San Francisco Sunday night and rested Monday in anticipation of the arrival of the San Diego Padres, who brought a deceptive 35–33 record that found them in fifth place, 7.5 games back. Under the leadership of new skipper George Metkovich, the Pads had recovered from their slow start, picked up the nickname "Bordertown Bombers," and became a force to be reckoned with. While sports writers in both communities billed the series as "ultra crucial," Gordon underlined those thoughts as he reminded his club that they faced a series far more important and far tougher than the one they just completed in Sacramento. Nobody needed to remind the San Franciscans of the effort required in order to retain their first place perch.

Would the series be a slugfest? Between the two clubs there were ten players batting over .300. The Padres had three outfielders, Rudy Regalado (.346), Bob Lennon (.316), and Dave Pope (.314), shortstop Billy Harrell

Bill Renna tagged the plate after he walloped his team-leading homerun, number eight, during the sixth inning rally that saw the Seals tie the score. He was greeted at home by Harry Malmberg (#4) and bat boy Mike Murphy (#55) as Sacramento catcher Cuno Barragan walked away (David Eskenazi Collection).

(.314), and first baseman Stu Locklin (.310). On the other hand, the Seals had two outfielders, Sal Taormina (.318) and Marty Keough (.309), second baseman Ken Aspromonte (.308), first baseman Frank Kellert (.305), and third baseman Grady Hatton (.304). At the same time, both teams were well stocked with effective pitchers fully capable of holding those big bats in check. Anticipation was high for all competitors.

According to Chip Aspromonte:

> Once I got to San Francisco I felt comfortable. I knew most of the guys who were optioned out with me like Marty Keough and a few others. Joe Gordon was our manager and he was an easy guy to work with. He molded the team into what he wanted and we had a good ballclub. Being on a good club is always a big help to individual players. I know it helped me a lot. When the teammates get along and the team wins it's always more fun to go to the park. It was one of those years when you're at home plate and just feel good swinging the bat and everything seemed to fall in line with you. Your strokes are better. I was seeing the ball better, and it probably seemed that I was pretty lucky up there, but believe me, the success that came was the result of a lot of hard work and some luck, I'm sure. That season was a big improvement from 1956 for me, and I was excited to think that my next stop could be the major leagues. But during the season all concentration was on improving and improving.

In addition to being Family Night at the stadium, Tuesday night's series opener was introduced by the antics of local entertainer Jackie Price, whose talents included shooting baseballs out of cannons and catching them while standing on his head.

Tuesday night's game was an exercise in frustration for the Seals. Gordon made good on his promise to rest Marty Keough and Grady Hatton and replaced them with Tom Umphlett and Jack Phillips. LHP Jack Spring faced former major league RHP Dick Brodowski, who decorated the scoreboard with nine goose eggs while whiffing eight and limiting the Seals to just six hits. All the scoring occurred in the third inning when the visitors collected two unearned runs thanks to errors by Aspromonte and Spring. Pearson, with two of the Seals' hits for the night, a bunt single and an infield single, took himself out of the game after the third inning due to a bone bruise on his hand, and Keough's night off was cut short when he was sent in as his replacement. The final score was Padres 2, Seals zip.

As if that weren't a big enough disappointment for the more than 10,000 in attendance, early in the evening the under-stocked concession stands ran out of hot dogs, hamburgers, peanuts, and even coffee, the best hand-warmer on those cold night battles at Seals Stadium.

Game two on Wednesday afternoon took a different route but ended in the same place, with another Seals defeat, this time 8–7. The Padres used the talents of 11 players to get 14 hits. Rudy Regalado and Ed Kazak combined for seven of them, while the home team sent 18 players, including five pitchers, into action and still fell one run short. To add insult to injury, the game was tied at seven in the top of the ninth when Bob DiPietro, with two on and two out, hit a sizzling single and drove in the winning run.

After the game Gordon held a rare clubhouse meeting before the players left and announced that he was fining pitcher Windy McCall $50 for throwing at Rudy Regalado four times as retribution for a collision at first base between the two on May 22, when McCall felt Regalado had deliberately collided with him. McCall complained that he had constant back problems ever since. It was the first fine ever levied by Gordon, who said it was "for prejudicing the interests of the club by taking out a personal grudge on the field." When interviewed the following day, McCall refused to comment and Regalado said he had no idea McCall was throwing at him.

On Thursday, same teams, same 8–7 score, different winners. Starter Fritz Dorish faced Pete Mesa. Things began tentatively for the hosts as Regalado singled in the first inning, extending his league-leading hitting streak to 18 games, while driving in the first run, putting the Seals behind before their first trip to the plate. The Seals plated two runs in the third, one in the fifth, but were still behind 5–3 when they went to bat in the seventh.

They quickly drove Mesa from the mound before he could get the first out. At that point the Padres inserted relief pitcher Ellis Kinder, age 42, a former major leaguer who had won 102 games and collected prestigious awards along the way. In his PCL debut the Seals failed to show him the proper respect and pummeled him for five runs that brought the fans to their feet and left the Padres facing the eighth and ninth innings down by three runs. They managed to eke out two more runs but still fell short as the game ended, 8–7. Reliever Bill Abernathie, who entered after Pearson batted for Dorish in the fifth, got his seventh win. Though the Seals were limited to eight hits, they made them count. Taormina, who started his seventh game of the season, smacked two doubles, drove in three runs, and scored the winning run when Aspromonte doubled down the left field line.

Joe Gordon tried a new strategy Friday night. He brought in 21-year-old rookie Walter Payne, who had signed his first pro contract with the Seals the day after he graduated with a degree in economics from Stanford University. Putting someone so wet behind the ears at the AAA level for his first pro game was against all protocol, but Gordon hoped it would give the Seals an edge because the Padres had never faced him before, had no advance scouting reports, and didn't know what to expect. After asking, "Who's Walter Payne?" the puzzled 6,631 fans in attendance sat quietly and wondered.

Clearly in over his head through no fault of his own, despite what was described as a good fastball and an even better curve, he was wild and yielded six walks and five earned runs before he left the game without logging an out in the third inning. Gordon gave the ball to Bert Thiel, but the Seals were already in a hole that got deeper. As they tried to climb out, Thiel allowed three more runs, and the Riverboat, now relieving more than starting, gave up the ninth run in the eighth before Abernathie took the ball and held tight in the last frame. The Seals played errorless ball but were only able to put together four tallies, three of them thanks to two Renna doubles and one on a solo homer by Sadowski.

Behind three games to one, the Seals knew they had to win all three remaining games or lose their second series of the season. Saturday, while Ken Aspromonte nursed a twisted ankle, the infield remained strong as Jack Phillips moved to second base and Grady Hatton manned third. It didn't change their luck, though, as starter Tommy Hurd left for pinch-hitter Albie Pearson in the sixth, trailing 5–3. Tommy Umphlett grounded out for Kiely in the eighth, and with the score tied at six apiece after eight, Dorish was brought in to hold the fort in the ninth. Instead, he gave up a huge homer to young outfielder Floyd Robinson that not only sucked the air out of the stadium and left the fans mute, but won the game. The Seals couldn't match it in the home half of the frame, resulting in another disappointing one-run loss, 7–6.

The confrontation series with the Bordertown Bombers was described as "one of the most destructive weeks in recent baseball history," but that didn't keep the 10,032 loyal Seals fans away from the stadium on a sunny Sunday in hope of seeing their team pull out of the doldrums in the double bill.

Unfortunately, the flood gates were still open for the Pads in the first game as they collected 15 hits and put eight tallies on the board while limiting the Seals to eight hits, two each by Keough, Aspromonte, Kellert, and Hatton, and one lonely run in the fourth inning. Jack Spring took the loss making his record 2–4.

The die-hard Seals fans finally got a long-overdue breath of fresh air in the last game of the "series of horrors" despite a four-zip Padres lead in the first inning. The Bay Boys inched back one run at a time and closed the gap to 4–3 after six. The locals had another shock when San Diego increased their lead to two with another tally in the top of the seventh.

But, as in the movies, the Seals got a second wind in the last half of the last inning of the day. In the bottom of the seventh their bats came back to life and heads rolled, the heads of San Diego twirlers, that is. Sadowski singled, and after Renna fouled out hitting for Kiely, Pearson beat out an infield single. Harry Malmberg kept the action alive as he smashed a double off the left field wall that drove in both runners. The score was tied at five. Left fielder Sal

Taormina approached the plate fully capable of hitting the long fly ball needed to score the winning run from third, but he was issued an intentional pass that loaded the bases and gave Aspromonte the oppor-tunity to be the hero. On a 2–1 count he hit a bullet to left that drove home Malm-berg for the winning run and earned a big face-saver for the home team.

After falling behind 4–0 in the first inning, the Seals inched their way back and defeated the Padres in the nightcap of the doubleheader when Harry Malmberg scored from second on a long fly off the bat of Ken Aspromonte (David Eskenazi Collection).

Despite the thrill of that comeback, the reality of the situation was that the Seals had lost the second series of the season, five games to two. With the off day on Monday the team, fans, and especially the press had time to evalu-ate the damages. Bob Stevens wrote, "The San Diego Padres, right at this little ol' minute the best equipped team in the league, did hor-rible things to the Joe Gor-don Athletic Club last week as they clobbered them five out of seven with a team batting average that dented the .335 mark. The Bordertowners did everything, however, except make the Seals quit.... It proved the Bay Boys are hard nosed."

During the Sacramento series Seals President Jerry Donovan had run into an old friend from the Mission District and invited him to attend some games at Seals Stadium as his guest. As the story goes, his friend laughed and emphatically replied that the games were boring because the Seals were too good for the league and there was never any doubt as to who would win. Donovan laughed and wondered if he had read the outcome of the San Diego series.

Although all the papers in the circuit agreed the Padres were the stiffest competition the Seals had faced all season, they also noted the league standings at the end of the series and fell back on that old adage "it's better to be lucky than good." In addition to the Pads adding three extra games in the win col-umn and the Seals adding the same amount on the loss side, the "right" com-bination of wins and losses among other clubs in the league allowed San

Diego to climb over the Seattle Rainiers into fourth place while the Seals occupied the same spot they did when the series began: in first place 2.5 games ahead of the Vancouver Mounties, with the Hollywood Stars in third. But the Padres had left their mark as a team to be feared.

Before the Padres left town Sunday night, Rudy Regalado, who batted close to .500 in the series, had extended his hitting streak to an impressive 22 games. That was behind them now. In front of them lurked Angels slugger Steve Bilko, currently engaged in a home run race with Joe Taylor of Seattle. Both had posted 16 to date.

The Seals flew to Los Angeles for their first series at Wrigley Field. Meanwhile, they enjoyed a well-deserved, though brief, rest on Monday while they awaited the last series before the July 2 All-Star Game.

The Seals roster was a little different for this duel with the Angels. Jack Spring, still recovering from what turned out to be a torn hamstring that was more severe than originally thought, went south with the team on the inactive list and was treated by the USC trainer. His spot was filled by 18-year-old LHP Bill Prout, son of former Seals first baseman William Prout, who was a teammate of Walter Mails in 1934. The youngster was sought by many scouts but signed by Joe Stephenson of the Red Sox the day after he graduated from Downey High School. His acquisition was intended to be temporary until Spring's return.

In his usual turn in the rotation, steady Harry Dorish started Tuesday's contest, which became contentious in the very first inning! After the Seals put one run across in the top of the frame and the Angels tied it up in the bottom when a line drive by Jim Baxes drove in Tom Saffell, the fireworks started. With one down and Baxes on first, Bilko doubled him to third. Bert Hamric was issued a free pass to load the bases, setting up a force out at any base. Roy Hartsfield strode to the plate and hit a whistling line drive to right field. Baxes broke for home with the crack of the bat while Pearson made a spectacular shoestring catch for the second out. He made a made a lightning throw back to the infield which Dorish intercepted and threw to Malmberg, who doubled off slow-running Bilko as he dove back into second. That made it three away, or so the Seals thought as they headed for the dugout. They assumed Baxes' run didn't count for two reasons: he failed to tag up after the catch and there were three outs when he scored. Thus, the game was still tied at one.

However, plate umpire Al Sommers said Baxes' run did count, explaining that there were only two outs when he crossed the plate because Bilko had not yet been doubled off second. Things got contentious until Gordon resolved them for the moment when he protested, and the next eight innings were played under the protest flag.

Although the Seals waged a fierce battle as they out-hit the Angels 11 to 10, four off the bat of Pearson that included three doubles, they fell short and lost the game, 8–5. Unlucky Dorish lasted six innings and took the loss as Abernathie (⅓ inning), Kiely (⅔ inning) and Payne (one inning) all got in some work. Soon thereafter they also lost the protest on the basis of Rule 7.10, which Gordon agreed with and accepted without further discussion. On the brighter side, the club didn't lose its hold on first place but everyone felt the pressure of encroachment from other teams.

After the struggle Tuesday, it took 11 innings to win Wednesday in a game where runs came in clusters. The Seals scored five unearned runs off former major league pitcher Tommy Lasorda in the second frame before being held scoreless until the 11th. During that time starter Tommy Hurd gave up one in the second thanks to Steve Bilko's 19th homer, a blast that is said to be in flight to this day. In the seventh the Angels scored four more times on a grand slam by pinch-hitter Jim Fridley.

In the top of the 11th the Seals once again proved why the local press dubbed them "the best overtime club in the business." All the Seals' runs were unearned, even the game-winner in the 11th when Umphlett started the action with a routine grounder to short but was safe at first as Wally Lammers made his third error of the game. He rushed his throw to first and the ball wound up in the Seals dugout, allowing Umphlett to advance to second. Aspromonte gave himself up with a sac bunt that sent the flying Umphlett to third. Renna was a quick out on a pop to second base. With two down Jack Phillips approached the plate and worked the count to 2–2 before he smashed a low liner up the middle, allowing Umphlett to score unchallenged. Reliever Leo Kiely didn't even work up a sweat as he got the final three outs in the ninth as the Seals won the game, 6–5, which made his record 9–0 out of the pen, 10–2 overall. Ironically all of the Seals runs were unearned. This victory gave the team its ninth consecutive extra-inning victory, its 14th one-run win, and brought the Seals' season record to 45–31, 14 games over .500.

Thursday San Francisco was out-hit by Los Angeles, 8–6, thanks to the home run bats of Steve Bilko and Jim Baxes, but the Angels didn't have Leo Kiely. And that turned out to be the difference. Starter Riverboat Smith made it to the eighth inning ahead, 6–3, when he was relieved by Kiely. Earlier Smith had given up a solo homer to Bilko, his 20th, before nailing him on called strike three in two subsequent at-bats. In protest of the second whiffing, Bilko flipped his cap in the air and was given the automatic heave-ho by the umpire. The normally soft-spoken, amiable player tried to get chest to chest with the ump to discuss it further when Los Angeles manager Clay Bryant got between them in an attempt to protect his player. Sixty seconds later, Bryant was also ejected.

Kiely came in with the bases loaded and promptly shocked everyone when he allowed a grand slam to Jim Baxes, putting the Seals behind, 7–6. When the Seals came to bat in the top of the ninth, Kiely shocked them again as the Black Cat picked up his weapon and turned into a tiger! With the game on the line Aspromonte walked, Phillips fouled out, and Kellert beat out a single that sent Aspromonte to third. Nini Tornay made the second out with a pop-up caught at third base. Then Kiely stepped up to the plate, worked the count full, and blasted a line drive double into left-center field, scoring Aspromonte and Kellert. Ironically it was his first extra-base hit of the season.

At the same time, things were exciting around the league. Rudy Regalado extended his hitting streak to 25 games as the Padres beat the Solons, 8–4; the Stars stung Seattle early and held on for a 7–1 win; and a fourth-inning triple play helped the Mounties top the Beavers, 6–1.

A small article in the *Chronicle* said third baseman Joe Tanner, earlier optioned to AA Oklahoma City as a result of recurring back problems, faced season-ending corrective surgery in the next few days, but would recover in time to join the Seals at spring training for the 1958 season.

The young high school graduate of one week, Bill Prout, made his debut Friday in what turned out to be a quick initiation into the disappointments of AAA play. In the first inning, after he walked the first two batters, none other than Steve Bilko crushed a three-run homer (#21). The saga continued in the second when he yielded a two-run dinger to Tom Saffell. Although both hits were homers in the Wrigley Field bandbox and would have been long fly outs in Seals Stadium, they still counted. By the end of the second heat the Angels had five runs on the board.

The Bay Bombers started chipping away at the lead. After Sal Taormina was hit by a pitch that left his hand black and blue, they played a little small ball that advanced him around the bases to tally the first run. Though they didn't know it, the Angels had scored all they were going to that day. Prout settled down and pitched four scoreless innings that included three strikeouts and three walks through the sixth. Bert Thiel took the reins in the seventh, and young Walter Payne pitched the eighth. After the Seals had put across two more runs in the sixth, Ken Aspromonte opened the ninth with his third homer of the season which left the team a run short of a tie. Final score: Los Angeles 5, San Francisco 4.

Shortly after that Payne went to AA Oklahoma City in the Texas League, then played in the lower minor leagues through 1961 when he retired from the game.

A sunny Saturday afternoon game provided the perfect backdrop for a game seasoned with seven homers, four for the home team and three for the visitors, in which the Seals ended on top of the 9–8 score. San Francisco's Bill Abernathie lasted into the eighth while Los Angeles starter John Jancse was the first of five pitchers the Angels needed in their losing effort.

Action started in the second when the Big Bomber, Steve Bilko, bashed a tremendous solo homer to left that many feared would hit a passing airplane. This was followed by a double off the bat of Bert Fridley, who watched from second as Bert Hamric crushed one into the center field bleachers that boosted the Los Angeles lead to 3–0.

The Seals waited until the fourth to put on the first show of their own as they drove in five runs until Jancse said his goodbyes and disappeared down the dugout stairs to the showers. Although two errors rendered three runs unearned, they were the result of solid hitting by the boys from the north that included back-to-back doubles by Grady Hatton and Frank Kellert that saw Hatton's hitting streak extended to ten games.

After Bilko hammered a solo homer in the bottom of the fourth making the score 5–4, the Seals punched back with another rally in the top of the fifth. With Marty Keough on first, cleanup hitter Sal Taormina proceeded to smack his second dinger of the season, followed by an even longer one off the bat of Grady Hatton that made the score 8–4, a tally that may have felt safe against any other team in any other park. But in the bandbox known as Wrigley Field, nothing was safe.

Things were calm until Keough clobbered his sixth homer of the season in the seventh. That was the ninth and final run for the Seals. After the seventh inning stretch Herb Olson smacked a homer that brought the Angels one run closer. But the eighth was different. When Baxes reached on a single followed by singles by Bilko and Fridley that that drove Baxes home, Abernathie took an early exit with two runners on and no outs. The din of the crowd declined considerably as the league's premier fireman, Leo Kiely, made his entrance for the 28th time. Unfortunately he allowed two hits that closed the gap to 9–8 before he got the third out. The ninth heat was scoreless for both teams, and the Seals clinched another one-run win.

That same day, the second triple play of the week occurred when the Solons turned a quick around-the-horn second inning-ender against the Padres. But, with their usual bad luck, the Solons were shut out, 2–0.

More than 9,200 fans showed up expecting an exciting series-ending double dip on Sunday, and, though bashers Bilko and Fridley had the day off nursing bumps and bruises, they weren't disappointed. There were 45 hits for the afternoon, as the Seals out-hit their hosts in both games (13–11, 12–9) in a day that ended in a split that gave the Seals the edge, four games to three, in the series.

Tommy Hurd earned his third win in game one when the deal was sealed by a ninth-inning three-run homer by Grady Hatton that made the score 9–5. A different Harry Dorish from the one who started the season in San Francisco left game two under fire in the third inning but escaped the loss, which went into the record books for Bert Thiel as the Angels won, 3–2.

At the halfway point of the season, everyone faced three days off for the Pacific Coast League All-Star Game slated for July 2 at Wrigley Field, with regularly scheduled play to resume with July 4 doubleheaders around the circuit.

The Seals held the lead they'd captured in mid–May, two games ahead of their season-long challenger, Vancouver. San Diego moved up to third place (behind by three games), with fourth-place Hollywood a half-game behind them, nipping at their heels. Seattle topped the second division in fifth, five and a half games behind the Seals. The 1956 champion Angels had slipped to sixth, six games behind. They were the teams in competition at that point. Portland had pulled itself out of last place and stood in seventh, 15 games out while the forlorn Sacramento Solons occupied the cellar, 25 games out with a dismal 21–57 record. Since 1903 the Solons had only won two championships, 1937 and 1942.

Meanwhile, away from the diamond, there was a lot of activity on several fronts. Locally, a new organization called the "Save the Seals Club" was formed by 500 members of the Southern Pacific Mainliners Club. Its spokesman, train conductor and group vice president Elmer Norton, announced their policies as follows: (1) stop the move of the Giants, which he said would substitute a poor major league club for a good Seals club; (2) the difference between the quality of play in the PCL and major leagues was minute; (3) the idea of pay–TV for ballgames was outrageous. Needless to say, aside from an initial postcard soliciting support, little else was heard from them.

In New York, developments were afoot to keep a National League team in that city. After one syndicate offered both O'Malley and Stoneham top dollar for their teams and was refused, a new plan was announced for public consideration. Former New York police commissioner George V. McLaughlin and other city officials advocated the formation of a new franchise called the "New Yorkers" if the Dodgers and Giants vacated the territory, giving the National League a ninth team which they hoped could be balanced later by the creation of a tenth team in another city.

Emil Sick, owner of the Rainiers, said in an interview with sports editor George N. Meyers of the *Seattle Times* that there was a strong possibility his club would withdraw from the Pacific Coast League after the 1957 season. He based it on the assumption that the Dodgers and Giants would move to California, which would disrupt the entire Coast League. He feared the remaining teams could "find ourselves playing at the mercy of the capricious intentions of Walter O'Malley and the Brooklyn Dodgers." Seattle General Manager Dewey Soriano said the Rainiers franchise, valued at $750,000, was the most viable in the league and should seek $3,000,000 in damages if any major league teams disrupted the PCL circuit.

League president Leslie O'Connor scheduled a meeting of team owners in Sacramento on Sunday, June 2, for the purpose of informally discussing their apprehension concerning the economic impact of what they called the coming "major league invasion," and demanded proper compensation for losses already incurred plus those yet to come. O'Connor aimed to calm things down a notch or two. One of the first items on his agenda was to label "premature and bogus" a report from an Eastern publication that said four PCL clubs had already filed suits amounting to a combined $6.7 million in damages: Seattle ($3,000,000) Sacramento ($1, 700,000), San Diego and Vancouver ($1,000,000 each).

At the same time, San Francisco sportswriters continued their support of efforts to acquire a big league team by pointing out the fan base and interest in the PCL were alive and well, noting the tremendous increase in attendance since 1956. In the last week of May alone the league drew 33,312, and had done almost as well in the week before that. Writers constantly emphasized the size of the potential fan base, marketing opportunities, and motel and restaurant accommodations readily available in the greater San Francisco Bay Area.

Meanwhile, on June 25, cold water was thrown on things when National League President Warren Giles warned all parties not to get too excited about the potential migration of two teams from his league. He elaborated that a House Judiciary Subcommittee on Professional Sports said there were many obstacles at that time, and he doubted very much that a move was imminent.

Six

July

July 2 PCL All-Star Game in Los Angeles
July 3–7 (Wednesday–Sunday) home vs. Portland
July 9–14 (Tuesday–Sunday) home vs. Hollywood
July 16–21 (Tuesday–Sunday) at Portland
July 23–26 (Tuesday–Friday) at Seattle
July 27–30 (Saturday–Tuesday) home vs. Vancouver

The 6,417 fans in attendance at the 15th annual Pacific Coast League All-Star Game at Wrigley Field in Los Angeles got their money's worth. The showcase for the league's best talent was an exciting exhibition which saw the South defeat the North, 3–1.

The team representing the North (Portland, Sacramento, Seattle, Vancouver), managed by Vancouver's Charlie Metro, consisted of the following starting players: 1B Ed Mickelson (Portland), 2B Bobby Adams (Portland), SS Buddy Peterson (Vancouver), 3B Hal Bevan (Seattle), RF Joe Taylor (Seattle), CF Al Heist (Sacramento), LF Lenny Green (Vancouver), C Roy Orteig (Seattle), and P Morrie Martin (Vancouver), who got the win. Other players included Nippy Jones, Jim Dyck, Charlie White, Spider Jorgensen, and pitchers Erv Palica, Earl Harrist, Marshall Bridges, and Bill Kennedy.

The team representing the South (Hollywood, Los Angeles, San Diego, San Francisco), managed by Clay Bryant (manager of the 1956 champion Angels), was composed of the following starters: 1B Frank Kellert (San Francisco), substituting for injured Steve Bilko, 2B George "Sparky" Anderson (Los Angeles), SS Wally Lammers (Los Angeles), 3B Rudy Regalado (San Diego), moving in from the outfield to man third for Baxes, RF Bill Causion (Hollywood), CF Marty Keough (San Francisco), LF Bert Hamric (Los Angeles), C Bill Hall (Hollywood), and starting P Bennie Daniels (Hollywood). Other players included Ken Aspromonte, Floyd Robinson, Dave Pope, Preston Ward, and pitchers Curt Raydon and Jim Hughes.

Perhaps the only disappointment concerned Steve Bilko, suffering from a groin injury, who limped onto the field out of uniform to take his bow when the players were introduced in pre-game ceremonies. Power-hitting Jim Baxes was also absent with a rib injury.

While limited to just six hits, the North made them count. The South's starter, Bennie Daniels, pitched better than his losing effort indicated. He gave up an unearned run in the second inning and was taken out of the game after the third, behind 1–0.

The North put the game to bed when Portland's Ed Mickleson belted a long homer in the sixth, followed by one more run thanks to singles by Hal Bevan and Al Heist and a fielder's choice play that allowed Bevan to score. At the same time, the South had nothing but goose eggs on the board through seven until Earl Averill slammed a solo homer in the eighth that made the score 3–1. The South recorded eight hits, as Aspromonte (2-for-2) hit a single and a double, Keough (1-for-1) hit a long single, and Kellert was 0-for-2.

During the All-Star break, Grady Hatton got everyone's attention in the Bay Area when he was asked by *Chronicle* sportswriter Bob Stevens what he thought about his first minor league experience and if he were surprised by the caliber of play in the Coast League so far. "Surprised? You're darned right I'm surprised. This is no patsy league by a very long shot! Honestly, I didn't expect the league to be this tough, nor this fine to play in, particularly the pitching. You run into a good, sharp, intelligent pitcher three or four times a week. Each club has them. Certainly we do, and that's why we're winning. After being here it's easy to see why so many big leaguers say, 'When I can't play in the big leagues any more I want to go only to one place, the Pacific Coast League.'"

Regular season play resumed with traditional doubleheaders on the Fourth of July. The Seals played the next two weeks at home, opening against weakened and floundering Portland, followed by the first visit by the much tougher Hollywood Stars before traveling to the Pacific Northwest, first to Portland, then Seattle.

The Portland Beavers, with a 30–48 record, returned to the City to kick off the second half of the season just as they had been there for Opening Day in April. Ironically, the team that was considered a hard-hitting club with challenging pitchers before the season began was still struggling. With new manager Bill Posedel they quickly fell into the lower division and lingered there through the entire first half.

Some players on the team who were known throughout the league were Earl Rapp, Ed Mickelson, and Sollie Drake. Outfielder Earl Rapp, age 36, who stepped up on the left side of the plate, had a good eye and pure power with the bat, always intimidated opposing pitchers, and was often a game-changer. First baseman Ed Mickelson, age 30, who previously had three cups of major league coffee with the Cardinals, Browns, and Cubs, was a dependable hitter who seemed to put a lot of pressure on himself in order to maintain a batting average in the .330 range. Durable Sollie Drake, back from a 66-game stint with the Cubs in 1956, played all 168 games in 1957, batted .290, and was a constant thorn in the side of the opposition. Veteran pitcher Bob Alexander struggled to the team's best record for the season, 14–13.

Thursday, July 4, was neither a time for celebration for the Portland Beavers nor a new beginning for the second half for them. If it weren't for the fact that the 12,576 fans at Seals Stadium had so much fun watching 16 innings of shutout baseball against the visiting Beavers that saw 19 Seals cross the dish to beat them 13–0 in game one followed by a 6–0 shutout in the finale, the press might have had a little compassion for the limping squad from the north that endured its 21st and 22nd shutouts of the year that day.

Tommy Hurd took the mound for the opener in which he sprinkled five hits, three walks, and two strikeouts as he achieved a complete-game victory that brought his record to 4–3. Actually, he spent most of the two-hour, 20-minute exhibition watching from the dugout while his teammates batted around and around, and the "ding, ding, ding" of Jack Rice's bell was music to his ears. The only downside to the game was a thigh pull by Marty Keough that caused him to exit early. With Eddie Sadowski the only batter to go hit-less, their assault was summed up in the box score as follows: Pearson (1-for-4), one triple; Keough (1-for-2); Aspromonte (3-for-5), two doubles, one triple, one RBI; Taormina (4-for-5), one double, one homer, four RBI; Hatton (2-for-3), one double, two RBI; Kellert (3-for-5), four RBI; Malmberg (4-for-5), one double; Sadowski, 0-for-4; Hurd (1-for-4), one RBI; and Umphlett, a late-inning replacement for Marty Keough, (1-for-2), one double, one RBI. Those who kept box scores at the park found their programs a mess before the second contest.

Riverboat Smith went the distance in the seven-inning nightcap, but came "that close" to giving up the shutout in the first inning. With two on and just one away, Louis Marquez hit a rope headed for the center field fence with Tommy Umphlett in hot pursuit. At the last second the tall, wiry fielder jumped up and grabbed the ball, then turned and fireballed it back to the infield as the runners held their bases and nobody crossed the plate. Although the Portlanders peppered a few doubles among singles, the Seals coasted to their tenth shutout of the season, 6–0.

Too smart to become euphoric over one luck-laden afternoon, they readied for Friday night's second start by Bill Prout, cleverly dubbed "Billy the Kid" by the sportswriters. In that outing, an authentic baseball game rather than the batting practice exhibition of the previous day, he impressed all onlookers. Although the Beavers out-hit their hosts, 8–7, Prout was in command all the way. One pitch in the sixth inning put a run on the board for the Beavers when Ed Mickleson walloped a long solo home run. Frank Kellert drove in all three runs for the victorious Seals, two in the second inning and one in the fourth. Sal Taormina continued to demonstrate his prowess at the plate, no surprise to anyone, as he went 3-for-4 including one double, and this man, often described by the press as having the ability to run just a step ahead of a tree, even stole a base!

In a post-game interview, Gordon praised Prout, saying he was pleasantly surprised by the kid's "stuff," which he said was sneaky-fast with smooth wrist action, and he felt Prout could win at the PCL level of play. Later Nini Tornay compared him to another youngster he had caught, bonus baby Eddie Cereghino from Daly City. He described Prout as faster with a better curve ball, and with every bit as much poise. Los Angeles manager Clay Bryant said Prout showed poise and intelligence and was a "real comer."

The most surprising news on Saturday was that the sagging Solons had sold one of their best players, veteran first baseman Nippy Jones, to their parent club, the Milwaukee Braves, to fill in for Joe Adcock who suffered a broken leg sliding into second base on June 24. Jim Westlake and PCL veteran Chuck Stevens took over at the bag, but they lacked the charisma Jones added to each game.

Before the game, Bob Feller conducted a baseball clinic at the stadium that was well-populated with participating youngsters under the watchful eyes of their doting dads who wanted to shake hands with the former Cleveland great. Once the game started, Rapid Robert, in his street clothes, was seen in the stands signing autographs during the early innings.

Harry Dorish and the Seals took their fourth straight from the Beavers, 9–2, as they out-hit them, 14–11. The lineup card looked different: catcher Haywood Sullivan, with the team in 1956 and 1957 spring training camp but starting the 1957 season in the AAA International League, was recalled to San Francisco in time for the final series of the month in Los Angeles; Jack Phillips was moved from third to second while Chip Aspromonte was down with a wrenched back; and Tommy Umphlett was still in center for Marty Keough. Shortstop Harry Malmberg led the team at the plate, going 3-for-5 as Dorish got the complete-game win, his eighth against six losses.

The article in Monday's *Chronicle* condensed Sunday's activities as follows: "S.F. Triumphs, 4–3 and Ditto." By taking the twin bill San Francisco probably made the Portlanders wish they could have stayed home because it was the beginning of a downward spiral that lasted throughout the season. Bill Abernathie got the complete-game win, number nine, in game one. After starter Windy McCall and reliever Bert Thiel were knocked around, Leo Kiely picked up win number 12 in the finale. Marty Keough took the field in the closer after a couple of recovery days and tripled for Ed Sadowski in the eighth. Phillips continued to fill the hole at second in Aspromonte's absence.

Because of the All-Star Game schedule at the beginning of the series, PCL teams forfeited the off-day on Monday to play the seventh game of the series. It was Family Night in Seals Stadium when the entire family went to the game for $1.25, the price of one general admission ticket. Jack Spring gave up just three hits, a single in each of the first three innings, and posted seven strikeouts in an exciting 2–1 victory. The Beavers drew first blood as they drove one across in their premier at-bat, and the score remained 1–0 until the Seals tied it in the sixth. Umphlett started the eighth with a double off the glove of shortstop Ed Winceniak, advanced to third on a Taormina sacrifice, then scored on Kellert's line drive to left. That was all it took to complete a seven-game series sweep for the Bay Area club.

The press announced that Ford Frick, the third baseball commissioner, who had served since Happy Chandler resigned in July 1951, had been re-elected for another seven years.

On another front, Portland skipper Bill Posedel gave an interview about his first impressions of Albie Pearson, saying he doubted all the good things he had heard about the young player could possibly be true. But they were. He added that, despite his sometimes getting confused on defense, Pearson had made him a believer and predicted he would go on to a successful major league career. By that point in the season Pearson had caught the eye and won the affection of the fans every place the team played.

When Hollywood came to town for a seven-game stint starting Tuesday, San Francisco's league lead had increased to four games over Vancouver, with San Diego and Hollywood back by six. The Stars were intent on closing that gap as much as possible. And they had a blend of players who could do just that: Carlos Bernier, Spook Jacobs, Paul Pettit, and pitchers George "Red" Witt and Bennie Daniels.

Without a doubt, Puerto Rican–born Carlos Bernier, age 30, was the most exciting and memorable player on the squad during that era. The speedy outfielder with a cannon for a throwing arm led the league in triples twice, stole over 500 bases in his long PCL career, and was always a dreaded opponent. Spook Jacobs, age 31, was masterful at second base and always found ways to cause trouble for the other side. Good clutch hitter Paul Pettit, age 25, was a versatile iron man who led the club with 158 games played that season, was primarily an outfielder who also played first base when needed. An interesting 19-year-old, Dick Stuart, was a backup at first base with a solid bat whose skill and colorful antics later took him to the major leagues, where he earned the nickname "Dr. Strangeglove." On the mound there were two young pitchers on their way to major league careers: RHP George "Red" Witt, who had a 1957 record of 18–7 with a 2.24 ERA to lead the staff closely followed by RHP Bennie Daniels, a workhorse who logged a 17–8 record with a 2.95 ERA in 229 innings pitched. The Seals knew this was a formidable team that could undermine their league lead, an event which they staunchly planned to prevent.

The series opener on Tuesday was quite an adventure for both clubs. Starter Tommy Hurd butted heads with Laurin Pepper for what turned out to be a back-and-forth ballgame that held the close attention of all 6,570 fans in the stands. Both made exits before the end of the game. Pepper was relieved by Ben Wade with one out in the second inning after the Seals placed four runs on the board. Chuck Churn came in in the seventh with two out and took the loss. Hurd pitched 8⅓ innings before Leo Kiely made his 30th entrance of the campaign and got his "bakers' dozen" 13th win in the contest that wasn't resolved until the 12th inning.

At the end of nine both teams had scored five times. Over three and a half hours after the first pitch, as the nail-biter went into the bottom of the 12th, things ended with a little comic relief ... at least for the home team.

With one away and the bases loaded (Pearson at third, Umphlett at second, and Aspromonte at first), all the infielders moved in close to prevent the winning run from scoring. Sal Taormina hit a weak grounder to Churn, who grabbed it but hesitated and pivoted from right to left before he decided to throw the ball to second base at the same time he noticed nobody was covering the bag. Finally, as he made a hurried throw to the plate, the ball bounced away from the catcher and Pearson scored. Game over. The victory prolonged their record of winning every extra-inning game of the campaign, and brought Kiely's record to 13–2 with a 1.19 ERA that gave him huge bragging rights, that is, if he were the type to brag.

When Carlos Bernier took himself out of the game in the first inning on Wednesday, complaining that he had reinjured the thumb he fractured June 18, the Seals probably thought that was the edge they needed, especially when skipper Clyde King completely reconfigured his defense. But the moment was fleeting. Umphlett, on base via the walk, scored the first run of the game in the third after a long single by Aspromonte got him to third before Taormina brought him home on an infield out. And that was all the scoring the Gordons did that day. Hollywood tied the game in the fourth, then added one more in the sixth, which was all they needed, but they scored twice more in the top of the ninth as a result of two critical Seals errors that made the final score 4–1. Bennie Daniels limited them to just four hits, one each by Umphlett and Sullivan and two by Aspromonte. Starter Riverboat Smith took what was described as a hard-luck loss.

Thursday afternoon, Prout faced PCL strikeout leader Curt Raydon.

Unfortunately Prout developed a blister on his pitching hand early, and when it popped in the fourth inning, he struggled with it until he had given up one unearned run thanks to a double play ball dropped by Aspromonte. With two away Gordon sent Bill Abernathie in to stop the bleeding, which he did.

Abernathie contained the visitors while the Seals tied the score in the seventh on an unearned run of their own. After Aspromonte extended his hitting streak to ten games with an infield single and took second on a Kellert single to left, Bill Renna narrowly missed grounding into a double play when Jacobs bobbled the ball at second allowing Aspromonte to score. In addition to those two hits, the Bay Bombers were limited to three more: two singles by Keough and one by Sadowski.

The tie was broken in the top of the ninth when Hollywood flexed some muscle. Spook Jacobs beat out an infield single, and, after both Jim Baumer and Bill Causion walked to load the bases, clutch-hitting Paul Pettit lined a single that scored two runs. Another single by Leo Rodriguez sent Causion to the plate. The Stars led, 4–1, and the Seals were unable to score in the bottom of the frame.

The pregame workouts Friday night were filled with energy and laughter from the Seals players, who were confident their two-game losing streak would be broken in the upcoming game. They signed a lot of autographs and graciously accepted the admiration of their adoring fans.

But the mood changed when the game started. Red Witt held them to four hits as on-rushing Hollywood shut them out, 7–0. Despite an enthusiastic crowd's pleadings, the Seals ran their consecutive innings without an earned run to an unbelievable 27. Ken Aspromonte's hitting streak died as he went 0-for-4. Haywood Sullivan doubled while Keough, Phillips, and Renna each singled. That was it for the night. It was also a hard night for pitcher Harry Dorish, who lasted five innings and was tagged for his seventh loss.

Saturday, July 13, was the Third Annual Old Timers and Hall of Fame Day at the stadium. The festivities began at 11:30 A.M. with the introduction of two former pitchers who had faced each other in a famous game played on May 1, 1920: Joe Oreschger (1892–1986, Boston Braves) and Leon Cadore (1890–1958, Brooklyn Robins). That game went 26 innings with both starting pitchers on the mound when it was called a 1–1 draw, and went into the record books as the longest game in major league history.

The Seals' host for the day, Walter Mails, said it was the first reunion between the two since that day. Walter Mails said those two pitchers had their names added to the San Francisco Hall of Fame as he introduced former Seals players Babe Pinelli, infielder Gus Suhr, and beloved pitcher Lefty Gomez. He read the list of notables present: pitchers Cack Henley and Bill Steen; infielders Roy Corhan, Eddie Mulligan, and Oscar Vitt; outfielder Ping Bodie;

trainer Denny Carroll; and player-managers Nick Williams and Bert Ellison. This was followed by a three-inning game that showcased 18 former San Francisco players: Ted Jennings, Gus Suhr, Al Wright, Brooks Holder, Augie Galan, Frankie Hawkins, Al Lien, Ferris Fain, Dolph Camilli, Reno Cheso, Jim Moran, Joe Sprinz, Ernie Lombardi, Billy Raimondi, Tom Seats, Will Leonard, Bob Joyce, and Seals president Jerry Donovan. Several played an inning or less and the lineups were supplemented by local semipro players. Fans chattered among themselves as if recalling games featuring some of the old timers they had just seen.

Jack Spring faced Laurin Pepper who had such a brief outing earlier in the week, in what turned out to be a somewhat "freaky" game. In the fifth inning, behind 1–0, the Gordons finally broke a drought and scored their first earned runs in 19 innings. After Marty Keough and Ken Aspromonte got back-to-back singles, Frank Kellert struck out and Grady Hatton pounded a double into deep center to score both runners. When Harry Malmberg laid down a perfect sacrifice bunt, Hatton took off and rounded third, heading for the plate. The pitcher fielded it and threw to the catcher, who literally laid himself out on the third base line, knocking Hatton to his knees and rendering him trapped in the no-man's land between third and home.

Gordon charged out of the dugout yelling "interference!" But umpire Chris Pelekoudas ruled otherwise and Hatton was called out. At that point a barrage of gear, bats, and whatever was not nailed down in the Seals dugout flew onto the field. After the dust settled and the litter was cleared, the score was tied at two.

The Seals scored the winning run in the eighth thanks to a Hollywood error. Hatton led off with a single to left, Bill Renna flied out to right, and Malmberg coaxed a walk from reliever Chuck Churn. Umphlett was put in at third to run for Hatton and Haywood Sullivan got the second walk of the inning, loading the bases. Pinch-hitter extraordinaire Sal Taormina came in to hit for Spring. He popped a windblown lazy fly a few feet behind third base. Dick Smith backed up, gloved it, but dropped it which was all the speedy Umphlett needed to score. The infield fly rule was called and Taormina was out, but the run counted.

Umphlett remembered:

> I don't remember many games after all this time, but there was one circumstance when I came in to replace our runner at third base. We eventually loaded the bases with a couple of walks and the hitter, Taormina I think, popped up a foul ball down the third base line. Now, if you're running the bases correctly, well, I was turned the right way and I knew that when the shortstop went out and caught the ball in foul territory down the third base line and dropped it he had to completely turn around to make the throw to the plate, and I just took a chance. As soon as he dropped the ball I took off

In the eighth inning Tommy Umphlett pinch-ran for Grady Hatton and scored on a windblown infield fly bobbled and dropped while catcher Pete Naton (#12) retrieved the throw home. Umpire Emmett Ashford watched (David Eskenazi Collection).

and beat his throw home and we won the game. Can't remember who we played against in that series, but I do remember that it was one of those different situations that come up where you can win a ballgame if you're alert and aggressive and do the right thing.

With the Seals behind in the series three games to two, the San Franciscans were ahead 3–2 in the ninth inning when Kiely came in to save it. Things may have been in jeopardy but for a spectacular catch by Renna who crashed into the left field wall with a loud thud and saved the day. The 3–2 triumph allowed them to save face to some extent. It was Jack Spring's fourth win against four losses.

On Sunday, although both contests were exciting one-run games, the 10,148 spectators were left scratching their heads wondering if the same two squads actually played both of them.

The opener, a true, unabridged slugfest, saw Tommy Hurd as the first of eight pitchers for the hosts, while Bennie Daniels led a parade of five hurlers

Catcher Haywood Sullivan tagged out Hollywood runner Lee Walls at the plate as the Seals lost game one of the double dip. On deck batter Bill Causion (#26) kept a close eye on the play (David Eskenazi Collection).

for the visitors. None of them could be described as effective, as a total of 38 hits and 35 runs went into the books and Hollywood won, 18–17, the most runs scored in a single game in Seals Stadium history.

The Seals apparently thought they had used their Sunday allotment of hits in the first game, as they managed only four in the 4–3 loss in the night-cap. Eddie Sadowski drove in all three Seals runs, first with a double with Kellert and Renna on the bases due to successive singles, then with a solo home run. It was one of the few times they lost a doubleheader that season. Even worse, they had lost five games of the seven-game set.

Once again the fates were on the side of the Gordons as they headed north to face Portland and Seattle still in first place by three games. But things had tightened up, as San Diego was behind by just 3.5 games and Hollywood by four. The gap between the two teams at the top and the two teams at the bottom had widened considerably. Portland, in seventh, was 22.5 games behind, and Sacramento sagged at the bottom, trailing by 24.5 games. On the way the Seals honored a pre-season promise to play an exhibition game against the Eugene Emeralds in the Class B Northwest League, which they won, 5–3.

In preparation for the remainder of season following the upcoming series with Portland, local sportswriters analyzed the needs and wish-lists of the Seals as they looked toward facing the top contenders in the league for the rest of the year. They more or less agreed that the "weakest link" was an unreliable and streaky pitching staff. McCall, said to have skated on thin ice since his arrival, was a candidate for option or release once a good replacement was lined up. The Seals could no longer afford the wait until next year attitude they'd used in the past. Boston was aware of the dilemma in San Francisco and wanted the team to finish their 54-year stint in the Pacific Coast League as champions. One of the rumors circulated was that the Seals would option a disappointing Windy McCall to Miami in the AAA International League, and Boston was looking into making a deal for another pitcher.

From Eugene the team flew north to face the Beavers for the first time in their home park, Multnomah Stadium, where they moved in 1956 after their long-time Vaughn Street Park home was condemned and demolished. The "new digs" was an old park built in 1926 as part of the Multnomah [County] Athletic Club for collegiate football and refurbished to accommodate baseball. Though it had one of the largest seating capacities in the league it was essentially considered a nightmare for pitchers thanks to the short left field fence, described as "reachable by Little League players" (*San Francisco Chronicle*, July 5, 1957.

The initial clash between the two teams on Tuesday night was between Bill Prout and Jack Carmichael, ten years his senior, and the first of four Portland twirlers. The game was scoreless through three innings when San Francisco broke the ice. With Hatton on third, Prout hit a single through the hole that scored him. But the Beavers tied it up in the bottom of the frame.

Things remained calm until the sixth when the Seals batted around. Prout made an out, Pearson walked, Keough flied out, and Aspromonte doubled, putting Pearson on third. Relief pitcher Ray Bauer issued an intentional pass to Frank Kellert, loading the bases. That was a game changer as Renna approached the plate with the bags full and his muscles flexing. Bauer carefully worked the count to 0–2 but his next offering was right in Renna's wheelhouse and he bashed it for a grand slam. The Seals added one more run to their total that inning before Prout made the third out. Portland managed to score twice more, but wound up on the short end of the 7–3 final. Prout allowed only six hits in his first complete-game victory. Gordon and the powers in Boston were glad they had kept him on the roster when Spring returned, as they had big league plans for the youth.

Wednesday night, game two turned out to be a real spectacle. After going back and forth, the score was tied at seven at the end of the regulation nine innings that saw starting pitchers Jack Spring and Bob Anderson depart early. The Seals went to the plate in the tenth inning intent on scoring a run to take the game. But it didn't turn out like that. It took three relief pitchers to get three outs as the Gordons hit everything in sight, ran the bases, and scored five times. Kiely came in, got the last three outs to end the game, 12–7, and collected his 14th win. The press described the Seals' rally as "an assault," "an explosion," "an eruption," and "an utter shambles," and all were right. By the time the final line score was assembled the Seals had accumulated 22 hits in the game and everybody contributed to that total: Pearson 4-for-7, Umphlett 1-for-5, Aspromonte 3-for-6 with a home run, Kellert 1-for-5 with a homer, Renna 3-for-5, Hatton 2-for-6, Malmberg 2-for-6, Sullivan 3-for-4, and Spring 1-for-2.

Jack Spring recalled, "Leo Kiely was a very unusual, highly effective pitcher for the team. We called him 'the vulture' because he swooped in and got the win after starters went the first seven. He was so good there was no way Gordon could not use him. I mean, the guy got over 20 wins out of the bullpen!"

The victory parade continued on Thursday. Seals sluggers continued their hitting rampage of the night before with a six-run binge in the fourth inning that gave Tommy Hurd a 6–4 lead and eventually the win. Unfortunately, he broke down with a split finger while batting in the sixth and was sent to the sidelines. In the bottom of the inning Leo Kiely came in and, despite two defensive bobbles from his teammates, held down the opponents. The Seals added one in the seventh off a Renna homer and another in the ninth for good measure, and walked away with 16 hits on their side of the ledger. That win put the Seals ahead in the series three games to none, kept them in first place ahead of Vancouver by four games, and locked the Beavers in the cellar. The San Francisco squad knew the race for the pennant was getting rougher as they would spend much of the remainder of the season combating the Mounties, Stars, Padres, and last season's champion Angels. They knew the opposition's hitting would be harder and the pitching much tougher.

For two hours and eight minutes on Friday night the Portland fans enjoyed their team out-hitting the visitors, 9–8, and outscoring them, 4–2. It was the first time they had defeated the Seals since Opening Day on April 12. They jumped to a 3–0 lead off Riverboat Smith in the first inning, then put goose eggs on the board through the seventh. They added one more tally the eighth when veteran Frank Carswell hit a solo home run. The only shining moment for the Seals came in the seventh when Renna blasted a long one over the left field fence with Frank Kellert on base.

After the game Gordon announced that Windy McCall, who had been skating on thin ice for a couple of weeks, had been sent to Miami in the AAA International League. "The Bull," Al Schroll, was recalled from Oklahoma City and expected any day. Other rumors "leaked" that the Seals were quite interested in putting together a contract with RHP Marino Pieretti, age 37, a veteran with eight PCL seasons plus six major league seasons in his resume. Ironically, the Italian born and San Francisco raised twirler, thought to be too small to sign as a youngster, was now considered a possible savior in the final months of the season as the squad faced the best teams in the Coast League. Although a lot of people were excited, nothing came of it.

Of the 6,384 fans in attendance Saturday afternoon, over half were thrilled Little Leaguers in full uniform which made the atmosphere in the park electric. But the chatter, heavier than usual in the visitors' dugout, was not about baseball at all. Instead they listened to an excited Joe Gordon as he discussed the fact that he had the best day of his life on the links when he shot a 71 earlier in the day. Feeling rejuvenated, he stationed himself at the short-stop spot with Red Sox second baseman Bobby Doerr at second during batting practice. The fans didn't realize it at the time, but they watched two future members of the Baseball Hall of Fame.

As soon as the umpire shouted "Play Ball," the spotlight turned to Harry Dorish, restored to early season form, as he scattered nine hits and pitched a complete-game 3–0 shutout. He was aided by eight hits off the bats of his teammates, including homers by Haywood Sullivan (who went 4-for-4) and Ken Aspromonte, doubles by Malmberg and Aspromonte, and a triple by Sullivan, who missed hitting for the cycle when he bashed a rope into center that was caught with great finesse by Solly Drake. Ironically, in an effort to rest Grady Hatton, Jack Phillips (6' 4") was inserted at third base in the late innings and made the defensive play of the game when he jumped high to grab a bouncer down the line off the bat of Ed Mickleson and threw it to second for a force play that ended the inning. The win brought Dorish's record to 9–7.

Sunday was "all Seals all day" as they took the twin bill, 7–2 and 5–1, which gave them the series, six games to one, and a 17–2 season advantage over the Beavers. Gordon continued his "lineup jiggling" for those two conflicts. He switched Marty Keough (2-for-4) and Albie Pearson (2-for-5) in the batting order, putting Keough in the leadoff slot and Pearson to the number two spot to see if it made any difference in their baserunning game. He also did the unthinkable when he moved catcher Haywood Sullivan from the traditional eight-spot in the batting order up to sixth.

In the first inning starter Bill Prout yielded two runs to the Beavers, all they would get in the game, before he ran out of gas and struggled through the fourth. Al Schroll took over in the fifth (his first appearance for the team since April 21). Leo Kiely entered the game with one out in the seventh and sealed the deal to log his 15th win. Fans and press compared him to Win "Pard" Ballou, a 40-year-old relief pitcher in the 1930s who went into games "cold" and saved a bucket-load of games for the Seals. The club won, 7–2, as they out-hit Portland 11–10, including a three-run homer by Ken Aspromonte and a solo homer by Harry Malmberg.

Marty Keough always praised Kiely's ability on the mound saying he was a supreme asset to the team that season. But he also laughed, saying,

> Leo Kiely was another guy I really enjoyed. That tall, thin pitcher drank more beer than anybody I've ever seen, and never gained any weight! At the motels he always had a bucket with five or six bottles of beer with a towel over it sitting in the pool to keep cool. I just couldn't believe he could do that and stay so skinny. And those days in the pool never sapped his energy or interfered with his skill on the mound. In game situations he wasn't one of those guys who threw real hard, but he had a good sinker and threw a lot of strikes. He was smart about it.

The series closer saw Jack Spring face Dick Fiedler in a game that was a hard-fought one-one tie in the fifth inning when Sal Taormina came to the plate with Kellert on third, Malmberg on second, and Phillips on first via an intentional pass. The *Chronicle* reported, "Two swings later the ball zoomed into left-center, everybody aboard fled home. The door to the basement flew open and Portland walked through it." Taormina stopped at second and later scored the fourth run of the inning on an error. For the rest of the game Spring sprinkled six hits and six strikeouts among Portland batters. Boston put Gordon on notice that the major league club was paying careful attention to his improvement and his ability.

The San Francisco Seals, in first place since June 11, were now a full five games ahead of the pack. Their next trip was their second to Seattle since the first week in May to face the O'Doul crew in Sick's Stadium, called "the baseball bungalow built by beer" in the Rainier Valley. Owned by Rainier Beer magnate Emil Sick, it was a cozy park that originally seated 11,000 until it was expanded to 25,400 to accommodate the major league Seattle Pilots in their only season in 1969.

In an article that appeared in every Coast League city, league president Leslie O'Connor announced that as of July 8, overall attendance was 1,072,247, an increase of 126,953 over the same period in the 1956 season. Five clubs showed increases: Vancouver (77,778), San Francisco (59,793), Los Angeles (44,213), Hollywood (25,479), and San Diego (1,601). Three clubs' attendance had declined: Seattle (41,759), Portland (14,270), and Sacramento (25, 882). Everyone agreed the Seattle situation was worrisome, especially owner Emil

Sick, who had made his concerns known at every opportunity and always blamed the uncertainty on what he and others called the "westward invasion" by the major leagues.

The visit to Seattle was scheduled as an abbreviated four-game set, Tuesday through Friday, and would be followed by a quick return to San Francisco without a day off to face the Vancouver Mounties for five games starting at two o'clock Saturday afternoon in Seals Stadium.

Originally Gordon wanted to send the riverboat gambler, Bob Smith (5–8), against flame-thrower Red Munger (6–6) in the opener. But when Smith turned up with a slight elbow problem, Gordon simply held him back a day and moved Prout up one day to make the start. The Seals had lost the last series four games to three, and were intent on avoiding a repeat performance. Instead they hoped to repeat the good week they had at the plate against the Beavers: Haywood Sullivan, .550; Ken Aspromonte, .452; Bill Renna, .448; Grady Hatton, .409; and Harry Malmberg, .367. But they knew it wouldn't last because the Seattle pitchers were immeasurably better than those they'd seen in Multnomah Stadium. In addition to Red Munger, their pitching staff included former Seals pitchers Larry Jansen and Duane Pillette, reliever Bill Kennedy, who appeared in 51 games and logged a 1.16 ERA, and Bud Podbielan, all veterans in their early to mid–30s.

Seattle had a strong team led by veterans. Bobby Balcena, 31, was a dynamic outfielder who had played minor league ball since 1948, mostly at the AAA level, with time out in 1956 for seven games with the Cincinnati Redlegs as the first player of Filipino heritage to make the majors before he returned to Seattle. First baseman Jim Dyck, 35, was an iron horse who also had a long minor league career, and his .310 average at the plate led the team in 1957. Versatile infielder Eddie Basinski, who played second, short, and third in 129 games, had spent nine seasons with Portland through 1956, then moved to Seattle. Veteran right fielder Joe Taylor, a speedster with a good arm, was always a threat at the plate as he batted a dependable .300 throughout the season. And there was a 24-year-old shortstop named Maury Wills who stole 31 bases in 1957 and later made a big name for himself in the big leagues.

O'Doul noted that the Seals were not the same team they faced earlier in the season. Their offense had improved once Gordon stopped playing the "matching players to position dance," with the biggest improvement in Ken Aspromonte once he found his niche at second base.

At the last minute the Seals' roster became one man short as Pearson flew home to be with his ill wife. Right field was manned by Tommy Umphlett. O'Doul started Charlie Rabe, optioned from parent club Cincinnati, who was in the midst of his best season that would end 16–10 with a

3.37 ERA. But nobody was surprised when Prout had the game of his life. Just a month after his high school graduation, his finesse and smoothness were resounding as he scattered four hits, allowed just one run, and struck out nine for the complete-game victory, his third. Rabe yielded only five hits, including two singles to Aspromonte, a triple to Phillips, and a single apiece to Sullivan and Renna. All the runs for the game were on the board after four innings with the Seals ahead, 3–1.

Prout was opening eyes around the circuit. His youth, lack of professional experience, and determined work ethic with the Seals gained well-deserved praise and respect. The press noted that Boston had high hopes for the rookie in their future and praised the way Joe Gordon, Glenn Wright and the entire coaching staff handled his development.

Wednesday was a different story as Seattle overshadowed the Bay Bombers in the hits department, 15–6, in the runs scored department, 8–2, and stopped their consecutive wins streak at four. Duane Pillette made Joe Gordon rethink letting him get away earlier in the season as he pitched a complete-game victory. Riverboat Smith, on the other hand, was the first of four Seals moundsmen who tried unsuccessfully to contain the bats of the Suds. Pearson was back in the lineup in the two-slot and went 0-for-2 for his night's work.

With the series tied at one, the Seals sent Jack Spring to face Red Munger on Thursday night. The Seals got a run in the second inning when Frank Kellert singled, advanced to third on Hatton's long single into the right field corner, and crossed the plate on a Bill Renna sacrifice fly. The Seals added three runs in the sixth thanks to defensive plays "almost made." Going into the seventh Spring had a four-hit shutout, all doubles—three by Joe Taylor and one by Ray Orteig. Both starters allowed seven hits. Kiely entered with two outs in the seventh and Bud Podbielan took the mound to start the eighth for the Rainiers. San Francisco won the game, 4–1, and took the lead in the series, two games to one.

Friday saw the tables turned on the visitors when they played a game that took just one hour and 40 minutes. Pitchers Harry Dorish and Larry Jansen carefully rationed hits to their opponents. The Seals got nine, including two doubles by Sullivan and one by Kellert, and the Suds got eight, including an Eddie Basinski homer. When Dorish tired in the seventh, Kiely made his appearance and things settled down. The score was even at three until the Seals scratched out a one-run lead in the eighth. Everyone applauded Seattle's outstanding defensive plays that kept the game close as they approached the bottom of the ninth behind, 4–3. The Rainiers rallied for two runs and won the game, 5–4, to tie the series at two. Kiely's win streak in relief was stopped at 14 as he got his first defeat of the season in that role (his previous two losses were as a starter), and the great fireman's record "plummeted" to 15–3.

An article in the *Los Angeles Times* reported on Wednesday, July 24, that Hollywood Stars president Bob Cobb had accepted the Sheriff Gene Biscailuz Award for the Stars' 14–10 win in the annual cross-town rivalry with the Angels in 1956. More newsworthy than the award was his comment to the crowd: "It looks like this is the finale of the Coast League, but I am delighted that the Brooklyn Dodgers are coming out here."

Although logic demanded that the Seals would be tired and sluggish after a crammed week and unique travel schedule that saw them awaken before the sun came up on Saturday morning, rush to catch a flight from Seattle to San Francisco, then be given a police escort to get to the park by one o'clock for the two o'clock game against Vancouver, they seemed energized. They played in the sunshine in front of 4,065 welcoming fans who witnessed what may well have been Bill Abernathie's best effort of the season. He pitched a complete game and limited the Mounties to six hits with no passes and four strikeouts as the Seals won, 3–1. He put the visitors behind the eight-ball immediately as he retired the first 11 batters he faced, while the two quick unearned runs they got off George Bamberger in the first inning was all they needed to claim the victory. It brought his record to 10–1.

In addition, that performance allowed Leo Kiely a view from the bullpen as a spectator as he enjoyed a well-deserved rest. Frank Kellert also watched the game from the sidelines thanks to an ankle injury received sliding into second in Friday night's game in Seattle. He never said anything until Joe Gordon and teammates observed him limping after the game. Versatile Sal Taormina guarded the bag at first.

The thing that got the headline in the papers was a tape-measure homer slammed by Bill Renna in the fifth, estimated at 550 soaring feet, and considered one of the three longest homers in the history of Seals Stadium. It was compared to a Steve Bilko bash in 1956 that flew over the left field fence and across the parking lot, and was later found on the roof of the Steeple Bakery. The other, also hit in 1956, was off the bat of Seals pitcher and power hitter Jerry Casale, who temporarily left the game for military service during the 1957 season.

The Sunday twin bill was more like a night at the fights than professional baseball. The largest crowd of the year in the Pacific Coast League (13,294), all of whom had apparently rented their 15-cent seat cushions, got their money's worth in the seventh inning of the first game. Umpire Emmett Ashford, known for self-indulgent antics that inserted him into more games than managers, players, or fans appreciated, made another of his infamous loud but inaccurate calls. With the Seals behind by a run, a rally that may have at least tied the game brewed when Ashford went through his gyrations as he called Marty Keough out at first. A barrage of cushions covered the field as Joe Gordon charged the ump to talk it over, at least until Ashford gave him the thumb amid thunderous boos and a second downpour of cushions. The game was delayed while hapless ushers cleaned up the mess. By the end of nine innings, however, San Francisco was still one run short and lost the battle, 3–2.

But it wasn't over for Ashford. In the first inning of the closer, after Haywood Sullivan, backed up by Gordon, argued about a pitch Ashford called ball four that pushed across a run to give the Mounties a 1–0 lead, Ashford tossed the pair with one grand heave-ho. Once again loud, unrepeatable comments permeated the atmosphere, and most of the last remaining cushions in the stands, enhanced by paper cups and assorted wrappers, littered the diamond. The only thing all that accomplished was another game delay.

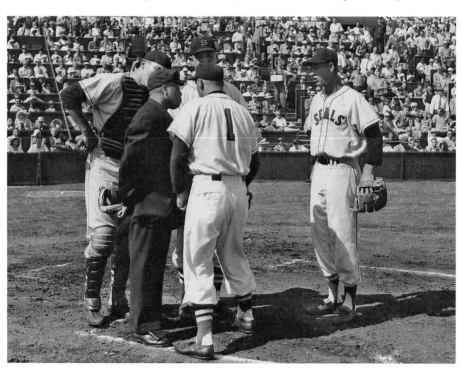

In the first inning of the seven-inning nightcap catcher Haywood Sullivan and Joe Gordon (#1) protested a questionable ball four call by Emmett Ashford that forced in a run giving the Mounties a 1–0 lead before Ashford tossed the pair. Infielders Jack Phillips (facing Gordon) and Harry Malmberg (up the line) add their two cents (David Eskenazi Collection).

The second of several "discussions" between Seals catcher Haywood Sullivan and home plate umpire Emmett Ashford during the twin bill (David Eskenazi Collection).

Throughout the seven-inning encounter the fans vehemently kept after Ashford's every move. As Seals players hit the baseball and scored runs that led to a 7–4 win, the fans gradually relaxed. Things finally ended when the Mounties couldn't catch up in the top of the ninth and the Seals bagged the win, 7–4. As a safety precaution, Ashford received an escort off the field by uniformed (and armed) police downstairs into the inner sanctum corridors as the few remaining cushions rained down on them.

Under normal circumstances, Vancouver would have left San Francisco and both teams would have had a needed and deserved off-day. But the late–July schedule was not normal, and the two teams faced each other in two more games, Monday and Tuesday. Monday night was a well-fought game in spite of a disparity in the hits department as the Mounties had 11, including five doubles, while the Seals were limited to five singles and one extra-base hit. Their only tally went on the board in the second when Phillips singled, went to second on a fly out by Malmberg, and scored on Eddie Sadowski's long double. The locals watched Vancouver trim their league lead to five games as starter Harry Dorish lasted until he was lifted for unsuccessful pinch-hitter Haywood Sullivan in the seventh, and relieved by Kiely for the rest of the ride. The final score was 3–1, and the series was tied at two. Vancouver clinched Tuesday's rubber game in short order before they left town to the relief of the locals.

The Seals finally had a day off on Wednesday to relax and contemplate August and the arrival of the surging Hollywood Stars for five games starting Thursday. The morning sports pages announced the reactivation of Carlos Bernier, out since July 10 with a broken right thumb, which automatically made them more viable contenders. His name on the Stars' lineup card always impacted the strategy of the opposition.

Meanwhile, away from the diamond, July was inundated with activity focused on a variety of things that had to be done in order to get big league baseball in San Francisco.

On July 3, columnist Art Rosenbaum wrote that, according to protocol, the official letter of intent to bid on a major league baseball team for San Francisco was in the initial drafting stages, and Mayor Christopher announced it would be submitted no later than midnight, August 15. In the meantime, a new brochure promoting assets that made the City a desirable place for major league baseball was created and sent to appropriate personnel of all big league clubs.

Concomitantly, architects and construction companies submitted bids to build a new major league ballpark, which was prematurely projected for completion in time for opening day of the 1958 season. The locations for such a venture were a source of local controversy which was eventually pared down to two areas, the South Basin site and the Bay View site, each with distinct pros and cons.

A week later, on July 10, the mayor of Hayward told the world that his East Bay city would make a bid for the Giants, and he planned to submit an elaborate plan to build a 90,000-seat ballpark with parking for 20,000 cars that could also be used for 49ers football and other sports. In addition, the complex was to include a 200-room motel that could house players, visiting dignitaries, and others. They suggested everything would be built to meet Horace Stoneham's specifications. Initial reactions were not as favorable as anticipated, and the idea eventually dried up and blew away.

Simultaneously, to add to the pressure, there was speculation that the Red Sox would side-step all the second-guessing by moving its own major league club to San Francisco and bring the American League to the Pacific Coast. But that rumor was quickly squelched when general manager Joe Cronin said there was no basis in that report, emphasizing that owner Tom Yawkey intended to remain in Boston. He added, "This is an awfully poor time for these rumors to arise. The San Francisco Seals are out there fighting to win the pennant. If anybody wants to write about baseball, write about the Seals. They're doing a dandy job and deserve support."

And, of course, there was the issue of pay–TV rights, which seemed to get more complicated by the day. That well-publicized bit of unfinished business involved offers to the city government from several pay-as-you-see television companies, as they were called back in the day. Seeing it as a lucrative market for the future, clubs were nervous about fan reaction to having to pay for ballgames they were able to get for free in the past. Stoneham said the deal did not hinge on the issue of pay–TV.

Thursday, July 18, was a busy news day for the Pacific Coast League. First, self-explanatory headlines in the green sheet of the *San Francisco Chronicle* read, "Stoneham: Our Last Year in N.Y." He stated emphatically that 1957 was the final season for his Giants in New York and pointed out that the imagined condition that linked the move of one New York team to the other had "no connection to reality." He had received National League approval to move to San Francisco no matter what Walter O'Malley and Brooklyn decided. He concluded by saying everything would be signed, sealed and delivered in a month or so.

The fans, who had either become immune to or cynical about the continual flow of promises, responded with more curiosity than excitement. Another proclamation that San Francisco would have a major league baseball team in 1958. Ho-hum. Of course, hundreds of details remained to be worked out.

In a lighthearted manner, an Oakland paper revealed that Oakland had strongly considered seeking a major league club of its own but nothing came of it. When the City Council earlier attempted to pass a resolution to bid for the Giants, it was defeated by one dissenting vote, and that dissenting councilman explained his action by asking the others, "What will you do if they say, 'Yes'?"

It seemed that the Bay View location, Mayor Christopher's preference from the start because of more moderate weather, was the logical choice to get the nod for the new park, and the Harney Construction Company foolishly stuck to an old promise to have the park ready for baseball on opening day of the 1958 season. They were the only ones who saw that goal as a possibility, and arrangements were underway to extend the lease on Seals Stadium through the 1959 season and longer if necessary.

Another news brief concerned an "unofficial report from New York" that the Giants had previously made arrangements to exchange their AAA farm team, the Minneapolis Millers in the American Association, with Boston for their AAA club in San Francisco. But the problems related to that aspect of the wheeling and dealing turned out to be more complicated than originally thought when Minneapolis later revealed it would make a bid of its own for the Giants' major league club that would include a new and expandable baseball park. But Christopher calmed down the media by explaining that he was positive Minneapolis had a ten percent chance at best to land the deal while San Francisco had a 90 percent chance of success.

On the lighter side, Walter Mails, always eager for the spotlight and never shy about expressing his opinions, put in his two cents: "The Seals are leading the Pacific Coast League. What more does a baseball fan want? Give us two more pitchers and we'll beat the Giants four games out of seven, every series. They can keep Willie Mays, too. My only worry is that after the Giants met the Seals, they'd want to steal Albie Pearson from us."

It seemed everyone had joined the "jump the gun" bandwagon when Hollywood Stars President Bob Cobb announced at an awards ceremony at Gilmore Field that the Pacific Coast League was in its final season and the future looked uncertain for the remaining six teams if the Dodgers and Giants moved to Los Angeles and San Francisco. He thanked the fans for their loyal support of the Stars for 20 years and wished the Dodgers well.

The guesswork and speculation about which players the Giants, if they were smart, would snag from the Seals squad to help them in the future was a hot topic of conversation, with everyone putting the name of his favorite in the hat. The fans and press agreed that a smart move for the Giants would be to purchase Albie Pearson, who could ease the transition for fans in their acceptance of the Giants. Imagine Pearson in the same outfield with Willie Mays. It kept the readers talking for a few days.

Once again the month ended without "definite-without-a-doubt" confirmation or a signed-sealed-and-delivered contract on the matter, although everyone caught the fever and felt much had been accomplished in July. With only six weeks left in the season, the pressure was on for Christopher and Stoneham to make a definite statement that everything was in place for the Giants to move in 1958.

SEVEN

August

August 1–4 (Thursday–Sunday) home vs. Hollywood
August 5–10 (Monday–Saturday) home vs. Los Angeles
August 11–14 (Sunday–Wednesday) at Vancouver
August 15–18 (Thursday–Sunday) at Portland
August 20–24 (Tuesday–Saturday) home vs. Seattle
August 25–28 (Sunday–Wednesday) at Sacramento
August 29–Sept.1 (Thursday–Sunday) home vs. San Diego

To the delight of both San Francisco and the parent Boston Red Sox, there were no dog days of August for the Seals. To the contrary, they faced seven abbreviated series interrupted by just one off-day slated for August 19. Gordon braced himself in anticipation of a hectic August as they were scheduled to face every team in the league, winding up the month at home with a visit from the San Diego Padres.

San Francisco was still the team to beat, and the first division clubs in the league were in hot pursuit. As July ended the Pacific Coast League looked more and more like a have and have-not situation. The race among teams in the first division tightened while it was a steep step down into the second division. The Seals still held first place (67–45), with Vancouver (63–49) and Hollywood (64–50) separated by two percentage points and tied for second, San Diego (62–50) in fourth, five games out, Seattle (59–56) fifth 9.5 games back, the 1956 champion Angels (53–57) 13 back in sixth place, Sacramento (42–72) 26 behind, and Portland (41–72), 26.5 games out. The bottom two teams spent the rest of the season battling to stay out of the cellar.

The powers that be in Boston conferred with Gordon and all agreed to some roster changes that required a fast game of musical chairs. The Red Sox purchased the contract of pitcher Murray Wall from AA Dallas (where Bert Thiel starred in 1956) and added him to the major league roster, then optioned veteran RHP Bob Chakales from Boston to San Francisco and told Joe Gordon to send Bull Schroll to Dallas to fill the hole created by Wall's absence. When he was finished scratching his head, Gordon complied.

140

Thirty-year-old Chakales, described as the player sent from "Beantown to Baytown," arrived the first day of August with seven seasons of big league relief pitching experience (1951–1957) with the Indians, Orioles, White Sox, Senators, and Red Sox on his resume. It was quite a trip as he was the opening day pitcher for the Senators against the Orioles a few months earlier. By the time he arrived he had a record of 0–2 with a disappointing 8.42 ERA in 17 appearances. He never returned to the majors and pitched at the AAA level until he retired after the 1959 season. But he helped the 1957 Seals.

In a rare weekday afternoon game, the abbreviated series against Hollywood began Thursday, August 1, as 2,991 fans enjoyed a sunny afternoon at Seals Stadium and saw the Seals drop a full game off their league lead when they fell, 3–1, and Vancouver beat the Padres, 5–1. Starters "Billy the Kid" Bill Prout and Ben Wade had good outings. Each yielded nine hits, and, with the exception of doubles by Harry Malmberg and Grady Hatton, all were singles. Prout gave up six walks and allowed one run in the fifth, sixth, and seventh frames. After Wade gave up a run in the first thanks to back-to-back singles from Marty Keough and Albie Pearson, and a double-play ball hit by Grady Hatton that allowed Keough to cross the dish, he settled down and pitched a solid game.

Prout left for a pinch-hitter in the seventh and Thiel finished his losing effort, which evened the kid's record at 3–3. For Seals fans, the most exciting events were the 21st and 22nd outfield assists by Pearson. Twice he chased down hits in deep right and shot the balls back into the infield quickly and accurately enough to cut speedy Carlos Bernier down on the base paths, first when he overran the bag at second and couldn't get back, and later at the plate. Bernier was always a key weapon for the Stars, and minimizing his threat was a big deal for the Seals. In addition, Pearson contributed two of the squad's nine hits.

Walter Mails, a great Albie Pearson supporter from the beginning, said he wasn't surprised in any way by those throws because "Pearson has the greatest outfield arm I've seen in Seals Stadium since Dominic DiMaggio." Every time Pearson showed his tools (hits, speed, throwing arm), the press wrote about it. It became a little joke that the press called him "Mighty Mite" so often that fans kidded that they couldn't remember his name half the time!

During that period, one of the regular items in the papers throughout the league was a sort of "Steve Bilko home run watch." Every pitcher, every team, and every fan was interested in the big man's power. As of August first his magic total was 34.

The game that night was one of the most frustrating outings of the season for the Seals. The headline said it all: "Stars Bury Seals 10–1 in Landslide." The Hollywood attack began in what became their 26-minute at-bat in the first inning. Thirteen men batted and nine scored, a couple of them assisted by errors by Kellert and Phillips, as they drove starter Bill Abernathie from the mound before the first out was made. It was the most runs scored in one inning against San Francisco all season. Reliable fireman Bert Thiel came in and doused the fire. Except for pushing across run number ten in the fourth, the visitors were limited to zeroes.

Red Witt took a no-hitter into the fifth inning, when a single off the bat of Haywood Sullivan ended that quest. He lost his bid for a shutout in the seventh, the result of a wild pitch and an error that allowed the Seals their only tally. The home team collected four more singles but was unable to put them together for runs: one more by Sullivan, two by Harry Malmberg, and one by Jack Phillips. After Umphlett popped up hitting for Thiel in the seventh, Leo Kiely made relief appearance number 38. Abernathie got the loss, his second against ten wins.

As bad as that game was for the Seals, the long-term results could have been worse. At least San Francisco received backdoor assistance from San Diego, who shut out the Mounties and prevented the second-place club from gaining ground. For some strange reason the press got analytical and tried to sell the idea that panic had set in among the Seals players who were so accustomed to winning. But the fans didn't buy it for a minute. Instead they were so euphoric about the success of their beloved Seals that they temporarily forgot what loomed at the end of the season.

Saturday's game was a fan-pleaser that ended with a bang! After getting a total of 13 hits in the first two games of the series, the Bay Bombers broke out of their little funk with 14 hits, mostly singles plus two doubles by Kellert (one with bases loaded in the third inning that drove in three runs), and a triple by Keough. The Stars logged a dozen hits and drew first blood off starter Riverboat Smith with three runs in the top of the third. Then the Seals came back with four in the bottom half thanks to a combination of two singles (Aspromonte and Malmberg), two walks (Keough and Hatton), and a line drive double by Kellert that rattled around in the left field corner and allowed the runners to circle the bases.

The Stars got two more runs in the top of the fourth. Behind 5–4, Smith hit the showers and Kiely entered the fray to shut down that inning. The visitors added one more in the seventh. After Malmberg singled in the eighth, Kiely was lifted for Sal Taormina, who doubled, and Malmberg scored. Then Taormina scored on a timely Keough triple. Abernathie came in for the ninth and gave up a solo homer which left the Seals behind 7–6 and set the stage for the fireworks.

Don Rowe had come on in the eighth when George Witt was not only out of gas, he was out of fumes. Rowe walked Jack Phillips on five pitches and

Sadowski, sent in to run for him, wound up at second after Aspromonte laid down a sacrifice bunt. Kellert kept the parade going when he proved his earlier double was no fluke and clobbered another one in the same place. Sadowski scored easily to tie the game at seven. Sullivan flied out to right and suddenly it looked like the teams would have to go into extra innings. But Renna approached the plate with two down, and, after striking out in his three previous attempts, he waited for a pitch to his liking and whacked the cover off the ball! The walk-off homer gave the Seals a dramatic 9–7 win. The only thing that kept the day from being perfect for the Seals was when Harry Malmberg was plunked on the elbow on a pitch from Ralph Mauriello that left him on the bench, soaking it in a bucket of ice for the final innings.

The Seals accomplished more than just a victory that day. San Francisco remained in first place with San Diego and Hollywood tied for second four games back, and Vancouver five games behind in fourth. The Seals broke out of a brief batting slump, ended their losing streak, and impacted Red Witt in a bigger way: it snapped his consecutive $29^{2/3}$ scoreless innings streak and a record of $53^{1/3}$ consecutive innings without allowing an earned run.

The series-ending doubleheader on Sunday was a split between two tired clubs that went into the record books as one of the longest doubleheaders in minor league history: six and a half hours. After starter Jack Spring was tagged for three runs in the first inning, he, Thiel, Dorish, and Kiely shut out the Twinks for ten innings while the Seals scored three runs, one inning at a time, to tie the score but fell short when Hollywood put across their fourth tally in the 12th to win the game, 4–3, and clinch the series.

Game two, scheduled for seven innings, also went overtime. After an ungracious welcome to the PCL for Bob Chakales when Hollywood scored five runs in the first inning and one in the second, San Francisco fought back with three in the first and two in the second before they tied the contest in the fourth. Bill Abernathie and Leo Kiely permitted just two more hits until the Seals scored the winning run in the bottom of the ninth. One of the highlights for the San Franciscans was a long home run by Marty Keough.

It was an exciting afternoon of baseball for 10,036 noisy fans who witnessed a total of 38 hits, divided at 19 in each game. Most accolades were tossed Leo Kiely's way for successfully holding down the fort in both games while he demonstrated his skills, which were considered unmatched by any other PCL pitcher. He collected his 17th win in game two. Australian Prime Minister Robert Gordon Menzies, on his way home from a conference of prime ministers in London, was in attendance and enjoyed his first American baseball game.

Though the Seals players were disappointed with the results of the Hollywood series, they had worked hard and felt good about various aspects of

Bill Renna rounds the bases after hitting a walk-off homerun to end the game. He is greeted by teammates Frank Kellert (#3) who scored ahead of him. On deck batter Harry Malmberg (#4) awaits a handshake (David Eskenazi Collection).

Manager Joe Gordon congratulates Marty Keough as he headed home after belt-ing one of his longest round-trippers of the season (David Eskenazi Collection).

it. They were tired but there was no time to indulge that because Monday was not an off-day; Steve Bilko and the Los Angeles Angels were on their way to town.

Only 2,474 fans turned out to see the big man Monday night in the series opener at the stadium. Bill Prout faced John Jancse and limited the Angels to seven hits as he struck out ten while yielding one unearned run in the first inning and one run in the fourth. The San Francisco Bombers scored in four different innings, two in the first, two in the third, one in the fourth, and one in the eighth, in spite of efforts by relief hurlers Bill George, Tom Lasorda, and Glen Mickens to shut them down. Big Steve Bilko got the collar, 0-for-4, compliments of "Billy the Kid" Prout.

On the other hand, his Bay Area counterpart, Bill Renna, had a big day. He went 3-for-4 as he drove in both Seals runs in the first on a long single and added a wallop in the third that bounced off the center field clock tower and landed in the parking lot behind the fence. Although no score was posted in the sixth, Albie Pearson almost got an RBI when he hit a long ball off the right field fence. While running it down, Hamric hit the wall hard and retrieved it quickly while Pearson tore around the bases and made the wide turn at third headed for home. But Hamric made an on-the-money throw to the cutoff man, who got the ball to catcher Dick Teed, who tagged Pearson out at the plate.

The team had a couple of upsets that turned out to be minor. Second baseman Ken Aspromonte was hit in the ankle by a batted ball during pregame workouts and missed the game. Later catcher Haywood Sullivan left the action early with a split finger. Both returned for the double-dip on Tuesday.

In Tuesday's face-off against the Angels, the 4,624 ticket holders witnessed what they described as the most unique 16 innings of baseball played at the emerald confines all season.

Game one lasted three minutes short of two hours as Tommy Hurd, who had missed two outings with a split finger suffered in Portland, went the distance and gave up just four hits to get his sixth win against three losses. The Seals were busy at the plate as they collected ten hits: Keough (1-for-4), Pearson (1-for-4), Aspromonte (2-for-3 with one double), Kellert (2-for-3 with one double), Renna (2-for-4 with one homer), Sullivan (1-for-3), and Phillips (1-for-4, a homer). The Seals won the game, 8–2.

Riverboat Smith dittoed the pattern set by Hurd in the nightcap. In a game that lasted only an hour and 30 minutes, he allowed just four hits as he whitewashed the Angels in seven innings, 5–0, and brought his record to 6–9. One of the most exciting plays of the day happened in the second inning when "Marvelous Marty" Keough, so named by the San Francisco press, hit an inside-the-park homer that was a catalyst for a four-run frame. Just when the reporters were writing that he couldn't get better, Keough went out to center field in the third and made an unbelievable catch of a ball that bounced around in the air as if it were on a magic carpet of wind, saving two runs. Aspromonte banged his second double of the day, his 38th. And Steve Bilko got lots of rest on the bench in the top of each inning as he went "one for all day."

Wednesday night the Angels won their only game in the series, 7–4. Harry Dorish gave up two homers in the fourth inning, to Hamric and Jenkins, before Sal Taormina pinch-hit for him in the bottom of the frame. Bill Abernathie, Bert Thiel and Leo Kiely (in his 42nd appearance) worked hard to keep the Angels within reach, but it was a mountain too high in spite of doubles off the bats of Aspromonte, Hatton, Renna, Phillips, and Pearson. The fans went away chuckling about a unique moment in the seventh when Steve Bilko bashed a line drive to center that everyone thought would land across the bay in Oakland! He broke into his home run trot. But, to his embarrassment, the flailing wind helped keep the ball inside the park, where it was retrieved by Marty Keough, who threw it to second and limited the big man to a 400-foot single, his only hit for the day.

On Thursday, the second two-gamer in three days, the Seals pulled out all the stops as they toppled the defending champions in both ends, 9–6 in nine innings, then 6–4 in seven.

Game one, with Jack Spring on the mound all the way, was a close contest in which the Angels scored three runs in the first inning on a two-run bash by Steve Bilko, number 35, and one more in the second. The Seals inched back with a single tally in the first followed by a solo wallop by Bill Renna in the second, the first of his three homers for the day. The score went back and forth until the fate of the Angels was sealed in the bottom of the seventh when the Gordons added three more, making the final score 9–6 and elevated Jack Spring's record to 7–5.

Game two was more of the same, well, almost. Starter Bob Chakales faced Tommy Lasorda and they both had good command until the fourth inning with the Seals ahead 3–0, when things changed. With two on and two away, Gordon brought in Leo Kiely, who allowed one run to cross the dish before he got the third out. In their turn at bat the Seals added two more runs that put them ahead for good. But the surprises weren't over. Kiely got into trouble in the sixth, gave up two runs, and for the first time all season, Gordon went to the mound and took the ball, relieving the great reliever despite the team being ahead by a 6–4 score. Bill Abernathie took the reins and got the final out in the sixth, then skated through the last three outs in the seventh. Two homers by Bill Renna (three for the day) and one by Marty Keough plus timely hitting by the Bay Nine contributed to the victory. The home team had won five of six games with one more remaining in the series.

Then an odd thing happened. It was taken for granted that because Chakales didn't pitch five innings to qualify for the win, the victory belonged to Kiely, who left with the Seals ahead. But the official scorer, using what the press called "rule book judgment," gave the win to Abernathie (12–2) on the

Veteran Grady Hatton took a big cut, made contact, and wound up at second base as catcher Pete Naton and the umpire look on (David Eskenazi Collection).

basis that Kiely worked a less impressive game in relief than did Abby. The decision left players and fans scratching their heads, but it stood.

Everyone joked before and during the game wondering about how many days in advance of this last game the Angels had their bags packed in anticipation of "escaping" from San Francisco. Despite the pregame attention given to Pearson, once the umpire cried "Play ball," all eyes turned to Bill Renna. He was John Wayne leading the cavalry, getting five RBI with his 21st homer in the second inning and his 22nd in the third with two on, as part of a 15-hit, 12–6 walloping of the Angels. Marty Keough contributed a four-bagger of his own; Albie Pearson smashed a triple and made two exciting catches in the outfield; Frank Kellert and Haywood Sullivan each doubled; Ken Aspromonte and Grady Hatton each contributed two singles; and Harry Malmberg and Prout each hit singles.

Bill Prout took the mound for the second time in a week despite a split fingernail still healing from his last outing, and faced off against John Jancse, who took a licking and did stop ticking in the first inning after the hosts plated seven runs. Lasorda relieved into the fifth, when he was lifted for a pinch-hitter after the Seals had increased their run total to an even dozen. Prout seemed tired in the ninth when he allowed a three-run homer to catcher Earl Battey before he retired the side.

After the game the Seals flew to Vancouver, British Columbia, and, without a day off, began a five-game stint against the red hot Mounties, who were coming off a seven-game sweep of the Sacramento Solons. The Bay Bombers had captured nine of their last 11 and were eager to keep their own streak intact. Going into the opener on Saturday night, the Seals squad (76–48) was five full games ahead of second-place Vancouver (70–52).

On August 12 it was announced that, based on a longtime study of PCL records during the 1903–1957 seasons, the Helms Athletic Foundation had selected as the All-Time Pacific Coast League Team: Frank "Lefty" O'Doul (LF, Seals, 1927), Joe DiMaggio (CF, Seals, 1935); Ike Boone (RF, S.F. Missions, 1929), Gus Suhr (1B, Seals, 1929), Jimmy Reese (2B, Oakland, 1929), Frank Crosetti (SS, Seals, 1930), Willie Kamm (3B, Seals, 1922), Art Koehler (C, Sacramento, 1923), Ernie Lombardi (C, Oakland, 1930), Frank "Jake" May (P, Vernon, 1922), Fay Thomas (P, Los Angeles, 1934), Larry Jansen (P, Seals, 1945), Larry Vickers (P, Seattle, 1906), and Vean Gregg (P, Portland, 1910).

In the Saturday opener Riverboat Smith pitched a four-hitter against Art Houtteman. Things started on a silly note when Smith yielded two unearned runs in the first inning and was then ordered to re-adjust his cap and tuck in his shirt before the game could continue. After Joe Gordon got in his two-cents' worth on the issue, the game moved forward and the Seals retaliated to tie the score in the second when Bill Renna bashed a homer with Grady Hatton on base. Things settled down until the top of the fifth. After Smith struck out and Marty Keough and Albie Pearson both held out for walks, Ken Aspromonte lashed a low liner that deflected off the pitcher's knee for a single to load the bases before Kellert grounded into a force play that scored Keough to put the Seals in the lead, 3–2.

The pace slowed again until the top of the seventh, when the Mounties got their third unearned run of the night. In the bottom of that heat, Houtteman was driven to the showers when Ken Aspromonte walked, Frank Kellert singled, and Grady Hatton drove them both in with a double that rattled around in right-center. The matter was settled when Renna launched a surging single up the middle that scored Hatton. Because reliever Morrie Martin was slow to apply the cork, Haywood Sullivan kept the parade going with a double that scored Renna. In the eighth San Francisco put its eighth run on the board when Keough tripled and scored on a Pearson double.

The local citizens of Capilano Stadium and Vancouver players alike were unhappy with the performance of recently appointed umpire Gordon Perkins and let him know it one pitch at a time. Finally, after subtly complaining about the calls throughout the game, catcher Toby Atwell was a little too animated in his disagreement in the eighth inning to suit Perkins, who gave him the thumb. When Charlie Metro charged the scene in defense of his player, he, too, was excused for the rest of the day. Then, just as had happened at Seals Stadium earlier in the year, Perkins was pummeled with seat cushions and everything fans could find to launch at him. The next day the press calmly described the event as a "riotous conclusion" that had no impact whatsoever on the Seals 8–3 win.

Sunday was a one-of-a-kind set. The initial encounter was the completion of the game suspended in the sixth inning on May 12 due to the six o'clock curfew imposed by Canada's Blue Laws. When the game was suspended, five outs remained, San Francisco was ahead, 3–2, with one out in the sixth after they had scored two unearned runs off Erv Palica in the second inning, and Albie Pearson added one in the fifth with a home run. When play resumed, Tommy Umphlett hit a triple, and a Ken Aspromonte sacrifice fly drove him home for the final run. In a game that technically took 91 days to get into the books, the Seals won, 4–2.

The regularly scheduled game was a pitching duel between Tommy Hurd and young Charlie Beamon, age 22, in which a total of 16 hits were allowed and three runs scored. After Hurd gave up a first-inning homer to Spider Jorgensen, he bore down and scattered five hits as he pitched shutout ball through the seventh. Marty Keough smashed his 11th homer to tie things at one in the fifth. Amazing defense by the visitors kept things close.

The press said Beamon "staggered all over British Columbia," and it took three double plays and a series of other breathtaking maneuvers to keep him from getting clobbered until he left in the sixth with two on and nobody out. Reliever Sandy Consuegra came in and retired the side, then easily finished the game and kept the Seals off the board. Leo Kiely came in for Hurd in the eighth, and was unable to prevent the second and winning run from crossing the plate in the ninth. Vancouver won, 2–1, and the clubs got a split doubleheader with no change in the standings for their day's work.

Monday, August 12, was another day off that wasn't. The Seals entered the game with their five-game lead reduced to four, as every game they lost to Vancouver cost them one full game in the standings. San Francisco came in second in this game, 3–2, in what turned out to be a bad night.

It started in the first inning. Leadoff man Marty Keough made an out, and Albie Pearson singled. Ken Aspromonte, batting in the three-hole, hit a grounder to shortstop Buddy Peterson which should have been an inning-ending double play. But he threw it to second baseman Owen Friend, who twisted around and threw to first, expecting that to be the end of the inning.

Although the ball beat the hard-running Aspromonte to first, the ump called Pearson safe at second, saying Friend failed to touch the base or tag him. Friend went ballistic! He shouted at the ump, jumped up and down on the bag, and threw his glove high into the air, followed by his cap, requiring automatic ejection. Manager Charlie Metro defended the play but not his player, and the unsympathetic umpire forcefully urged him to leave the field or be ejected. Metro returned to the dugout.

Despite key defensive plays in the third inning and again in the fifth, the Seals were unable to get the calls they needed to get the desired outs to protect Jack Spring's game. To add insult to injury, none other than Friend got a timely single in the eighth that drove in what turned out to be the winning run for the Mounties and the sixth defeat for Spring.

The Seals, aware that the Mounties were closing the gap between the two clubs, knew they had to win Tuesday. Instead it turned out to be another disappointment. Starter Bob Chakales held his own against Morrie Martin through five scoreless innings but Mounties first baseman Jim Marshall walloped a homer in the sixth, followed by a triple by Owen Friend, who was driven in by a Joe Frazier single. The Mounties scored again in the seventh and eighth, when Bill Abernathie came to the rescue.

Big Cuban reliever Sandy Consuegra took over for the Mounties and hoped to save Martin's shutout. But the Bay Bombers had other ideas. With Malmberg on second and Sadowski on first, Tommy Umphlett lined a long single up the middle that sent both runners across the plate at top speed, making the score 4–2 and averting the whitewash. Unfortunately it wasn't enough runs to give the Seals a win, and they lost their third consecutive game, 4–2.

The few positives the press could find in addition to five shutout innings from Chakales were the continuing hitting streaks by Ken Aspromonte (ten games), Harry Malmberg (seven games), and Walloping Willie Renna (12 games). While the Seals' lead declined one day at a time, San Diego was on a six-game winning streak, Portland edged visiting Sacramento, and Steve Bilko's 38th homer helped Los Angeles defeat Hollywood. Chip Aspromonte, who had led the league in hitting for most of the season, remained on top while his closest contender, Rudy Regalado, continued to hit above .300 but needed a prolonged Aspromonte slump to possibly catch him. It didn't happen.

With the end of the season in sight, there was talk about voting for the Manager of the Year Award. San Francisco columnist Art Rosenbaum reported that Hollywood President Bob Cobb praised manager Clyde King of the Stars, saying King deserved the honor hands down for having "done the best job under adverse circumstances," namely numerous player injuries throughout the campaign. But San Franciscans argued that, without question, the award belonged to Joe Gordon. According to Albie Pearson, "Gordon was more than a manager. He was a guide and teacher for the younger players like myself. I mean, he chewed us out when we needed it and praised us when we earned it. He always said we should play hard so we would have no regrets when we look back." Others agreed that he had instilled the same "we can't lose" attitude he learned with the Yankees into his Seals team.

Wednesday they played the final game of the set and possibly the last confrontation ever between the two contenders. The Mounties, formerly the Oakland Oaks, and the Seals shared a rivalry that went back 54 years to 1903 when the Pacific Coast League was launched. Their across-bay rivalry had been a mainstay of the league and was known to baseball fans well beyond the geographic boundaries of the PCL and well beyond the years in which it existed.

The largest crowd in the history of Capilano Stadium (10,404) brought the paid attendance for the series close to 40,000, plus an additional 2,000 non-paying fans who watched from the hill behind the right field fence from time to time. It was a noisy event from Don Ferrarese's first pitch to Seals leadoff hitter Albie Pearson, through seven nail-biting innings. Things quieted briefly after Haywood Sullivan clobbered a huge home run that sucked all the air from the park, which turned out to be the Seals' only hurrah of the day. Vancouver wore down Bill Prout in the bottom of the inning. The youth had struggled all night against the hitters in addition to poor balls-and-strikes calls from plate umpire Chris Pelekoudas, as they posted four tallies. Leo Kiely was called in to put out the fire. In addition to Sullivan's clout, the Seals were held to three singles, one each by Tommy Umphlett, Frank Kellert, and Bill Prout. The streaks by Aspromonte, Malmberg, and Renna were ended.

Ironically, years later members of the team remembered that series in Vancouver as the most disappointing of the season and the most motivating at the same time. They never took their place at the top of the pack for granted, or gave less than 100 percent in any game. But there was a certain feeling of invincibility because they had led the league for so long. Those days in British Columbia served as an eye-opener about one of the givens in pro baseball: any team can be beaten on any given day.

Pearson remembered the impact Gordon had on his 1957 season and his subsequent big league career.

Joe Gordon was a psychologist. He understood the pressures on the younger guys like me [age 22] and chewed us out when [we] needed it. And the older guys liked him because he respected their experience. When we lost in our last series in Vancouver near the end of the season we were pretty mad at ourselves. He called a team meeting and reminded us that we were still in first place and the pennant was ours to lose. I still remember that.

Their next stop was Portland, 30 games in the cellar. Earlier that day longtime baseball man and Beavers General Manager Joe Ziegler (since 1954) had been fired in a unanimous decision by the board of directors in a move that had been under consideration for a long time. The final straw was the day they arrived, when Ziegler sold veteran southpaw Bill Werle to San Diego, which left the team with just one LHP.

The Seals looked forward to the five-game series against the Beavers in Multnomah Stadium because the left field fences were close and the home team didn't present anything near the challenge and competition they had faced in Vancouver. Best of all, it was the last series on this road trip.

They took a four-game losing streak and a two-game league lead into the series opener. Many said that game was a direct reflection of their hunger for an overdue win. Sportswriters had a field day in which words like "rampage," "rant," "warpath," and "buried" were used to describe the Seals' assault in which they posted six runs in the first five innings and garnered 13 in nine, recorded 15 hits overall, and stranded an additional ten runners on the base paths. In spite of all that, the game actually turned into a contest when Portland tied the score with a six-run rally in the fifth on a string of long singles topped off by a huge homer by Earl Rapp that ended starter Harry Dorish's day with just two outs in the inning. As usual, Leo Kiely was summoned to save the day, and he did as he held the Beavers scoreless. Meanwhile, the San Franciscans added seven more tallies: two in the sixth, one in the seventh, three in the eighth, and one in the ninth, and Kiely collected his 18th win.

And there was more good news for the Seals. Hollywood defeated Vancouver, Steve Bilko's 39th homer led Los Angeles past the Padres, and Seattle beat Sacramento. San Francisco's lead was three games.

The contest Friday night started nearly 30 minutes late due to an Old Timers Game that delighted the fans. Riverboat Smith was the hero of the night as he scattered six hits in a 9–0 whitewash, the fourth shutout of his eight wins. Solly Drake led off with a solid double in the fourth inning but died at second, which left Smith with a one-hitter through 6⅓. On three occasions he "encountered a little trouble" maintaining the shutout, but he pitched his way through each of them.

Ironically, after the team had scored 21 times in the first two games, they were shut out 1–0 on Saturday. The game was a good one that left fans talking long after it was over. Starters Tommy Hurd and Bob Alexander allowed a combined eight hits, five for the hosts and three for the visitors (Hatton two, Malmberg one) as they posted goose eggs on the scoreboard in every half of every frame until the Beavers scored one in the bottom of the eighth and the Seals were unable to match it. Hurd went the distance and took a disappointing loss.

The Seals, eager for the flight home after Sunday's doubleheader, looked forward to an actual off-day Monday before clashing with the Seattle Rainiers on Tuesday. But first, they had unfinished business in Portland: two games to play.

The Beavers beat them 3–1 in the nine-inning opener that evened the series at two games apiece. Portland's Don Kaiser simply outpitched Jack Spring who needed assistance from Bert Thiel and Bill Abernathie. Portland posted three runs in the third inning, which was all they needed. Two of those runs were the result of a two-run triple down the third base line by Ron Bowen, who briefly played for the Seals in 1953 after he was signed out of a semipro tournament. Kaiser held the Seals to seven hits that included doubles by Bill Renna and Frank Kellert as he kept them scoreless until an eighth-inning homer by Tommy Umphlett ended his shutout bid.

Umphlett later said he remembered helping the team but couldn't recall any round-trippers. "I wasn't a home run hitter, but got my share of singles and doubles, hit behind the runner, and things like that. They tell me I hit four home runs that season in that big ballpark [Seals Stadium], but I really don't remember any of them. Odd, too, because since I hit only four I should at least be able to remember one!"

Things turned around in the closer when the Seals came out of the gate swinging and didn't stop until the game was over. Both starters, Bob Chakales and veteran Dick Fiedler, kept things scoreless through the first three heats. Then the Bay Bombers exploded for four runs in the fourth, three in the fifth, one in the sixth, and one more in the seventh as they knocked around relief hurlers Derrell Martin, Ray Shore, Dick Marlowe, Jack Carswell, and John Carmichael.

Chakales, who got his first win in a Seals uniform, was in command the entire game as he permitted the Beavers a small comeback when a triple by second baseman Ed Winceniak drove in one run. They followed with one more in the fifth and that was all she wrote. It was no surprise that Bill Renna's two long home runs brought the fans to their feet. The first, off Ray Shore, estimated at 410 feet, landed in the center field bleachers. Not to play favorites, he bashed another one, his 24th, off John Carmichael in the seventh. Portland was unable to stop the hitting or catch up with hits of their own, and the Seals took the second game 10–2.

The standings didn't change. The other three double bills in the league ended in splits and the Seals remained out in front by three games.

After a relaxing day off Monday, 3,154 fans welcomed the team home Tuesday night to begin a five-game stint with Lefty O'Doul's Seattle Rainiers ending with a doubleheader on Sal Taormina Night on Friday. Although the Suds had slipped to fifth place, 12 games behind the leaders, they always presented tough competition and had topped the Seals ten times in their previous 19 encounters.

Before the game it was Leo Kiely Night as teammates and fans celebrated the amazing season logged by Mr. Bones. In addition to numerous gifts from local merchants, he received telegrams from the folks back home in New Jersey and a check from his teammates in appreciation of his prowess on the hill that helped them win so many games.

To even the season series at ten games each, Gordon sent LHP Riverboat Smith to the mound for Tuesday's opener to face old friend RHP Duane Pillette, who had continued his winning ways in Seattle. The game was scoreless until the bottom of the sixth inning, when the home team ruined Pillette's two-hit shutout. Speedy Tommy Umphlett beat out an infield single and went to third on a rope single through the hole by Ken Aspromonte, who moved to second when Bill Renna walked, loading the bases. Haywood Sullivan waited for his pitch, a juicy fastball down the middle, and walloped a grand slam which brought everyone in the park to their feet. The sports pages said, "[Sullivan's] fifth homerun of the year rattled among the cars in the parking lot and the Riverboat had completed another successful cruise."

The flip side of that coin was that when the Suds put one tally on the board in the seventh, it ended Smith's streak of 31 innings without allowing an earned run. But the Seals took a 4–1 victory from the O'Douls, and Smith's season record was again even at 9–9.

In other games that day, the Angels took two from flailing Portland, and the Bilko watch continued as the slugger clobbered homers number 44 and 45.

On Wednesday it seemed as though the fans had just settled in and gotten comfortable when the 1–0 clash was over and hard-luck Tommy Hurd had lost a game in which he allowed just three hits and no earned runs. In fact, his mates had been able to push across only one lonely run in his last 23 innings on the mound. It was his deceptive fifth loss, and the second as a result of an Albie Pearson misplay.

The only tally occurred in the sixth inning when Maury Wills slapped a high fly to short right that was misjudged and dropped by Pearson. By the time he gathered his wits and got the ball back to the infield, speedy Wills was at second. After additional sloppy defense that was not scored as an error, Wills was at third and was then driven home by a sacrifice fly off the bat of Seattle relief pitcher Bud Podbielan. And that was that.

Ironically, the luck of the Seals held firm. Thanks to San Diego taking a twin bill from Vancouver, the Seals lead grew to four games. Elsewhere around the circuit Los Angeles beat Portland as Bilko slammed number 46, giving him the career record for the Angels franchise with 138, and Sacramento defeated Hollywood for their third consecutive win.

A three-run homer from Haywood Sullivan brought the capacity crowd to its feet as teammates Harry Malmberg (#4) and Bill Renna (#23) wait to congratulate him as the catcher stands back.

Before the start of the game Thursday night, the stands were abuzz with chatter about an article in the paper concerning Horace Stoneham's arrival in San Francisco earlier that day. He and Giants vice president Chub Feeney brought a detailed agenda to discuss with Mayor Christopher that was rumored to include a bid to purchase the Seals.

Others discussed an article in the morning paper that suggested for the second time that Horace Stoneham should purchase the contract of Albie Pearson for the Giants since rumors abounded that he was "not on the radar" for Boston's future and would be sold or traded after 1957 anyway. The logic was that he would certainly be a magnet for the Seals' die-hard fans who resisted the upcoming change. Even better, he could help the team on the field because of his skills and familiarity with Seals Stadium and the San Francisco breezes.

Fritz Dorish faced whip-armed former major leaguer Marion Fricano. That night Joe Gordon experimented with his roster and penciled in Keough at first base to give a well-deserved day off to tired Frank Kellert who, after appearing in 144 of 147 games thus far, had seen his batting average drop from .305 to .283 in the last 21 games. There was a bit of irony in that situation. Kellert's father had driven 1,700 miles from Oklahoma City to check things out. After a couple of games when he saw his son log some hits without showing power, he was overheard advising Kellert to "loosen up and get to swingin', lad." Everyone enjoyed having him around.

The Seals started things off with a bang in the first inning when Pearson clobbered his fourth homer into the bleachers. Umphlett doubled and advanced to third when Keough flied out to right. Aspromonte held out for a walk and stole second. Umphlett scored on a ground out by Hatton, and a long single by Bill Renna plated Aspromonte. The excited 3,046 fans enjoyed the 3–0 lead given to Dorish.

But the Rainiers turned things around in the top of the second. Bobby Balcena walked and Maury Wills doubled, moving Balcena to third. And then the sad fact that Keough was not a first baseman set in. Ray Orteig hit a high wind-blown pop fly that he caught in spectacular fashion at the rail of the Rainiers dugout, but in his haste to nail Balcena at the plate he threw the ball to Haywood Sullivan with his outfielder's arm. It flew six feet over Sullivan's head into the stands and Balcena and Wills both scored.

Balcena annoyed the Seals again in the sixth. Jim Dyck doubled, then scored when Balcena singled, tying the score at three. The Gordons didn't have any runs left in them that day, but the Suds came up with two more tallies in the seventh thanks to a couple of hits combined with an error by Grady Hatton. At that point Dorish was replaced by Kiely. The 5–3 loss brought Dorish's record to a surprising 9–11.

The slated double dip on Friday night to end the series was preceded by Sal Taormina Night. Dubbed "The San Jose Milkman" (he worked for the Marin Dell Milk Company in the off-season), Taormina was beloved by Seals fans. During the ceremonies he was described as a rugged, personable pinch-hitter deluxe, gifted with such tools as courage, desire, and tenacity, and had been a beloved factor in the scheme of San Francisco baseball for over ten years.

In the theme of the evening, as Jack Spring faced Red Munger, the Seals took charge from the first pitch to leadoff batter Albie Pearson as they put two runs on the board. Their hit parade continued and by the end of the third inning they were ahead, 8–2. By the end of the game the Bay Nine had scored ten runs while limiting the Suds to three. In the course of the rout, Eddie Sadowski smashed three of the Seals' 13 hits, all triples, that earned him four RBI for his night's work. When all was said and done, Spring added another complete-game victory.

The seven-inning finale was a quick 75-minute affair in which pitchers Bob Chakales and Larry Jansen allowed a combined seven hits, four for the Seals and three for the Suds. The difference was a solo home run by Marty Keough in the fourth. Chakales gave up no walks as he garnered his second win in the 1–0 battle.

Amid the celebration for Sal Taormina and the two Seals victories in the season's last confrontation with Seattle, there was a note of sadness. It was announced that coach Glenn Wright would miss the remainder of the season after being diagnosed with a bone cancer that required immediate surgery. Catcher Nini Tornay, who had been functioning as Wright's right-hand man for the last several weeks after his own injury, took over all of his coaching duties.

The squad then took an hour and a half bus trip to Sacramento to face Tommy Heath and the Solons in a five-game encounter, Saturday through Tuesday.

The Seals' barrage of the Sacramento club continued in game one. In addition to doubles by Bill Renna and Eddie Sadowski, Kellert returned to his station at first base refreshed and back to his old form at the plate and led his team to victory with homeruns 15 and 16, that yielded three RBI. Both teams garnered ten hits, but starter Bill Prout scattered the ones he allowed to the Solons in his complete-game 10–4 win. It was one of those rare games in which Ken Aspromonte took the collar as he went 0-for-5. By that point the league-leading hitter had become such a dependable and integral part of the squad that his going hitless in a game rated headlines in the sports pages.

Home runs parted the waters and opened a path that permitted the Seals to take both ends of the twin bill Sunday, first by 4–3 and then 4–2. It was their 12th top-and-bottom sweep of double-deckers of the season and increased their league lead to 4.5 games. In the first game Riverboat Smith, aided by Bill Abernathie for the last two innings, sailed to his fifth consecutive win and tenth of the campaign thanks to homers by Frank Kellert and Eddie Sadowski.

The second game was a different story. Starter Tom Hurd limited the Sacs to three hits, two singles and a solo home run to Thomas Agosta, padded with six walks. San Francisco got four runs with just five hits: second homers of the day by Kellert and Sadowski plus a soaring triple by Bill Renna that drove in two runs in the fifth inning after Malmberg and Umphlett had both singled. This outing brought Hurd's record to 8–5.

While Steve Bilko crushed homer number 50 for Los Angeles, the Solons turned the tables on the Seals Monday night when pitcher Bud Watkins held the Seals to six hits as he and Harry Dorish faced off in a pitchers' duel in the fourth game of the set. Though the Seals fought back in the ninth inning, they came up short and lost, 2–1. It was just the fourth time Tommy Heath's squad beat the Seals in 19 contests.

The last game began on a down note for the San Franciscans as Sal Taormina, who had been dealing with back spasms without complaint for over a week, was sent home early to undergo medical tests to determine the cause.

Edmonds Field was the site of a 5–0 Seals win that was spiced with a bit of rancor as 1,738 spectators saw a unique PCL event. Early in the game umpires St. Clair, Carlucci, and Steiner accused Chakales of having resin (an illegal substance) on the leg of his uniform pants and ordered him to take them off for inspection. Naturally he protested vehemently when the umpires allegedly told him to "change his pants or get out of our lives forever." He made the change and returned to the mound for a stunning outing that limited the Solons to nine hits and no runs. The complete game brought his record to 3–1. Nobody knows what happened to the pants, and other than initial teasing from teammates, the incident was not spoken of again.

The club enjoyed a day off on Wednesday and readied for the five-game tilt with the much tougher Padres at Seals Stadium that began Thursday. "Billy the Kid" Prout faced 36-year-old veteran Vic Lombardi in a game that turned out to be quite a battle. With San Francisco in the lead, 4–1, in the top of the sixth inning, Prout ran out of gas and allowed the Pads to score four times to take a 5–4 lead. Despite his best effort, the youngster was unable to get the third out and Gordon called on his favorite fireman, Leo Kiely, to put a lid on the trouble, which he did in his usual efficient fashion. Things changed quickly in the bottom of the seventh when the Seals rallied, loading the bases with two outs, and pinch-hitter Grady Hatton cleared them with a perfectly placed single to right.

Kiely was dissatisfied with his performance that day, which he later described as "shaky," but he got the job done for the team and ended up in the record books for his trouble. The win, number 19, 18 in relief, set an all-time record for relief pitchers in professional baseball at that time.

Veteran Bill Werle, a well-respected, side-arm fireball pitcher, evened the series on Friday with a 5–2 victory. In charge from the first pitch, he shut out the Seals until the bottom of the ninth. After posting four runs in the third inning off Tom Hurd thanks to a close call against the Seals on a double play attempt that would have ended the inning and kept the game scoreless, it was 4–0 and the home team couldn't catch up.

In an unusual move in the fifth, when the Seals had a scoring opportunity with Hurd due at the plate, Joe Gordon reactivated catcher Nini Tornay to pinch-hit. But Tornay, who had not batted in a game since May 12, hit into an inning-ending double play.

Relievers Bert Thiel, who blanked the Padres for three innings without a hit, and Bill Abernathie, who gave up a run in the top of the ninth, kept things within reach as the Seals came to bat in the ninth. Werle took the hill for the final three outs with his whitewash in tact. However, sloppy defense that let him down coupled with San Francisco tenacity saw the Seals stage a comeback drive that brought the fans to their feet, but they fell short and lost the game, 5–2.

The following day it was announced that fan favorite Ken Aspromonte had been recalled by the Red Sox and was scheduled to leave for Boston after the double dip on Sunday, September 1. He remembered, "My batting average had slipped a few points for about a week before the recall happened. I got impatient with myself and stressed over it. Up to that time I saw the ball so well that everything seemed to come easily. Thankfully Joe Gordon noticed that I was putting pressure on myself and he talked to me and helped me get back on track."

Although Buddy Peterson (Vancouver) was his closest challenger at that point, he only remembered keeping an eye on the progress of San Diego outfielder Rudy Regalado. At the end of the season, Aspromonte's .334 average earned him a spot in the record books as the 1957 PCL batting champion, the first for a Seals player since outfielder Gene Woodling did it in 1948 with a .385 average in 146 games.

The team completed the series with the Padres on the first day of September in front of 9,247 spectators that brought the season's paid attendance at Seals Stadium over the 300,000 mark. The team put on a good show in the twin bill on a sunny and surprisingly warm fall Sunday afternoon in San Francisco.

Jack Spring was masterful in the opener and gave the fans a lot to cheer about. He scattered nine hits and limited the visiting club to just one run in the eighth inning and one more in the ninth for a complete-game win that made his record 9–7 Although Frank Kellert went hitless in three trips, everyone else made contact and they pushed across eight tallies on ten hits. They scored in the third, fourth, fifth, sixth and seventh innings while Spring kept the door shut on the Padres to that point. Bill Renna went 3-for-4 with two singles and home run number 27 that zoomed high and long; Harry Malmberg hit his first triple of the season; and Ken Aspromonte, who was given a standing ovation in his first at-bat for the day, went 2-for-3 with a long double.

Bob DiPietro manned first base for the Padres and the local fans welcomed the chance to watch this old friend play at Seals Stadium one more time, even if he did drive in San Diego's second run in the ninth with a mighty wallop over the left field fence, his fifth home run of the season. Pitchers Dick Brodowski and Dolan Nichols were unable to contain the Seals. When all was

Big Bill Renna reminded fans he could run as he beat out an infield single. San Diego first baseman Bob DiPietro (#11) waits for the throw to the bag (David Eskenazi Collection).

said and done they had put eight tallies on the board to win, 8–2, and the squad was on its way to winning yet another twin bill.

The second game was a nail-biter from first to last pitch, as each team logged seven hits and both pitchers went all the way. Bob Chakales went toe-to-toe with veteran Vic Lombardi as the Padres scored a run in the first inning. The home team responded with two in the bottom of that inning, and led 2–1 until the fourth, when they added one more. The Pads were held at bay until the top of the seventh, when they rallied and got Rudy Regalado around the bases one base at a time until he scored their second run. In addition to triples off the bats of Frank Kellert and Ken Aspromonte (who had a four–RBI day), Chakales helped himself with a long single as he logged his fourth consecutive win. In his final trip to the plate in a Seals uniform, Aspromonte received a well-deserved, prolonged standing ovation from a grateful crowd who thanked him for giving them an enjoyable season.

Shortly afterward he said his goodbyes to his teammates as they flew

Ken Aspromonte scores his last run in his final game in a Seals uniform before heading to Boston to begin his major league career. Also pictured are Frank Kellert (#3), San Diego catcher Earl Avrill (#15), and the umpire (David Eskenazi Collection).

south on the first leg of a 13-game road trip that took them to Hollywood, San Diego, and Los Angeles, and he flew east to join the Boston Red Sox.

Meanwhile, away from the diamond, the month began with an announcement that Horace Stoneham had convinced his Board of Directors that the move of his team from New York to San Francisco was in the best interest of the club. On August 20 the Giants Board of Directors voted (8–1) to move their franchise to San Francisco in time for the 1958 season. Stoneham and George Christopher issued simultaneous statements approving the deal. As expected, there were hundreds of details on both ends to be ironed out before things could be finalized.

In the interim the Coast League considered all options about its own future. The Dodgers and Giants would legally draft those territories for themselves leaving the Los Angeles Angels and Seals virtually homeless. Because that could be the beginning of a domino effect that would have negative financial repercussions on all six remaining PCL teams, the major league clubs would be required to reimburse each of them for all losses. While that was a given, calculating the value of each one individually was expected to take some time.

Portland and Seattle initially applied for membership in the AAA American Association but were persuaded to remain in the PCL with Sacramento, San Diego, and Vancouver while the league looked for three cities that could support PCL baseball to bring the league back to eight franchises. Some of the more likely places under consideration were Fresno, San Jose, and Salt Lake City.

While the press focused on such details as city finances, bond issues, and miscellaneous issues related to the construction of new ballparks, the fans in San Francisco yawned and left all that to the experts. Instead, they counted down the last games of the season one at a time as they approached the demise of their beloved San Francisco Seals.

On one of his trips to the west coast in the final week of August, Stoneham indicated that he had negotiated to purchase the Seals and relocate them as a AAA affiliate of the Giants, but no current Seals players would be part of that deal. He said he and Boston GM Joe Cronin had talked and he was certain an amicable agreement could be reached whereby the Red Sox organization would relocate Seals players within their organization.

Despite the fact that it was announced that Willie Mays had put his Harlem home on the market in anticipation of the move to San Francisco, public reaction to news connected to the New York–to–San Francisco move was still mild as the uncertainty still loomed. *Sports Illustrated* compared it to the delirious reaction in Milwaukee in 1953 when that city became the new home of a major league club, and described the Bay Area reaction as "restraint that was almost self conscious." One interpretation was that cosmopolitan San Francisco already considered itself major league. Another was that, because of the Seals' existing affiliation with Boston, they more or less expected an American League team. *Newsweek* added that all the Giants had to do to be accepted by Bay Area fans was to field a winning team.

Meanwhile, citizens in Brooklyn, a proud city of roughly three million people, all of whom were said to be diehard fans of "Dem Bums" who had finally won their first World Series in 1956, vehemently resented and protested the very idea of moving their historic and beloved team 3,000 miles away. They wrote letters to every local and state official they could think of in protest, marched at city hall with banners begging them to build a new park for the Dodgers to keep them in Brooklyn, and flooded officials with letters and phone calls emphasizing that the team was the heart and soul of their community.

EIGHT

September

Sept. 2–5 (Monday–Thursday) at Hollywood
Sept. 6–8 (Friday–Sunday) at San Diego
Sept. 9–12 (Monday–Thursday) at Los Angeles
Sept 13–15 (Friday–Sunday) home vs. Sacramento

The team was tired by the end of August and still faced a tight schedule during the month of September. After completing the series in San Diego on Sunday, September 1, they immediately bussed up Interstate 5 to Hollywood to face the Stars on Monday for their second twin bill in as many days. The San Franciscans knew the five games in Hollywood were pivotal to the outcome of the season, as the Stars were six games behind the Seals and 2.5 behind the second-place Mounties in the standings. With just two weeks left in the season, every game was a crucial must-win for those three contenders.

In a bit of dramatic irony San Francisco's longtime rival Vancouver (transplanted from Oakland) was in hot pursuit of the pennant, just 3.5 games back, and the pressure was on both clubs as they counted the remaining games of the season with the pennant essentially still up for grabs. It brought out the fans and made for exciting baseball.

In addition, Joe Gordon had to deal with the loss of Aspromonte It not only took the most stable bat out of the lineup, but also left a gaping hole up the middle that destabilized the steady double-play combination of Malmberg to Aspromonte to Kellert. They knew each other's moves so well and were well respected for their defense. Aware that Boston's minor league director Johnny Murphy was having difficulty finding a replacement, the frustrated manager got creative. He initially tried agile catcher Eddie Sadowski and then third sacker Jack Phillips at second with an option to try reliable Grady Hatton. He also brought 40-year-old veteran Lou Stringer on board for a few games.

At least Sal Taormina returned to the team in time for the flight to Hollywood after spending two days in traction at St. Luke's Hospital to release pressure on his back that caused painful spasms. He was warmly welcomed back by all.

Both clubs went to the ballpark ready to do battle. Gordon had restructured his club's lineup with Eddie Sadowski in the leadoff spot playing second base in the opener. Prout started against Bennie Daniels and gave up two runs in the first inning. Back-to-back solo home runs by Eddie Sadowski (number seven) and Marty Keough (number 13) tied the game at two. The Stars went ahead 3–2 in the sixth before they exploded for five runs in the seventh. Even Leo Kiely was unable to squelch the onslaught as Carlos Bernier clobbered a three-run homer that dashed Seals' hopes of catching up and sealed the 8–2 triumph for the Stars. Lou Stringer made his debut in a Seals uniform when he struck out for Kiely in the ninth.

Well aware that this put the second game in a must-win category, Gordon sent Harry Dorish to the mound against veteran Fred Waters in what turned out to be a 32-hit, 16-run adventure in the scheduled seven-inning closer. By the end of the game his lineup card was a scribbled mess! Eddie Sadowski, still at the top of the batting order, started in right, but finished manning second after non-starter Albie Pearson doubled for Malmberg in the sixth and remained in the game in right. Stringer started at second but was later pulled for pinch-hitter Grady Hatton who struck out then replaced Malmberg at short. Marty Keough was rested with a game off while center field was covered by Tommy Umphlett. And Bill Abernathie, Bert Thiel, and Riverboat Smith all saw action before the game ended. Only four players finished the game where they had started: Bill Renna, Frank Kellert, Jack Phillips, and Haywood Sullivan. In five innings in long relief, Thiel allowed the first batter in each of those innings to reach base only to be erased by double plays.

The hard-fought conflict went back and forth and was tied at six after seven innings. Three more innings passed with the tie unbroken until the Seals staged one of the most important rallies of the season in the 11th. The fireworks started when Hatton singled and went to third on a powerful double off the left field fence off the bat of Renna, and Kellert was intentionally passed to load the bases Third baseman Jack Phillips hit an "excuse me" fly to short right that allowed Hatton to scamper to the plate, giving San Francisco a 7–6 lead. Not satisfied after his two-run homer in the fourth, Sullivan slammed a double that scored both Renna and Kellert and put the game in the Seals' pocket. The Stars went down fighting and managed to plate one before Smith got the final out and the 9–7 victory.

While Steve Bilko clobbered homers 53 and 54 as Los Angeles crushed Portland 12–0 Tuesday night, the Seals had another rough outing in game three. Starter Tommy Hurd played catch-up from the first inning, but fell short by the score of 5–3 as the surging Stars pulled within five games of the lead. Despite the efforts of Jack Spring in relief, a two-out two-run double by Leo Rodriguez in the seventh was all the Stars needed. Sal Taormina made his first appearance back in the lineup when he walked for Harry Malmberg in the seventh. Hurd, whose luck was still shaky as his team had yet to score more than four runs in a game for him, left the game in the sixth with things deadlocked at three, and Spring took the loss.

Earlier that day San Francisco got word from Boston General Manager Joe Cronin that pitcher Bob Chakales, catcher Haywood Sullivan, and outfielder Marty Keough had been recalled and were scheduled to report at the end of the PCL season. Pitchers Leo Kiely and Bert Thiel, also recalled, were told to report to Boston's 1958 spring training camp.

On the lighter side was an event that started badly in San Francisco but ended well in Hollywood. Apparently before the club left for the airport for the trip south, Leo Kiely's traveling bag, with all his clothes inside, was stolen from Tommy Hurd's car during the game. An angry Kiely fretted until he could shop for new duds that allowed him to arrive at the park before Wednesday's game looking like a real "man about town," to the surprise of his teammates. He was told two little kids had committed the crime and the mystery was solved. Later he told a reporter, "Well, it's not so bad after all, I guess. I got a good deal on the new drapes, and now I'll be the best dressed as well as the most completely broke man on the club."

The morning papers reported that in game four San Francisco had coasted to a 9–6 conquest of the Stars thanks to the complete-game effort of Riverboat Smith, who survived eight walks and three threats from the enemy, as his tenacity and stubbornness took him to his 11th win of the season and evened the series at two. They were aided by Stars starter Red Witt, who was wild from the start and left with two outs in the second inning behind by four runs. The four relievers who followed him yielded an additional five runs. In the three-run fifth, after Renna singled and Hatton tripled, Frank Kellert bashed his 29th homer and logged RBI number 100 and 101. In the seventh Bill Renna contributed his 29th homer and posted his 99th RBI.

Thursday's game was attended by 6,354 Hollywood loyals who went to see the Stars' last hurrah at Gilmore Field which was dramatically described by Bob Stevens: "It had to be, from all considered angles, the most dramatic game of the dying campaign and end of the dying Pacific Coast League." But Hollywood didn't go quietly!

A 26-year-old former All-American halfback from Mississippi Southern, Hugh Pepper, handled the Seals better than any other hurler that year as he came "that close" to a perfect game. He not only held them scoreless through eight innings while his squad scored six runs off Bob Chakales, but he allowed just one man to reach base, Frank Kellert, on a walk in the second. The park was essentially silent as he took the mound and fans held their breath with each pitch he threw. After Harry Malmberg made a routine groundout to short and Sal Taormina flew out to short left hitting for Kiely, who had come in to get two outs in the eighth, the crowd was on its feet screaming with excitement when Eddie Sadowski belted a clean single up the middle. The game ended on a pop foul to first base by Marty Keough. That game, originally written about as one of the best games played in the 19-year history of Gilmore Field, was, over time, reduced to the status of just one of many one-hitters in the PCL annals.

Gordon was still juggling his players to find the best combination to fill the hole created by Aspromonte's departure less than a week prior, when he got a second jolt. During pregame workouts Harry Malmberg suffered a shoulder injury that put him out of action. With his back to the wall, Gordon moved Sadowski to Malmberg's spot and put Lou Stringer at second. When he notified Boston of the situation, Cronin announced that young Bay Area infielder Pumpsie Green would be returned to San Francisco from Oklahoma City in the AA Texas League, and was slated to report for the series in Los Angeles.

But first things first. The Seals went to Lane Field for an important weekend set against the Padres, Friday through Sunday. The Padres had been a thorn in the side of the Seals all year, always a difficult competitor. At this point in the season they were in fourth place, a full dozen games behind San Francisco. The Seals swept all four games.

In Friday's opener Jack Spring out-pitched Vic Lombardi as he logged a shutout through seven innings and, despite giving up a three-run homer to Preston Ward in the eighth, garnered his tenth win. The Seals scored first and last in the game. Kellert blasted a solo homer (number 21) in the second, and Bill Renna drove in Albie Pearson in the ninth for his 100th RBI, a goal he achieved for the first time in his career. That was preceded by a busy eighth when Kellert doubled and Jack Phillips clobbered his eighth homer over the right field wall. The Seals won, 6–3, but the race with Vancouver remained the same as the Mounties defeated the Hollywood Stars, 2–0.

Saturday afternoon, 21 minutes into the conflict with the Seals in front 1–0, things were stalled when an unexpected cloudburst resulted in a two-hour delay thanks to the sudden downpour that quickly soaked the wooden seats of Lane Field and reduced the diamond to a muddy quagmire. Fans who sought shelter joked that any lingering termites in Lane Field had probably drowned! After a long and restless hour, Joe Gordon and San Diego General Manager Ralph Kiner were seen down the right field line in an animated, jovial conversation. They shook hands and suddenly Gordon threw his hands in the air and took off running down the third base line, turned and dove, then slid in the water and muck with his arms outstretched in front of his face all the way to home plate. Then he casually got back on his feet amid a flurry of laughter and cheers. When questioned after the game, he explained he did the prank for just one reason: Kiner bet him he wouldn't!

When action finally resumed, Bill Prout held the Pads to a 2–2 tie into the eighth inning when he stumbled and was picked up by Leo Kiely. The score remained unchanged at the end of nine, already nearly four hours after the first pitch. The Seals loaded the bases in the top of the tenth, and after putting a double in the books earlier, Pearson smashed the most exciting hit of his young career, a grand slam that won the day for the Seals, 6–2, as Leo Kiely added win number 20 to his total.

The Seals took both ends of the Sunday double-dip, 2–0 in 12 innings and 9–6 in their final game in Lane Field while 3,748 San Diego loyals witnessed the event.

In the three-plus-hour game one, the scoreboard was littered with goose eggs at the end of 11 frames in what was described as a riveting pitching duel between Riverboat Smith and 22-year-old Mudcat Grant. Riverboat was the victor when the game ended in 12 innings. It was his 12th win of the season and seventh in his last eight starts. He scattered five hits, struck out nine, and posted his fifth shutout of the season. The Seals scored twice in the top of the 12th, and the final tally was a solo homer by Bill Renna.

The seven-inning second game was another story. By comparison it was a slugfest in which the Seals logged 14 hits and the Padres 13. It was marked by a 15-minute argument that erupted during the Seals' six-run rally in the fifth inning when Frank Kellert hit what was called "a foul line splitting" double. When the dust finally settled both Padres manager George Metkovich and starter Bill Werle had been given the heave-ho, and when reliever Pete Mesa was called he initially refused to come out of the bullpen. The game ended 9–6 for the Seals. Starter Tom Hurd, aided by Jack Spring and Leo Kiely, earned his 21st win.

The group relaxed, joked with each other, and discussed off-season plans on the easy two-hour bus trip north to Los Angeles to take on the Angels at Wrigley Field before going back to San Francisco to complete the season over the weekend. At that point their 97–62 record still led the league by the same 3.5 margin they had maintained since the Mounties temporarily decreased it to two games on July 27. Hollywood, still third, had slipped to nine games behind; Seattle had moved into fourth, a game ahead of San Diego; and the 1956 champion Angels were sixth, behind by 21 games. The seventh and eighth spots, far below the pack, were owned by Sacramento (39 back) and Portland (42 behind).

The Seals entered the five-game set anxious to "seal the deal" and get back to Seals Stadium. To the skipper's relief, Pumpsie Green had already arrived and was waiting for them. In game one he had an impressive outing.

He was 2-for-2 with a single, double, and two walks, stole one base. Defensively he displayed agility and quick feet and hands at second base. It was complemented by an outstanding effort from Bob Chakales, whose complete game allowed the team to post its fifth consecutive win and ninth out of the last 12 contests.

Other runs were driven across by Marty Keough's triple, Frank Kellert's double, and timely singles by Renna, Sullivan, Phillips, and Chakales himself as the Seals led the way after their four-run first inning. The final score was 7–4.

Tuesday was the site of yet another doubleheader. Game one, scheduled for seven innings, saw Jack Spring pitch one of his most determined efforts against young Larry Sherry as he held the Angels to four hits, struck out nine, walked five, and helped his own cause with a single in four trips to the plate, earning a complete game win. Steve Bilko, who had been moved by manager Clay Bryant from the cleanup slot to the leadoff spot in order to give him more at-bats in his quest for 60 home runs, got two of those hits but both stayed inside the yard.

The Seals managed a baker's dozen in the hits department. They scored one run in the third inning when Albie Pearson singled home Marty Keough, and added another in the fourth when Frank Kellert doubled and was driven home on a single by Grady Hatton. In what was slated to be the final inning, Keough doubled then went home on Pearson's third single of the day. Ahead 3–1 in the seventh, the impossible happened as flawless infielder Grady Hatton made not one but two errors, allowing two runners to reach base. Steve Bilko then launched his second hit, a long single that drove them home and tied things up. With a second game still to be played, the Seals made short work of the tie when, with two away in the top of the eighth, Bill Renna walloped a two-run homer, his 29th, that gave the visitors a 5–3 victory.

Tommy Lasorda took the mound for the Angels in the second game against Harry Dorish as Gordon once again altered things. Green, moved from second to short, was at the top of the lineup card, followed by Pearson, Umphlett, Kellert, Renna, Phillips, Sullivan, and Stringer, back at second, hitting eighth with Dorish at the bottom.

After the Seals logged a run in the first inning when Tommy Umphlett hit into a fielder's choice that scored Green, and followed up with one more in the second when Jack Phillips bashed his ninth round-tripper, the energy shifted to the home team. With the scoreboard showing the Seals ahead 2–1 entering the fifth, Dorish lost steam after the score was tied at two. He was pulled by Gordon with one down and the bases loaded as Steve Bilko approached the plate. Leo Kiely was called and put out the fire when he surprised Bilko with a strikeout pitch, then got the final out to retire the side.

Kiely and Lasorda battled each other into the bottom of the ninth without a score change when second baseman Sparky Anderson, who had played every game of the season, reached out and smashed a long single that scored the winning run. The Angels won, 3–2. It was a complete-game, four-hit victory for Lasorda that brought his record to 7–10 and added a fifth loss to Leo Kiely's ledger against 21 wins.

Wednesday morning, in search of relaxation and fresh air, Joe Gordon, trainer Doc Hughes, and a couple of players hired a boat and spent a few hours ocean fishing off the coast of Long Beach. It was reported that they brought back a good catch of bonita which they sent with their compliments to a local restaurant that prepared a nice seafood meal for members of the press.

That night the Angels took charge from the start and slowed the Seals' quest for the pennant with a 3–1 victory. The report in the paper the next day said, "The Seals were prodigal in defeat. They outhit their southern tormentors, 6–4, messed up a half a dozen scoring chances, left nine men to die on the trail, and got only one back-to-the-home-base." With the end of the season just days away and the pennant not yet clinched, it was not their plan to stall at 99 wins.

Fortunately, that night Portland defeated Vancouver 5–4 in a hard-fought conflict in Vancouver that caused the Mounties to miss a golden opportunity to gain valued ground. While the Seals struggled in Los Angeles, Lefty O'Doul and the Seattle Rainiers enjoyed a laugh a few miles away as they humiliated Hollywood, 20–2.

Things were not so funny for the Bay Nine, however, as they had a rare experience: back-to-back-to-back defeats. This time Tommy Hurd and Connie Grob took shutouts to the fifth inning that ended when Hurd made a throwing error on a Sparky Anderson bunt and compounded it with a wild pitch to Tom Saffell. All in all, it took ten innings and a solo homer by Bob Jenkins to beat them, 3–2, but Los Angeles defeated them in the series by the same margin.

Concomitantly, but never used as an excuse, the Seals struggled with a minor epidemic of Asian flu that left Harry Dorish, Haywood Sullivan, Bill Renna, Eddie Sadowski and even Joe Gordon in weakened states. Their work was not finished yet. Their goal was still within reach as they headed for the airport right after the game for a quick flight home to the comfort and support of the local fans and Seals Stadium. On the way they energized each other, knowing any combination of a San Francisco win and a Vancouver loss would seal the championship for them, the 11th for the organization in its 55 consecutive years in the Pacific Coast League.

They deplaned in San Francisco around 1:30 A.M. and were greeted by over 300 cheering fans. They looked forward to a day of rest and recuperation from the flu as they faced a busy weekend. While Vancouver battled Seattle to end the season, the Seals caught a break as they faced Tommy Heath and the Sacramento Solons who, at 39 games back, were trying to stay out of the basement currently occupied by Portland, 40 games behind. The Seals intended to win the championship for their loyal fans during that series.

When they got to the park the next day they found a pile of newspapers on the benches in front of the lockers, all opened to the sports section as usual. There was an editorial column that focused on the wonderments of the team and pointed out specific accomplishments of the players. It was a goodbye to the club that had developed dozens of players over the years, had provided sanctuary for former major leaguers who still had a lot of baseball to play, and had become part of San Francisco families for generations. But these players had other things on their minds.

Although Sunday was originally slated as San Francisco Appreciation Day, the players had discussed it and Grady Hatton approached Joe Gordon in his office with the idea of having Glenn Wright Day instead. Their coach had just returned home from St. Luke's Hospital, where he had surgery that removed a malignant tumor in his throat and jaw and faced a long recovery. Hatton told him that every player agreed to donate a day's pay for their respected friend. They all agreed Wright had gone above and beyond for the team as the former shortstop worked tirelessly with players when they slumped, helped infielders adjust to each other's habits, and helped runners on ways to get the best lead off to steal bases and avoid being picked off base.

Gordon talked to his players before the first game of the series, which happened to be Friday the 13th, and congratulated them for the many things they had accomplished as a team and individually over the course of a busy season. Then, in his usual fashion, he quickly reminded them not to take the ailing Solons for granted. After all, while the Sacs were still fighting to avoid a basement finish, the Seals still needed a win to clinch the pennant.

During the pregame workouts the stands along the third base line and the Seals dugout were littered with admiring autograph-seeking fans. Although the idea of actually having major league baseball in 1958 was appealing to the majority, the longtime Seals loyals considered their loss a high price to pay. In fact, throughout the Bay Area newspapers received letters to the editors asking why the Seals couldn't stay and play in the Coast League with home games at Seals Stadium during Giants road trips. Although that sold newspapers, it was never a viable cause and was never taken seriously. Local luncheon clubs also supported the idea of keeping the Seals who they felt would draw well in spite of the presence of major league baseball. But it all went for naught.

While action in Vancouver between the Mounties and the Rainiers was nip-and-tuck for a dozen innings, the Seals sent Riverboat Smith to the mound in a face-off with 38-year-old veteran Earl Harrist, who had a 5–12 record. The long and the short of it was that the Seals sacked the Solons 3–0 in a two-hour event witnessed by only 4,438 vocal fans. Smith limited the foes to four hits, pitched a complete game for his eighth win in his last nine starts that brought his season record to 13–10, and ran up a string of 21 scoreless innings.

Although the Solons threatened in the first inning, the slate was wiped clean by a double play. With two on base and one away in the third, a double play once again ended a potential rally. The harder the frustrated Solons fought, the more Smith reared back and gave them his best stuff one batter at a time until he put them down one-two-three in the ninth. All they got for their night's work was a line of nine zeroes on the board.

The Seals scored solo runs in the first, second, and sixth innings as everybody contributed to the team's 12 hits. Doubles by Eddie Sadowski, Marty Keough, and Pumpsie Green in addition to a single each, plus two hits by Frank Kellert and long singles by Haywood Sullivan and Albie Pearson, were capped off by an excuse-me single by Smith and a stolen base by Green that gave the fans plenty to yell about. Although they didn't know it, the winning plays of the game had come in the first inning when Eddie Sadowski doubled, went to third on a Marty Keough fly to deep right, and scored on a passed ball by catcher Cuno Barragan.

As the team exited the field after the last out fans gave them a five-minute standing ovation, knowing everything hinged on the score of the Mounties game. Joe Cronin had called from Boston to congratulate them and stayed on the telephone for 40 minutes until the Mounties were defeated, 4–3, in the 12th inning. He congratulated Joe Gordon and the team as he heard loud laughter in the background. He then said he wanted Marty Keough and Bob Chakales, scheduled to pitch the next day, on the first plane to Boston.

Ironically, the last time the Seals won the PCL pennant, 1946, when they beat Casey Stengel's Oakland Oaks by four games, the Seals had Lefty O'Doul at the helm. This time they played their pennant-clinching game against former skipper Tommy Heath. The important thing to the organization was that they were leaving winners. It was a bittersweet conquest as all welcomed the honor of first place and the banner that would fly over the stadium. But the older players knew it was the end of a long baseball tradition in San Francisco that they hoped would not be forgotten.

"SEALS WIN FLAG!" was the two-inch headline above the name of the Saturday morning *San Francisco Chronicle*. The event gave new meaning to the ominous date "Friday the 13th." Fans were ecstatic and proud, honked horns and waved at passing cars all over town. Moreover, the excitement was felt throughout the Bay Area and the rest of the league. The team went to the park for the afternoon game a little bit the worse for wear after celebrating their success of the night before. Three games remained in their season.

Although everyone knew Saturday's game didn't mean anything in the standings as far as the Seals were concerned, Gordon still wanted his team to make a good showing on the field. The problem was that Marty Keough and slated starter Bob Chakales were already on their way to Boston, and third baseman Jack Phillips was out with a wrist injury. He juggled the players around the infield and outfield in his own inimitable style and created what was dubbed "a patchwork lineup" in the sports pages: Sadowski at short, Green at second, Pearson in center field, Kellert at first, Renna in left field, Sullivan in right field, Umphlett at third, and Tornay behind the plate. The top three in that lineup offered the same get-on-base ability and speed Gordon appreciated, and the rest had the power to drive them around the bases.

But the first thing he did was name Bert Thiel as the starter, his first start since May 12, when, to his surprise, he was added to the bullpen staff where he patiently and successfully performed all season. The skipper said he had earned that start as a reward for his hard work. Initially Thiel saw it differently.

> I especially remember when Gordon told me to start the game the Saturday after we won the pennant. It was the game before the last game of the season and didn't mean nothing. I found it insulting at first. But I took the ball with the feeling that I wanted to go out there and do my very best to show the people who left me in the bullpen that they were wrong and I could still be an effective starter. I pitched one heck of a game that we won 3–2 in 11 innings. And I went all 11 innings, not like they use pitchers today.

After the Seals scored once in the first inning and the Sacs tied it in the fourth, everybody was scoreless until the 11th when Al Heist belted one of the longest homers of his career to put the visitors ahead, 2–1. In the bottom of the inning the Seals did what they always did and took the game back. Albie Pearson singled to right and was advanced to third when Bill Renna managed an infield single. Sal Taormina batted for Haywood Sullivan, and his ground ball was said to have rolled up the middle over the mound and dissected second base before it dribbled into short center and died.

While infielders tripped over themselves trying to get to the ball, Pearson scored to tie the game. When Nini Tornay slapped a single to right, Renna stormed across for the game-winning tally. Thiel was at his best as he scattered six hits through 11 frames for the complete-game victory that brought his record for the season to 5–4 with a 2.79 ERA in 109⅔ innings pitched, most of them in relief.

Saturday night Joe Cronin arrived in the City by the Bay with orders from Boston to spare no expense as host of a proper celebration for the players, coaches, members of the press, and all the wives in honor of their good season and the championship. They had a long, relaxing dinner at DiMaggio's on Fisherman's Wharf. That's when the players were told the 1957 *Look* magazine All-Pacific-Coast League Team had been selected and would be officially announced when the magazine hit the newsstands the following week. Three Seals players were among the nine-man roster: second baseman Chip Aspromonte, center fielder Marty Keough, and pitcher Leo Kiely. Other members of the honored team included Vancouver left fielder Lenny Green, Seattle right fielder Joe Taylor, San Diego third baseman Rudy Regalado, San Diego catcher Earl Averill, and Hollywood RHP George Witt.

Sunday, September 15, 1957, was more than the last day of the season in San Francisco. With the pennant in hand and victory celebrations temporarily on the back burner, it was a day of remembering, reminiscing, and honoring the long history of a beloved team that had been part of the Bay Area ambiance as a charter member of the Pacific Coast League since its inception in 1903. Most of the 15,484 fans in attendance had lived and died with the Seals their entire lives. They brought their cameras and extra film and took photos of the stadium and the players throughout the afternoon.

Although two games were scheduled for the season-ender on Sunday, it turned out to be a day of sentimental fun and games and neither team cared about winning. That turned out to be a good thing because the record books have the Seals taking the short end of both games, 5–4 in the first and 14–7 in the second.

Game one was a ballgame that the Solons needed to win to clinch seventh place. The press later reported that the Seals didn't have their hearts in it, but that didn't seem accurate. Starter Jack Spring pitched the entire game. As the Seals entered the bottom of the ninth behind 5–3, he readied himself to return to the hill if his club could tie the score. Unfortunately the squad rallied, but fell one run short.

Between games president Al Glass of the Mission Merchants Association, aided by "Miss Miracle Mile," Jeri Hanson, presented small gifts to the players, honoring their request for an abbreviated Fan Appreciation Day. When this was completed, Sal Taormina stepped up to the mike in front of home plate and explained how coach Glenn Wright, who had devoted nearly 40 years of his life to baseball, was recovering from serious cancer surgery and faced a long, challenging road ahead. He explained that the players had already donated a day's pay to help with Wright's recovery, and then his teammates joined with members of the Solons and the umpires in the stands as they collected a few thousand dollars.

The final ceremony before the second game started was the announcement of the winner of the "Most Popular Seal" contest. During the final eight weeks of the season ballots were distributed throughout the Bay Area, and fans wrote the name of their favorite player and deposited them by the turnstiles as they entered the ballgames. The winning player received a free trip for two to the World Series between the New York Yankees and Milwaukee Braves. Giants broadcaster Lon Simmons was brought in as Master of Ceremonies for the big announcement. When he said the winner was Sal Taormina, the fans were as thrilled as Sal was surprised. The standing ovation didn't stop until the humbled veteran, obviously moved, stepped up to the microphone and quietly said, "Thank you."

The final game of the season and the era was a seven-inning laugher deliberately staged as a time to have fun. The tone was immediately set when the Seals exited the dugout and took their positions in the field, with Joe Gordon at his old spot at second base. With that, Tommy Heath ran out of the visitors' dugout on the first base side and protested because Gordon was not listed on the lineup card, but gave up when the umpires laughed. Former high school pitcher Albie Pearson took the mound, Pumpsie Green trotted out to right field, Eddie Sadowski went to shortstop before he and Gordon later switched positions, Frank Kellert played first base for one at-bat before he was called back to a standing ovation and replaced by Sal Taormina, Bill Renna went into left field, Haywood Sullivan played center, and Nini Tornay was behind the plate. In the sixth frame, Gordon left the field and replaced himself with Harry Malmberg. After Pearson gave up four earned runs in the first inning he was yanked for Bill Prout, who yielded nine more runs through the fifth. Finally the closer, Grady Hatton, gave up just one run in the sixth and none in the seventh.

During the adventure, Pearson rotated to most positions, and Joe Gordon even pitched, but not for long. When his pitch to former Seal Jimmy Westlake was called a ball by umpire Chris Pelekoudas, an "irate" Gordon stormed the plate. After a two-minute back and forth, the ump and the pitcher laughed in a "let's see if you can do better" mode, then changed places, which brought loud laughter from the crowd. After one pitch from Pelekoudas in full umpire garb minus chest protector that had the fans rolling in the aisles, they went back to their proper spots and play resumed. Albie Pearson took the loss on the mound that gave him a pitching record of 0–1 with an ERA of 36.00 in the record books for 1957.

As the fans exited Seals Stadium as the home of the San Francisco Seals for the last time, they remembered former players who graced that field and went on to major league careers: Frankie Crosetti, Smead Jolley, Dario Lodigiani, Augie Galan, Larry Jansen, Lefty O'Doul, Tony Lazzeri, the three

DiMaggio brothers, and others. They remembered the Seals-Oaks cross-bay rivalry. They remembered ten other pennant-winning seasons. They remembered cold nights and sunny days watching the team struggle through tough losses and well-deserved wins. They remembered how being a fan of the San Francisco Seals had enriched their lives, and they anticipated the arrival of major league baseball.

On September 16 the Art Rosenbaum column reported on the Seals' last day accompanied by a photo of Joe Gordon captioned "the last manager" and one of Albie Pearson captioned "the last pitcher." And in the box score for that day the umpires were listed as Pelekoudas, Mutart, Orr, and Gordon. Throughout the second game, action was regularly halted by fans running onto the field seeking autographs and handshakes.

When the last out was called the fans gave the Seals players a standing ovation as they exited the field and disappeared into the clubhouse for the last time. Was their applause for the Seals' championship in their final season, the success of the best minor league in professional baseball history that faced reconfiguration and would never be the same again, the pending arrival of major league baseball, or all of the above? It was a moment of mixed emotions and much to think about. The Seals shook hands with many fans as they slowly made their way to the open doors in center field and left the park and memories of the Golden Era of the Pacific Coast League behind.

Looking back, the players I was able to interview had memories of their own about that season nearly 60 years ago.

Ken Aspromonte: Once I got to San Francisco I felt comfortable. I knew most of the guys who were optioned out with me like Marty Keough and a few others. Being on a good club is always a big help to individual players. I know it helped me a lot. When the teammates get along and the team wins it's always more fun to go to the park. In my case, it was one of those years when you're at home at the plate and just felt good swinging the bat, and everything seemed to fall in line. Your strokes are better. You're seeing the ball better, and it probably seemed that I was pretty lucky up there, but believe me, the success that came was the result of hard work and some luck, I'm sure. That season was a big improvement from 1956 for me. I just made a lot of good contacts and I think I got close to 180 hits [171]. That was a lot more than 1956 [154] because I was out for about a month with an appendectomy. So I missed a lot of at-bats and had to get back into the groove a little bit when I came back.

Joe Gordon was our manager and he was an easy guy to work with. He molded us into a good ballclub. Gordon wanted us to have fun. He was one of those fun guys himself as a player and was the same way as a manager. He just let us go out there and play our own game, unless we asked for help with something. He was a great second baseman in the major leagues and I wish he would have pulled me aside once in a while and given me tips about footwork or other elements of playing second. I wish he would have taken me under his wing a little bit and said, "Look, this is how we play second base, and this is how we do this and that."

But in those days there really wasn't much instruction like there should have been, especially at that level of play. Look at Tommy Umphlett. He could have been an excellent outfielder for a major league ballclub if someone would have worked with him with his hitting at the minor league level. But at that time we were more or less on our own and all that it accomplished was that when we got to the major leagues it was that much more difficult for us up there because we had to learn things on the job that we should have been taught in the minors. The outfield was crowded at Boston with Piersall, Jensen and Williams, and I wish they would have traded Tom to give him the opportunity to break into a big league outfield. And that happens to a lot of guys when clubs hold on to them as a backup in case of injury at the top and they wear themselves out in the minors and then nobody wants them. Personally, I had a great fondness for Tom. He was a real good guy. We roomed together on the road during those days and talked a lot of baseball and got along well. He was very quiet and low-key.

Actually, the Coast League was a tough league. I remember Vancouver, San Diego, Hollywood and Seattle all had good ball clubs, very competitive, and we did well against them. All the teams were made up of guys looking to make it to the majors and a lot of old timers that came back down from the major leagues who wanted to play a little longer. I can't remember all their names but most of the older guys had at least a couple of seasons in the major leagues and some had long careers up there. And there were tough pitchers, too, like Vic Lombardi and others who were almost ten years older than I was at that time.

We respected their experience. It didn't matter if those guys threw a fast-ball 90 miles per hour or 80 miles per hour because they knew when to throw it and where to put it. They were in and out, high and low, not afraid to knock you down. In fact I got knocked down quite a few times in the PCL because I was the league-leading batter. It's a pride thing and made me feel good ... well ... as long as it didn't actually hit me!

It was a great time in San Francisco. It was a great city in those days. We really loved it there.

Jack Spring: I think the 1957 Seals was one of the great minor league teams of all time. We had Big Bill Renna, Albie Pearson, Marty Keough, Grady Hatton, Ken Aspromonte [who] was on his way to the big leagues, Frank Kellert, Ed Sadowski and Haywood Sullivan behind the plate and some good but no-name pitchers who were on their way. But I'll tell you, that was a really solid AAA baseball team and by far the best minor league team I've ever played on. Later they talked about the 1960 year in Spokane, the Dodgers affiliate, the year after I retired, as one of the great minor league clubs but I really think the '57 Seals were better.

Before that 1957 season I had already been in the majors, well, briefly. I went to spring training with the Phillies in 1955 and that was a time when big league clubs were allowed 28 players (three extra) for the first 30 days of the regular season and they took me with them as one of the three. I made my major league debut pitching in the old Polo Grounds. Actually I pitched only twice that season.

Looking back it was kind of funny. The first major league game I ever saw was when I was in the bullpen! Robin Roberts pitched opening day and he got into a little jam in the ninth inning and they had me and somebody else in the bullpen get up, and I think when Roberts looked down our way and saw what was going on he struck out the next two guys. But after two appearances they sent me back to Syracuse for the rest of that year.

In 1956 they moved their AAA team to Miami and I went there, which was quite an experience because one of my teammates there was Satchel Paige. He was quite a character, never at a loss for words and told lots of stories about himself. When I went to play winter baseball in Venezuela the Red Sox drafted me and I went to spring training in Sarasota with them. I had a really good spring and again I went north with the team. I was there 30 days and, as I recall, I had pitched just one inning, struck out two out of three hitters I faced and they said they were sending me to San Francisco.

At that time Pinky Higgins was the manager and he explained that it was kind of a rough deal but was out of his hands. At that time Boston was a notoriously tough ballpark for left-handed pitchers and they didn't use too many because of the short porch in left field ... and teams loaded up with right-handed hitters when they played there and that was sort of the excuse for sending me out. Of course that changed years later when they built the green monster out there.

But I wouldn't trade the experiences I had with the team, my teammates, or playing with San Francisco in that particular season for anything. It was a wonderful time.

Grady Hatton: We had such a good club that the fans came out in droves and showed excellent support for us. They were outstanding ... and noisy. They saw us as a bunch of good guys who got along well and they liked that.

The Pacific Coast League was a unique place to play, and special, too.

Even though it wasn't the majors, it had what was called Open Classification status since 1952, I think, which made it a step above other minor leagues in everyone's eyes at the time. The Seals were one of the landmark teams in the league. Earlier Joe DiMaggio and others like him put both the Seals and the league on the map. When he was there it was the beginning of so many good Seals players going on to the major leagues. And as a tribute to all that the Red Sox really wanted us to win the pennant because a lot of folks were sad about having to lose their club. It was a great season for all of us.

Marty Keough: Years after that season, when I was riding to the airport with Tommy Lasorda and somebody else, we were talking about those days. Tommy said, "You guys had a great team in '57 but I beat you guys five times." I know we played the Angels a lot but there's no way he beat us more than once when our errors helped him out. So I said to him, "Tommy, I can't even remember you pitching. All you ever did was yell at everybody."

Tommy Umphlett: I think anybody who played in the Coast League that season considered it one of the best and most challenging experiences of his career.

Albie Pearson: So many seasons have passed that it's sometimes hard to remember too many things. But it was a happy year for the players and the fans. I especially remember the game on the last day of the season because I played every position. It was all part of the plan to have a little fun with the fans. We had clinched the pennant on Friday night so Joe Gordon had everybody out of position to start the game and we kept changing spots. Joe even went out on the mound and threw a few pitches, well, until he and the umpire got into an argument over his calls. The way they both acted it was obvious they were not serious, just kidding around, so they traded places for a few pitches. The fans got a kick out of it. Everybody did, except maybe the batter at the plate.

When I pitched to one batter, their third baseman who later played briefly for the Yankees but I can't remember his name, he smacked a home run off me! That put me in the Coast League record books in the pitching column with a 36.00 ERA.

Bert Thiel: We all knew the 1957 team was built to win, period. I don't think Boston looked at it as ending with a winner for the San Francisco fans. At the start of the season they apparently still didn't know for sure whether '57 or maybe '58 would be the last year. Either way, Boston had underestimated the Coast League when they took over in San Francisco in

1956 and wanted to make a better showing in '57. So they picked up a lot of veterans towards the end of our careers and financially I don't think it cost them too much. I was 31 that season and thought I had a lot of baseball left in me. But very seldom do you get veterans and rookie ballplayers who blend that well together, you know. It was really a good experience for all of us.

And that league was great. We had nice long series every place because the league was set up so we played seven games in a series, five games and a doubleheader on Sunday, and then Mondays off for travel or whatever. It was a good schedule, and we got to spend some time and take a look at every city where we played when we weren't on the field.

Because I'm from northern Wisconsin I liked Vancouver a lot. I'm an outdoor guy and liked the outdoors. Seattle was always special because my brother was a career military man stationed at Fort Lewis in Washington and he would come and stay with me when the team played there. It broke everything up to have him there.

Before I went out there I read about the Coast League and learned a little bit what Open Classification, and discovered it was more important to the teams than individual players. We didn't care about that stuff. We just wanted to play ball. But I remember guys didn't want to leave that league to go to the big leagues. They were making more money in the Coast League then they ever would make in the big leagues. They enjoyed the travel, the cities, and the weather in the league and many refused to go up. I know that's what [Steve] Bilko did."

Bill Renna: Being raised in the Bay Area I was no stranger to the Coast League. I'm now 87 and hanging in with good health. I go to the gym three days a week to strengthen my back after spinal cord surgeries. My memory is good and I remember the season with the Seals very well. It was a special time.

The Seals were in San Francisco for a long time, and they had developed a great reputation and following that went from generation to generation. The fans were really great. The Pacific Coast League was the third major league because there was controversy whether or not it should be classified as a third major league. It was much better than the other two AAA leagues, believe me. I played in the International League and the American Association, and the PCL was a big step up. There was no comparison.

As the guys came in I remember thinking it was going to be a good year. We had Grady Hatton, Frank Kellert, Harry Malmberg, Ken Aspromonte, Albie Pearson and others. I remember Pearson had a great arm but threw kind of sidearm and the ball kind of veered off to the left like it was a curve ball. So I played catch with him all the time to try to help him get in the habit of throwing over the top so it would be more direct and bounce straight when it hit the ground, making it easier for the receiver to catch it. He worked at it but never really mastered the over-the-top throw.

One of my best memories of that season was Sal Taormina, an older veteran just like me, who also played the outfield. He was a great person and we got to be close friends. We both lived in San Jose and commuted to home games together. He drove one day and I'd drive the next. From then until now, whenever former players from that team have run into each other at games or whatever over the years, we were always glad to see each other and reminisced about fond memories of that season.

* * *

As the author who has carried memories of that season and those players in a very special place and now realize my grandchildren are older than I was back in those days, I decided it seems only fitting that the final words about the San Francisco Seals should come from the "invisible" member of the squad, broadcaster Don Klein, who was actually the father of Seals baseball broadcasts. As the link to the Seals for those of us who couldn't attend every game, he not only did play-by-play coverage, but he also allowed fans to know players better on all eight teams as well as understand the importance of the Pacific Coast League itself.

Hearing his voice again after so many years was a thrill that brought back a flood of memories for me personally. He is sharp, articulate, and proud to have been a part of the last few years with that team in that league. The history of the Seals would not be complete without noting his contribution. Don Klein was one of a kind, a San Francisco icon who left a lifelong impression on this fan and so many others. In tribute to his 50-plus years spent covering the Seals, Stanford football, and the San Francisco 49ers, he was inducted into the Bay Area Radio Hall of Fame in 2007.

This is his story.

Don Klein: Well, I played softball, and in grade school I pitched. I just wasn't much of an athlete, but always loved sports.

I started in radio when I was a senior in high school, Roosevelt High in Seattle. I was hired because of an interest in sports that I had, and because I knew the station owner who wanted to get the high school football games on the air and said he'd like me to do them.

I really learned football that way because I broadcast three high school games a week over a period of several weeks which amounted to 30–35 football games. The rest of the time when we did college games we did 12 and when we did the 49ers we did 16. So that old experience had me do twice as many and I got into the real swing of it.

Then the war came along and I was out of broadcasting through 1945 when I served in Naval Intelligence as a Japanese Language Officer. When the war ended and they gave us a chance to disembark from the navy or go to Japan in the post-war period as a liaison officer, I passed it up because I wanted to get back into civilian life. I took my discharge in Hawaii and, to make a long story short with the Seals, the team trained there with Paul Fagan. He had his [pineapple] ranch in Maui and before the season he brought the team over there to train at the ranch and then they returned to Honolulu and played against semipro teams there for about a week. Lefty O'Doul was the manager at that time and he had a great following in the islands and so did the entire team, as a result of that.

My wife and I were living in Honolulu when I left the military after the war, and I got an idea. Let me backtrack to explain this. Well, I had played around as a kid, imitating a Seattle broadcaster named Leo Lassen and playing with baseball board games and broadcasting baseball games to myself. So I felt I wanted to do a thing called "re-creation." We got permission from Paul Fagan. Curiously enough, he would start the first week or so of the season with San Francisco and then he was never there during baseball season. He spent the summers on his ranch on Maui. So we phoned him and said we'd like to do the broadcasts if he'd give permission, and we'd recreate Sunday afternoon games. He said, "Fine, fine." The games were played in Coast League cities and we got the information by phone in Honolulu and sent the games out in Hawaii and the San Francisco area.

So we started out that first year in 1946 and did a Sunday game. Sponsors sold out right away so we added a Saturday game which also sold out right away. After a month into the season we decided we would add a Tuesday and Friday night game. And by mid-season we had the whole thing sold and we did every game. They were quite popular and well received in the Bay Area. Well, Paul Fagan sat over in Maui and that was how he kept track of the Seals—through me. And I didn't know him personally and actually never met him. We made the arrangements by phone.

So after that I did all the Seals games for two years and then a guy, a big-time contractor in Honolulu, came in and said, "Hey, those Seals games are great and all that, but I'm a Red Sox fan. Can you do the Red Sox games?" So we did one major league game a week, called it "The Game of the Week," and invariably one of the teams in each game was the Red Sox. That's all the guy wanted.

And anyway, lo and behold, I was recreating in the football season in

1948 after the baseball season was over. I was recreating a Notre Dame and somebody football game. It was halftime and a person came in and said, "Don, can you come and take a phone call from San Francisco?" I had a color guy working with me to cover things. So I picked up the telephone and it was Paul Fagan and Lefty O'Doul on the phone. "Don, how would you like to come to San Francisco and broadcast all our baseball games?" It was right out of the blue.

What had happened was, Jack McDonald, who had been the Seals broadcaster in the states for a long time, got caught in a sponsor switch. He had been plugging Lucky Lager beer as per his contract. In those days the sponsor bought into half of the program or a quarter. They didn't sell "spots," you know, like they do now. Well, everyone really identified him with the Lucky Lager plugs, until Regal Pale bought the rights to the San Francisco Seals and they refused to go along with Jack McDonald for that reason. They thought it would be better to go with a new broadcaster. So I was "clean" in that regard. They asked me to fly to San Francisco to talk about it, which I did the following week, and you can imagine how I felt. My gosh, I was 25 years old and got that big chance. We left the islands after living there for three years and thoroughly enjoyed it.

So I went there, worked for station KSFO in San Francisco. [Author's note: This story was written about before, that Klein went to the broadcast booth and was about to describe the San Francisco Seals baseball games after having broadcast the last 280 of them without ever seeing them play!]

Everything was done in Hawaii as recreations. Anyway, we made quite a hit doing live home games with the Seals and recreations of road games. For them I used more sound. For instance, when the batter got a hit, I had a little drummer's totem block and when you hit it with a drumstick near the microphone it sounded like the bat hitting the ball. And when the pitched ball hit the catcher's mitt I would tap that against the back of a leather chair right beside me. We even put in the background noises. We had made some recordings that sounded like ballpark announcements: "Tickets to the next Portland game (or whatever road team we were playing) are on sale now," and other things, being careful to use the right team for the place we were playing. The one that always got them was, "Will the fan down the left field line please remove the jacket from the wall." And we played that one at a higher volume so you could really hear it over the air.

From that I went on to do the Stanford games for 25 years and became very close to Bill Walsh. In 1981 Bill had been coaching the 49ers into his third year and asked me to go over there. I thought about it long and hard and even called Lon Simmons, who had done them for a long time (I was sports director at CBS) and asked him if he would do it. I wanted to stay with Stanford because I had a lot of friends there and so forth, but he said he didn't feel comfortable changing.

Funny story. As a little kid, as much as I liked baseball, I was always star-struck with the idea of broadcasting the Rose Bowl. That had been my ambition more than the World Series or Stanford or anything else. And I actually went to the Rose Bowl for two years and broadcast the play-by-play nationally on NBC. That was a real thrill, you know. So then Bill Walsh came over and asked me to do the 49ers I told him how thrilled I was to have done the Rose Bowl games and looked forward to continuing that, and he said, "Well, Don, I think we're going to go to the Super Bowl." He had been with the team for three years. The first year they were 2–14, the second year they were 2–14, and that year they were 6–10 in 1980. And now he thinks he's going to the Super Bowl in 1981? But anyway, I went over to them and they actually did win the 1982 Super Bowl. How about that? Then the dynasty evolved.

Going back, I mentioned Leo Lassen. I grew up in Seattle listening to him announcing games. He was a Seattle legend in sports broadcasting. He was a fantastic man on detail and I learned baseball by listening to him. He would explain the meaning of little moves during the games. And later six of the eight Pacific Coast League broadcasters grew up in Seattle, and I guess you could say we were "trained" by listening to him. Let's see, there was, of course, Leo in Seattle; Rollie Truett was the Portland broadcaster; Tony Kester did the Sacramento Solons; Bud Foster was in Oakland; Al Schuss was in San Diego, and myself. Hollywood and Los Angeles had different ones. And we all say the same thing that I'm telling you now. We all learned our baseball by listening to Leo Lassen. He had a terrible voice, very nasal and high, and people always used to say we were lucky to have him in Seattle because he would never make it in the east with that voice.

I retired after 30 years with CBS. But I did continue broadcasting the NFL games until 1990, a couple of Monday night games and some playoff games in late December.

Going back real quick, I was broadcasting a high school football game in Seattle on Friday afternoon, my first year out of high school, before a Washington-Minnesota game the next day, and it was to be the "Game of the Week," and Bill Stern, who was my hero as a youngster, came out to broadcast it. I did the Friday game and my boss said they were having a banquet for Bill Stern and he's going to give a speech and suggested he and I attend and I would meet him. This was one of the great thrills of my life because he was an icon of broadcasting at that time. He was fantastic. So we get there and my boss says, "Bill, I'd like you to meet a young man coming up in broadcasting here, Don Klein." And Stern looked at me and said, "Were you the fellow broadcasting the high school football game yesterday?" When I said that was me, he said, "Well,

I heard you and you did a great job. How would you like to come with me to Hollywood and do broadcasts for NBC?" Well, I was standing there stunned.

What had happened was, at the stadium they had one of those old trucks used as a hot dog stand and coffee, and the guy in the truck had my broadcast on. Stern had gone for coffee or something and heard me and stayed there and listened. I was just out of high school so I told my dad about it. He had always been quite proud of me, but he said, "No, no way. You're too young to go to a thing like that. You have to get your education first." So I wrote and declined his offer. Well, I didn't expect any contact with him after that, but he wrote such a beautiful letter, very thoughtful and sincere, and I used that letter to get my first job in Hawaii after the war.

But let me tell you an amazing thing about that. In the late sixties he came out to do a Stanford game for television and I thought I'd go say hello, and was told he was up on the roof of the press box. So I went up to him, he was standing there alone, and I said, "Bill, I'm sure you won't remember me," and before I could finish the sentence, he looked me right in the eye and said, "You're the young fellow I talked to many years ago up in Seattle." Imagine that, after all that time. I was really overcome and will never forget that. That story I just told you was written in the *Chronicle* at one time.

I was hired to do the Seals broadcasts, I was also doing publicity about the team. So, whenever they had a story to give to the press I would give it to the beat writers and columnists, and I wrote the releases at the start of each series, discussing and recapping what happened in the last series with that team and a statistical recap of past events.

During that time I had two big stories that I took to the press. One had to do with Paul Fagan. He was unique and had lots of ideas. Some were wild ideas and some worked. He was insistent that the Coast League would become the third major league and was so disappointed when it didn't happen. Making the Coast League a major league was his great ambition. Anyway, during the early 1950s he decided the organization wasn't making enough money on peanut sales. So, at one of the press meetings before the game, I had to tell them that Fagan had banned peanuts from Seals Stadium. He said it was because for the price, the cleanup costs were too great and they were losing money on that deal. "Ban the Peanut" became a national story, and peanut farmers were upset. They went up in arms.

The other story I remember concerns Joe Brovia, one of the great players of his day, a great home run hitter and a really great guy. He was one of these guys who wore his pants down to his ankles, revolutionary to say the least at that time, and he didn't pull his pants up to his knee like everyone else because he said he was more comfortable his way. Well, one thing Paul Fagan insisted upon was that anyone in uniform had to have a handkerchief in his pocket in case he needed to blow his nose. And the other thing was that he insisted that everyone had to follow the standard uniform dress code, which meant Brovia had to wear short pants. He told Lefty O'Doul to have him "pull those pants up or he's outta here."

Of course, it drove O'Doul nuts. Brovia was huge, a legend with the Seals fans. So I had to face the press and tell them Brovia had been traded to Portland. They couldn't believe it because there was no reason for the trade. But I had to tell them Fagan's reason was because his uniform pants were too long.

The Seals were such a class organization. Their facilities were always immaculate and sort of a step above the others in the league. Fagan paid them very well, often on the same footing or better than players in the major leagues. He paid Lefty O'Doul more as a manager than a lot of major league managers were making because he wanted him to stay in San Francisco. In the 1949 season Fagan built a real nice broadcast booth to replace a pretty run-down and almost falling-down one that had probably been there since the park was built.

I remember there were no broadcast booths in Oakland, and I sat right behind the plate in the first or second row announcing play-by-play right among the fans. They were all around me. So during one night game there a fan came up from behind me, he was more than a little drunk, and he stammered, "Hey, Klein, will you get me a ticket to the game you're watching?"

I remember some exhibition games in San Francisco, let's see, I remember in 1949 when we beat the 1948 Cleveland Indians with Lou Boudreau at the helm in a couple of games before the start of the season. Remember, they had won the World Series in 1948. The Seals and other teams in the league beat other big league teams. In Fagan's mind it just proved that clubs in the Pacific Coast [League] could compete with major league clubs and deserved major league status.

Tommy Heath, the jolly round man, knew baseball very well and he was a very likeable guy who got along well with his players. It wasn't easy following Lefty O'Doul. He was so well loved. But Lefty's problem was that he liked to play golf too much when he should have been thinking about baseball and ways to win more games. Eventually, as the club fell lower and lower in the standings, he and Fagan had a falling out. Fagan objected to Lefty playing golf too much. But my goodness, he managed the team for 17 years. Joe Gordon had a great major league career and Eddie Joost was a great shortstop who I believe played with Connie Mack, but was pretty tense in his managing duties.

To bring it home to the Seals and how I felt about the club, there was a great difference in one aspect. The Seals were home-grown. They were all local players. You could go right down the roster and it gave the fans that local feeling. Of course, some of that changed when the Boston Red Sox took over but they smartly kept some of the old-time favorites. The bottom line was that the fans, though they resisted the fact that none of the Giants players were what you'd call local, eventually got used to it and realized how lucky they were to have a major league baseball team.

Meanwhile, away from the diamond, a few days before the end of the 1957 season Pacific Coast League President Leslie O'Connor held a news conference which more or less rehashed the results of a meeting of PCL team owners on June 2. He reiterated the frustration of the entire league and once again threatened a lawsuit against major league baseball unless PCL teams received adequate compensation for all losses incurred by the uncertainty of the major league movement to California. He said the alleged $50,000 paid to the cities of the American Association and International League when Baltimore, Kansas City, and Milwaukee became major league franchises would not be enough, and predicted that in addition to losing San Francisco and Los Angeles, Hollywood would be eliminated and possibly San Diego, and it seemed doubtful Sacramento could continue to support a PCL team. In addition, Emil Sick had threatened to move his team from Seattle if two big league teams moved west, which could leave the PCL with as few as two teams, Portland and Vancouver. However, other league owners talked with Sick, who later announced that Seattle might stay in the league even if two teams moved west.

A few days later the Los Angeles City Council approved a proposal by an 11–3 vote authorizing the city negotiator, Harold C. McClellan, to make a firm offer to Walter O'Malley, and the plot thickened in New York as far as the Dodgers were concerned.

Nelson Rockerfeller had been active in a Keep-the-Dodgers-in-Brooklyn movement that attempted to discourage the organization from leaving the area. He even offered to help finance a new stadium in downtown Brooklyn, and city officials learned they could legally condemn the land desired by O'Malley at the corner of Flatbush and Atlantic Avenues, the site of the Flatbush terminal of the Long Island Railroad. At one point Rockerfeller said he was willing to buy the Dodgers just to keep them in New York, but that idea was flatly rejected by O'Malley.

In mid–August, when Stoneham announced his club would move to San Francisco no matter what O'Malley and the Dodgers decided, fans in Los Angeles became angry at O'Malley's continued lack of a commitment to anything. They didn't like being left hanging in midair while things had progressed to another level in San Francisco.

Finally, in response to a city council report stating Los Angeles just had a 50–50 chance of getting the Dodgers, Mayor Poulson warned Brooklyn to get off the dime and issued an ultimatum to O'Malley: if the Dodgers don't make a decision by the first day for drafting minor league territories, October 1, another major league club may draft the territory. He created a desired sense of urgency that other big league clubs were interested in the area and could beat them to it.

And Mayor Christopher adamantly stated that all the hedging from Los Angeles was not in their best interest, emphasizing that if they presented a serious bid for the team, not even Nelson Rockerfeller could keep the Dodgers in New York.

"In about as much time as it takes to say, 'It's a deal, Seal,' Paul I. Fagan, owner of Seals Stadium, and Mayor George Christopher yesterday reach a telephone agreement over the lease of the 16th and Bryant streets plant to the New York Giants next baseball season," wrote Bob Stevens on September 27. After weeks of negotiation, Fagan agreed to lease the stadium at $125,000 a year plus five percent of ticket sales after all required deductions, and he would pay the annual property tax. On September 29, two weeks after the end of the Pacific Coast League season, the Giants and Dodgers played their final games as New York teams.

Prior to the agreement Stoneham had visited Seals Stadium and said he saw potential to increase the seating capacity of the stadium from 18,075 to approximately 22,000–22,500, which would accommodate a draw of a million fans for their initial season in San Francisco.

At the same time, the New York businessmen tried to get another major league franchise into their city. They courted owners of the Cincinnati Redlegs, Pittsburgh Pirates, and Philadelphia Phillies, and if rumors are accurate, they even considered talking William Wrigley into selling the Chicago Cubs. As we now know, their ideas never came to fruition.

During the ensuing month of discussions that some might describe as "serious wheeling and dealing," Commissioner Ford Frick got into the act by predicting the Dodgers would play in Los Angeles in 1958. There was a lot of give and take between O'Malley and the City of Los Angeles over the location for a new park to be built for the Dodgers at a place called Chavez Ravine that resulted in arguments over oil and mineral rights for the property until both sides consented to a 50–50 agreement.

On the tenth of October the announcement was made that the Brooklyn Dodgers would be known as the Los Angeles Dodgers for the 1958 season. Although there remained "i's" to be dotted and "t's" to be crossed for both the Giants and the Dodgers, the westward expansion of major league baseball for 1958 had become a reality that came full circle when a capacity crowd of 23,448 witnessed the first major league baseball game in Seals Stadium as the San Francisco Giants defeated the Los Angeles Dodgers, 8–0, on Opening Day, April 15, 1958.

Epilogue

At the end of the season, each Seals player received a $400 bonus for winning the championship.

The first major league game in San Francisco was played on April 15, 1958, when the new San Francisco Giants hosted the new Los Angeles Dodgers in Seals Stadium at the corner of Sixteenth and Bryant on Opening Day.

The Pacific Coast League began a new era without the Los Angeles Angels, who became the Spokane Indians, the Hollywood Stars, who returned to Salt Lake City, and the San Francisco Seals. Instead, the league was composed of the Phoenix Giants, San Diego Padres, Vancouver Mounties, Portland Beavers, Salt Lake City Bees, Sacramento Solons, Spokane Indians, and Seattle Rainiers.

By the 2013 season the league had expanded to 16 teams divided into four competing divisions of four teams each: The American North (Omaha Storm Chasers, Nashville Sounds, Iowa Cubs, Memphis Redbirds); the American South (Round Rock Express, Albuquerque Isotopes, New Orleans Zyphers, Oklahoma City Red Hawks); the Pacific North (Reno Aces, Salt Lake City Bees, Colorado Springs Sky Sox, Tacoma Rainiers); and Pacific South (Sacramento River Cats, Fresno Grizzlies, Las Vegas 51s, Tucson Padres).

According to the terms of the westward movement of the Giants, Phoenix became their AAA affiliate and the Minneapolis Millers became Boston's AAA club. It was considered a geographically convenient arrangement for both organizations.

As for the Seals, the players were scattered in different directions and the name "Seals," though not officially retired, has never been used again.

In 1958, pitchers Ted Bowsfield (0–0), Al Schroll (0–0) and Riverboat Smith (4–3) started with Boston but spent most of the season in AAA Minneapolis; Leo Kiely spent the first of two seasons with Boston but did not come close to his glory season with the Seals when he came in second in MVP voting behind Steve Bilko; Ken Aspromonte played six games with Boston before he was traded to the Washington Senators, later continuing his career as a minor league manager before he was at the helm of the Cleveland Indians from 1972 to 1974; Albie Pearson was the 1958 American League Rookie of the Year with Washington, then played with the Los Angeles Angels; Marty Keough played games with the Red Sox but was never able to gain a permanent spot in an outfield manned by Jackie Jensen, Jimmy Piersall, and Ted Williams and completed the year in Minneapolis; and Bill Renna appeared in 39 games with the Red Sox, returning to the PCL in 1959 with San Diego before he retired.

Ten more players spent the full 1958 season in Minneapolis: pitchers Tom Hurd, Jack Spring, Bert Thiel, Harry Dorish, and Bill Abernathie, plus position players Frank Kellert, Harry Malmberg, Eddie Sadowski, Joe Tanner, and Tommy Umphlett. And a few Seals remained in the PCL: Sal Taormina was picked up by the Phoenix Giants, while Nini Tornay and Bob DiPietro moved to the Portland Beavers to play under their former manager, Tommy Heath. Jack Phillips went to the Buffalo Bisons in the AAA International League, and Grady Hatton was player-manager of the San Antonio Missions in the Texas League, which began a ten-year managerial career. Haywood Sullivan missed the entire 1958 season due to back surgery, but later went on to bigger things as part-owner of the Boston Red Sox.

Coach Glenn Wright retired from the game and won his bout with cancer. Joe Gordon managed the Cleveland Indians in 1958, then the Detroit Tigers in 1960 when the two franchises exchanged managers during the season.

After a dozen years in the Pacific Coast League, 1954–1965, colorful umpire Emmett Ashford was promoted to the American League as the first black umpire in the majors.

The San Francisco Giants played in Seals Stadium for the 1958 and 1959 seasons while Candlestick Park was readied. It opened on April 12, 1960.

Seals Stadium was demolished in 1960. But the seats and light towers remain part of the Pacific Coast League at Cheney Stadium, home of the AAA Tacoma Rainiers in Washington.

The 1957 San Francisco Seals Roster

The 1957 Seals club was quite a group. Typical of the Coast League, there were young prospects on the cusp of their own major league careers, a handful of local favorites from the pre–Red Sox era, and major league veterans brought in to fortify the team. While some played the final years of their pro careers in Seals Stadium, others went on to bigger and better things. As with any club in any era, some players passed through on their way to other teams, but were not part of the permanent roster. They are mentioned in the text but are not included in this section. Sadly, during the 50-plus years since that season, several players have passed away.

Manager

Gordon, Joe "Flash" (1915–1978) became the 18th manager in Seals history when he replaced Eddie Joost, who was fired on July 9, 1956, when the team was mired in seventh place. He returned to the Seals in 1957 to win a pennant for San Francisco.

The California native was a four-sport athlete signed out of the University of Oregon by the Yankees. He manned second base for the Oakland Oaks in the PCL in his rookie season before he made his mark in the major leagues. After 1,000 hits in 1,000 games in New York, he was traded to the Cleveland Indians for Allie Reynolds and played there from 1947 to 1950.

An agile and speedy player known for his competitiveness, steady defense, and batting prowess, Gordon was an eight-

Manager Joe "Flash" Gordon (Mark Macrae Collection).

time All-Star who earned a long string of awards, including American League Most Valuable Player in 1942. No stranger to the helm, he managed the Sacramento Solons in 1951–1952. Dubbed "a lively leprechaun" with a quick temper, he was known as a players' manager by his teams.

After his stint with the Seals, he managed Cleveland in 1958 until the Tigers and Indians traded managers mid-season in 1960, moving Gordon to Detroit. He followed this as manager of the Kansas City Athletics in 1961 and the Idaho Falls Angels in the Pioneer League in 1966, before spending his final year in the game at the helm of the expansion Kansas City Royals in 1969.

Joe Gordon was inducted into the Baseball Hall of Fame in 2009.

Coach

Wright, Forest Glenn "Cap" (1901–1984), called "Buckshot" with the Pirates because his throws were hard though not always accurate, was born in Archie, Missouri, where he learned to play the game on the sandlots before he pitched at the University of Missouri, and later made a name for himself at shortstop.

From 1924 to 1935 Wright played 1,119 major league games with the Pittsburgh Pirates, Brooklyn Robins/Dodgers, and Chicago White Sox. On May 7, 1925, when the Pirates played the Cardinals, he made an unassisted triple play. He retired with a .294 career batting average and four 100+ RBI seasons.

He was known as "Cap" in San Francisco, a tag he acquired many years earlier when he was traded to the Brooklyn Robins, later renamed the Dodgers, and captained the 1930–1933 squads. He was proud that he was named shortstop on the first All-Star team selected by *The Sporting News* in 1925. As Joe Gordon's coach and right-hand man, he gained the respect of the players and was loved by the fans for his sparkling and friendly though reserved personality and his willingness to talk baseball with them.

Glenn "Cap" Wright (Mark Macrae Collection).

William "Bill" Abernathie (Mark Macrae Collection).

Near the end of the 1957 season he was diagnosed with cancer that required jaw surgery. He bounced back with gusto, and from 1958 to 1974 he worked as a scout for Boston before he retired.

Players

Abernathie, Bill "Abby" (1929–2006) RHP, from Torrance, California, signed with Cleveland and collected accolades in his first two pro seasons with records of 17–14 and 19–8 with the Tucson Cowboys in the Arizona–Texas League (1948–1949), before he progressed to the Dayton Indians under skipper Dolph Camilli (1950), the Dallas Eagles (1951), and the AA Indianapolis Indians (1952), where he posted seven complete games and a record of 11–9 in 164 innings pitched. At 23 he was rewarded with a promotion to Cleveland at the end of the season and made his debut on September 27. Unfortunately it backfired. He lasted just two innings in a no-decision that resulted in a 13.50 ERA.

He returned to Indianapolis in 1953, was traded to the Brooklyn Dodgers on October 1, and went to AAA Montreal for the 1954 season. But after one game he enlisted in the U.S. Marine Corps. Though he was away from pro ball for two years, he played baseball with the Marines. When he returned in 1956 he met Boston scout Tom Downey, who referred him to the Seals, who offered him a contract.

As a late-season arrival he logged a 6–4 record with a 2.63 ERA in 68⅓ innings. In 1957 he had seven starts and 38 relief appearances, and logged three complete games with a 13–2 record thanks to his tenacity and pitching command. In 1958 he saw action with four minor league teams at the AA and AAA levels before he retired. In ten minor league seasons he posted a 100–74 record. He then spent 19 years as a deputy sheriff in San Bernadino and retired with the rank of Lieutenant.

Aspromonte, Ken "Chip" (1931–) from Brooklyn, grew up playing sandlot ball and was signed out of Lafayette High School by Boston scouts Neil T. Mahoney and Bots Nekola at age 18. He played his way to the AAA Louisville Colonels in the American Association before he missed 1954–1955, when he served in the U.S. Army.

He joined the Seals in 1956 and became a fan favorite when he hit .281 in 141 games despite being switched between third, short, and second defensively. Early in 1957 Gordon set his position at second. He relaxed and had the best season of his entire career: 171 hits in 143 games, a league-leading 35 doubles, and the PCL batting title at .334. He was called to Boston on September 1 and made his major league debut the next day.

Between 1958 and 1960 he saw action with Boston, Washington, and Cleveland. He was selected by the Los Angeles Angels in the 1961 expansion draft, spent 1961–1962 with the Angels, Indians and Braves.

Ken "Chip" Aspromonte (Mark Macrae Collection).

He landed with the Chicago Cubs in 1963, but finished the season with their AAA affiliate in Salt Lake City and was released.

Not yet finished, Aspromonte spent 1964–1966 with the Chunichi Dragons and Taiyo Whales in the Japan Central League, where he posted .273, .323, and .432 batting averages. When he returned to the U.S., he managed two minor league teams in the Cleveland organization, 1969–1971. He was promoted as skipper for the flailing major league club and led them to fifth-, sixth-, and fourth-place finishes from 1972 to 1974, during tumultuous times in the organization.

He was inducted into the National Italian American Sports Hall of Fame in 2011.

DiPietro, Bob "Deep" (1927–) is a San Francisco native who said he loved baseball before he could walk. Shortly thereafter he became a fan of the Seals. He caught the

Bob DiPietro (Ray Saraceni Collection).

eyes of scouts when he patrolled the outfield and manned first base at Lincoln High School.

After playing baseball during his stint in the Army, he signed with Boston scout Charlie Wallgren in 1947, then did so well in his rookie season with the San Jose Red Sox in the California League (.312, 24 doubles, 6 triples, 21 homers in 140 games) that everyone thought he'd reach the big leagues in no time. He finally arrived for a four-game cup of coffee in September, 1951, but returned to the minors with the Louisville Colonels for two seasons before joining the Seals in 1954. "Deep" smiled through personal tragedy in the 64th game in 1955, the best year of his career. He was batting .371 when he attempted to stretch a double into a triple and broke his leg sliding into third. It ended all hope of returning to the major leagues.

In 1956 he was one of the three veteran players kept by Boston when they took over the Seals franchise, but his batting average slipped to a disappointing .268 in 126 games. With the acquisition of Frank Kellert in 1957, he was limited to six games before he was sold to the San Diego Padres. Although he planned to retire from the game at the end of that season, his friend Tommy Heath, then with Portland, asked him to play first base for the Beavers, which he did through 1959. He then retired from the game. In 13 minor league seasons he appeared in 1,480 games and logged a respectable .282 career batting average on 1,341 hits in 4,756 at-bats. He was a good teammate and fan favorite at every stop in his career.

Dorish, Harry "Fritz" (1921–2000), RHP from Pennsylvania, was brought to the Seals as a reliever, but Gordon wanted this stocky pitcher in the starting rotation. The off-season plumber had an impressive resume. He played ball in the U.S. Army during World War II, followed by ten seasons with four teams in the American League —

Harry Dorish (Mark Macre Collection).

Boston, St. Louis, Chicago, and Baltimore. Considered by some as the first true relief pitcher of the postwar era, he led the American League with 11 saves in 1952 and was second with 18 in 1953, both seasons with the White Sox. He pitched 834⅓ innings in 323 major league games, posting a 45–43 record with what, under 1969 rules, would be 44 saves and a 3.83 ERA. In addition, he held a unique place in the record books as the last American League pitcher to steal home, on June 2, 1950. He later found it funny and laughingly explained that the record was only as permanent as the designated hitter rule.

Dorish was honored by Joe Gordon with the role of opening day starter in 1957. His congeniality, sense of humor, and success made him an instant favorite with his teammates and the fans. In 28 starts he led the team with five shutouts, and his 3.32 ERA belied a deceptive 9–12 season record.

Harry Dorish, at age 36, had hopes of returning as a major league player, and compared himself to one of his heroes, Sal Maglie, who pitched in the majors until age 41. But it didn't happen that way for him. After 1957 he remained active in the game for 30 more years as major and minor league pitching coach, minor league manager, and scout.

Hatton, Grady (1922–2013), a third baseman from Texas, played his first minor league game in 1957 with the Seals at age 35, after 11 years (1,284 games) in the majors with the Cincinnati Reds, Chicago White Sox, Boston Red Sox, St. Louis Cardinals, and Baltimore Orioles. He was a versatile asset to the Seals on and off the diamond.

The shortstop/captain of the University of Texas Longhorns led the team to two championships and was named All-Southwest Conference three times, 1941–1943, before he enlisted in the U.S. Army Air Force during World War II. While stationed at the Greensboro Overseas Replacement Depot in North Carolina, he played for the Tech Hawks baseball team,

Grady Hatton (Mark Macrae Collection).

where he was rated outstanding, and was sent to play in the National Semipro Tournament where he met Cincinnati scout Pat Patterson and signed a pro contract. Hatton said he had the money in his pocket when Commissioner Landis voided the deal because it was illegal to sign players in the service. After he left the military in February 1946, Hatton drove from North Carolina to Cincinnati, re-signed with Patterson, and went directly to the big league club. He batted .271 with 14 home runs and 69 RBI in his rookie season.

With the Seals he hit .317 in 118 games, and got 120 hits with just 21 strikeouts. He next turned to managing, beginning as player-manager of the San Antonio Missions (1958–1960), led the Oklahoma City 89ers to the pennant twice in three years (1963–1965) at the helm, then managed the Houston Astros from 1966 to 1968. He followed that with service as a coach with Houston, then scouted for the San Francisco Giants for many years. He's a Southern gentleman and a true baseball man.

Hurd, Tom "Whitey" (1924–1982) RHP born in Danville, Virginia, signed with the Chicago White Sox out of high school, then spent three years with the U.S. Army during World War II, was an agile, 5'9", 155-pound infielder, but was sent to the mound when his weak bat betrayed him. The blue-eyed blond had a dry sense of humor off the field camouflaged by his aggressive and competitive play between the white lines, even in his youth. He worked his way up the minor league ladder until 1954. At that time he was with the AAA American Association Charleston Senators when his contract was purchased by Boston on July 25. He was 30 years old. Though he was a starter in the minors, he was a reliever with Boston from 1954 to 1956. In 99 appearances he logged a 13–10 record with a 3.96 ERA. His most memorable performance was on Labor Day, 1956, when Washington hosted Boston. He was

Tommy Hurd (Mark Macrae Collection).

called to action in the first inning already behind, 4–0, and completed the game for the win.

He was 33 when he arrived at Seals Stadium and found himself back in a starting role Unable to bring his wife and three school-age daughters, he lived in a local hotel where two other pitchers in the same boat also roomed: Harry Dorish and Bert Thiel. The trio became close friends and enjoyed life in the Coast League.

In 174 innings pitched in 29 games with the Seals in 1957, he compiled a record of 8–6, with a 3.36 ERA. Hurd remained in the minors at the AAA level through 1960 and retired after ten minor league seasons. He then worked as a machine operator in a steel plant in Waterloo, Iowa.

Kellert, Frank (1924–1976), first base, was a tall, rangy, likeable player from Oklahoma City who pitched at Classen High School and Oklahoma A&M, where he caught the eye of scouts but didn't sign. Instead he served in the U.S. Army Air Force from 1942 to 1945. In 1942 he was a survivor

Frank Kellert (Marc Macrae Collection).

when his transport ship was torpedoed by the Germans and 1400 GIs were lost. In 1946 he returned to college and completed his degree in animal husbandry.

In 1949, at age 24, he signed with St. Louis Browns scout Fred Hawn and was quickly converted to a first baseman in his rookie season in Lynchburg in the Class B Piedmont League. By the time he got to the Seals in 1957, his big league career was behind him. From 1953 to 1956 he appeared in 122 games with the Browns, Orioles, Dodgers, and Cubs.

The best year of his career was 1954 with the San Antonio Missions in the AA Texas League: he posted 41 home runs and 146 RBI. Kellert said his favorite year was 1955 with Brooklyn when he appeared in 39 games, batted .325, and was used as a right-handed pinch-hitter in the Dodgers–Yankees World Series. In Game One he was the batter at the plate when Jackie Robinson stole home. The "safe" call was controversial. When the press asked what he saw, he said he thought Robinson was out. Branch Rickey was

furious and called him disloyal to the Dodgers.

He was a smart and classy player, a huge asset to the Seals. He retired in 1959 after he appeared in 1,280 minor league games and compiled a .289 career batting average.

Kiely, Leo "The Cat" (1929–1984), a tall, wispy southpaw from New Jersey who gave it away the minute he spoke, had been around the game since 1948 when Boston scout Bill McCarren found him playing CYO baseball and signed him. It took him little more than three seasons to get to the majors. He moved from the Wellsville Nitros in the Class D Pennsylvania–Ontario–New York League, to the Scranton Red Sox in the Class A Eastern League, to the Birmingham Barons in the AA Southern Association, and the Louisville Colonels in the AAA American Association, before he completed 1951 in Boston.

He served in the U.S. Army during the Korean War, 1952–1953, and was the first major league player in Japanese baseball when he pitched for the Mainichi Orions in the Pacific League. After he mustered out of the military in 1954, he returned to the American League until July 31, 1956, when he was optioned to the Seals and logged a 3–1 record. Gordon was impressed with his tenacity and cunning and eagerly welcomed him back in 1957, then used him in relief with Bill Abernathie and Bert Thiel as part of the most effective bullpen in the league. Nobody doubted he was the premier reliever in the PCL and maybe all of baseball that season. In 146 innings he compiled an amazing 21–6 record, with 20 wins in relief, 14 of them consecutive, and a 2.22 ERA. He was the first reliever to log 20 wins in PCL history. For that effort, he came in second to Steve Bilko (who hit 56 homers) in the MVP voting. In six minor league seasons he posted a 63–36 record with a 3.33 ERA.

He spent 1958–1960 with Boston and

Leo "Black Cat" Kiely (Mark Macrae Collection).

Richard "Marty" Keough (Mark Macrae Collection).

Kansas City and then retired with a 26–27 record.

Keough, Marty (1934–) dubbed "Marvelous Marty" by San Francisco sports writer Bob Stevens, became a fixture in professional baseball as a player and long-time scout. He was born in Oakland and raised in Pomona, where his abilities were noted early. He was named ALL-CIF Southern Section footballer in his junior year when Pomona High School won its only football championship, and the *Los Angeles Examiner* selected him as Southern California Prep Athlete of the Year in 1952 before he signed with scout Tom Downey as Boston's first six-figure bonus baby, something he doesn't like to talk about.

Two seasons later he joined the AAA Louisville Colonels (1954–1955). In 1956 he made his three-game big league debut at age 22 with Boston before he joined the Seals. Joe Gordon, ecstatic to get him, de-

scribed Keough as "a team player who knows a hundred ways to beat you," and his all-out style of play won over the fans right away. But his season ended abruptly after just 79 games when he broke his ankle in Portland on August 6, when he was batting .315. He returned to the Seals in 1957, made the PCL All-Star team, appeared in 139 games and was recalled to Boston at the end of the season. His colorful personality and aggressiveness on the field endeared him to fans.

Through 1966 he appeared in 841 games on the rosters of the Red Sox, Indians, Senators, Reds, Braves, and Cubs, but always in a backup role. His final season was in the PCL with the San Diego Padres at age 33. He managed their Tri-City Padres rookie team in 1970 before he began a long career as a respected scout with the St. Louis Cardinals and celebrated his 40th year in that capacity in 2011.

Malmberg, Harry "Swede" (1925–1976), a shortstop regarded as the glue and the anchor of the team, was born in Fairfield,

Harry Malmberg (Mark Macrae Collection).

Alabama, and raised in Pittsburg, California. He played basketball and baseball in high school and then served in the U.S. Navy as a 3/c radioman on an aircraft carrier in the South Pacific during World War II. When he returned home he signed with Cleveland and began his 15-year minor league career at shortstop. He made it to the AAA Pacific Coast League with the San Diego Padres in 1951, moved to the AAA Indianapolis Indians from 1952 to 1954, when his contract was sold to Detroit. In 1955, he played 67 games for the Tigers, batting .216, and returned to the AAA Charleston Senators in 1956 and batted .293. When Detroit optioned him to San Francisco in 1957, he happily joined the Seals as it allowed him to be close to his family in Antioch. Fans and teammates agreed he was the most valued man on the club. At age 31 he played 151 games, batted .277, and the Malmberg-Aspromonte-Kellert double-play combo was one of the best in the league.

He spent 1963–1964 coaching with Boston, before he managed in the minors through 1975. One of his memorable accomplishments came at the helm of the Elmira Royals in the Eastern League, 1970–1971. After the team finished in the cellar in 1970, he took them from worst to first in 1971. Fifty-five of their wins were one-run-games. He retired after managing the Birmingham A's in 1975, and continued selling cars as he had done in the offseason for many years. He also coached youth baseball, which he loved, and found time for hunting and fishing.

McCall, John "Windy" (1925–), LHP, grew up on the sandlots in the Mission District and was a good-hitting outfielder on the Seals Juniors semipro team in weekend games at Seals Stadium. After early graduation from Balboa High School he played center field at the University of San Francisco before was signed by Dodgers scout Charlie Wallgren.

Unaware that he needed permission from baseball, he joined the U.S. Marine Corps Reserve before reporting to a team, and earned Branch Rickey's ire. After

John "Windy" McCall (Mark Macrae Collection).

World War II, in 1946, he again signed with Wallgren, by then a Red Sox scout, and went to Roanoke in the Piedmont League to start his career. He played outfield until manager Pinky Higgins gave him a chance to pitch, and he opened people's eyes. He posted a 17–9 record with a 3.78 ERA and helped his team win the league championship.

In spring training 1948, the talkative and friendly McCall was tagged "Windy" by Ted Williams. He then made his big league debut against the Yankees. It was a disaster. He was pelted hard, lasted just 1⅓ innings, and at the end of the day his season ERA was computed at 20.25. He went to Louisville and spent the rest of his career between the major and minor leagues, pitching mostly in relief. His most successful season was with the Seals in 1953, when he pitched 150⅔ innings and compiled a 12–7 record with a 3.05 ERA, after which and the New York Giants bought his contract for $60,000. He remained there for three seasons until early 1957, when, after hurling three innings in five appearances, he returned to the Seals at age 31 to bolster their bullpen.

Pearson, Albie "Mighty Mite" (1934–) a 5′5″, 140-pound outfielder from Southern California, was popular throughout his career. He had good tools, worked hard, and held his own with the big boys. He signed out of Pomona Junior College at age 18 in 1952 and by 1956 he was with the Seals. But after 31 games, despite batting .297, new manager Eddie Joost sent him to Oklahoma City in the AA Texas League for the rest of the season, where he hit .371. When he returned in 1957 he and Marty Keough formed the potent one-two punch with their bats and speed. Albie, the small player with the big number "30" on his back, used his size to collect 85 walks as he posted a .297 average.

With the Seals gone, Boston traded him to the Washington Senators in January 1958. It was his big break and he made the

Albert "Albie" Pearson (Mark Macrae Collection).

most of it with a great season, getting selected 1958 American League Rookie of the Year. In 1959 he was traded to Baltimore. After he was selected fourth by the Los Angeles Angels in the 1961 Minor League Expansion Draft, he scored the first run for the franchise. In 1966 he was released after just two games. Albie Pearson appeared in 988 major league games, drew 477 bases on balls, and logged a .270 career average.

He then tested the waters in such other ventures as disk-jockeying and pro golf. Religion was always prominent in his life and in 1997 he and his wife, Helen, founded Father's Heart Ranch in Southern California, which cares for neglected, abused, and abandoned boys aged 6–12. He said baseball gave him the means to follow this dream.

Phillips, Jack (1921–2009), a first baseman from Clarence, New York, was a 6′4″, blue-eyed blond who excelled athletically at Lancaster High School and Clarkston University, where he led the basketball team in scoring three consecutive seasons and

Jack Phillips (Mark Macrae Collection).

was heavily scouted on the baseball diamond. He signed with the Yankees in 1943, but after just seven games in Newark in 1944, he served in the U.S. Navy from 1944 to 1947. He returned to Newark in 1947 until he made his major league debut with the Yankees that August and spent nine seasons with the New York Yankees, Pittsburgh Pirates, and Detroit Tigers.

His first year with the Yankees, 1947, was special as the Yankees won the American League pennant and took the World Series from the Dodgers in seven games. Phillips appeared in two World Series games and earned the coveted ring. Later, with the Pirates on July 8, 1950, he landed in rarefied air in the record books when he hit an "ultimate grand slam" (a game-winning grand slam) and joined just twenty-two immortals in that category.

When he joined the Seals in 1957, at age 35, he was no stranger to the PCL. He had been in and out of the league from 1952 to 1954, and was voted PCL Most Valuable Player with the Hollywood Stars in 1954. He spent the next two years, 1958–

1959, with the AAA Buffalo Bisons, and then spent 1960–1964 at the helm of four minor league teams and retired.

Phillips then coached the Clarkson University Golden Knights for 24 years. In 1992 Jack Phillips was inducted into the Clarkson University Hall of Fame.

Pillette, Duane "Dee" (1922–2011), RHP born in Detroit and raised in San Diego, was a 6' 3", wiry, second-generation baseball pitcher (age 34 in 1957) whose father, Herman Pillette, had a brief big league career, then pitched in the PCL until he was 49. Against the advice of his father, who called baseball "a game of bums," Duane signed out of the University of Santa Clara in 1946 and began his pro career at the AAA level. By the time he joined the Seals in 1957 he had pitched five-plus AAA seasons and eight years with the New York Yankees, the St. Louis Browns/Baltimore Orioles, where he struggled with chronic

Duane Pillette (Doug McWilliams Collection).

arm and elbow problems, and the Philadelphia Phillies.

In 1952, on the same St. Louis Browns
staff as aging Satchel Paige, he pitched
205⅓ innings and listened to many of
Paige's stories including some about his
father, who knew Satchel well. Ironically,
Pillette and his dad are linked in the
record books in a dubious way. They are
the only father-son pair to suffer the most
losses in a league one season: Herman, 19,
Detroit Tigers, 1923; and Duane, 14, St.
Louis Browns, 1951.

Pillette was number two man in the
Seals' 1957 starting rotation and was having a good year with a 4–1 record (2.91
ERA) when, on May 21, Gordon explained
they needed to make room for younger
players and would have to let him go. As
a gesture of respect, Boston gave the Seals
permission to allow Pillette to make his
own deal with another team or to be
traded. Disappointed and somewhat confused, he made a deal and went to Seattle
for that season, then remained in the PCL
with Portland and Salt Lake City until he
retired in 1960. For many years he regularly attended PCL reunions.

Prout, Bill "Billy the Kid" (1939–), LHP,
was a San Francisco native and a second
generation Seals player, the son of former
Seals first baseman William Prout, who
was a teammate of Joe DiMaggio and Walter Mails in 1934. The star pitcher at
Downey High School who caught the eye
of several scouts was signed by Red Sox
scout Joe Stephenson the day after he graduated, and joined the Seals in June to fill
in for injured Jack Spring for a game or
two.

He was such a surprise that he stayed
all season, pitched 124⅓ innings in 19
games (17 starts) and logged a 6–6 record.
He began his sophomore year, 1958, in the
AA Southern Association and ended it
with the AAA Minneapolis Millers, where
he was reunited with several teammates
from the 1957 Seals. Though he struggled

Bill Prout (Ray Scarceni Collection).

as a starter in 165 innings and posted a
combined 7–12 record.

Despite being plagued by elbow problems, Prout had the best year of his career
with Memphis in 1959. He underwent
surgery after the season and was never the
same after that. He continued in the Eastern League, American Association, and
Three-I League through 1964 and was
primarily used in relief. Off the charts in
1965, he reappeared in 1966 with Reynosa
in the AA Mexican League. Prout then retired from the game at age 27. In seven
minor league seasons he compiled a 46–
48 record with a 4.52 ERA in 751⅓ innings
pitched. These stats do not include his
season with Reynosa, where records are
not available.

Renna, Bill "Big Bill" (1924–), a 6'3",
muscular outfielder from California, was
a three-sport high school athlete still remembered for his football feats and awards
at Santa Clara University (1947–49). He

Bill Renna (Mark Macrae Collection).

also played baseball under coach Paddy Cottrell, who was a bird dog for Yankees scout Joe Devine, who signed him when he graduated. After three minor league seasons that included two games with the Seals in 1951, Renna spent 1953–1956 with the Yankees and Philadelphia/Kansas City A's. He recalled that he was initially overwhelmed playing with teammates Mickey Mantle, Yogi Berra, and Phil Rizzuto, and was platooned in left field with Gene Woodling under manager Casey Stengel in his rookie season when he hit .314 in 61 games.

After the 1956 season, the Yankees, who had re-acquired him in June slated him for minor league duty but struck a deal with Boston to send the 1956 Seals' leading hitter, outfielder Gordy Windhorn, with pitcher Eli Grba and $10,000 to the Yankees for Renna. Although he began 1957 beleaguered by a slump, he eventually made the trade a winner for the Seals as he played 138 games which would have been more except for injury, drove in 105 runs, walloped 29 homers, and batted .281. He was the Seals' counterpart to Los Angeles slugger Steve Bilko.

He returned to Boston in 1958–1959 as a pinch hitter, then retired. In seven minor league seasons he played 741 games with a .287 career batting average. He appeared in 370 games in parts of six major league seasons and logged a .239 batting average.

Sadowski, Ed "Eddie" (1931–1993), catcher from Pennsylvania and one of a dozen children in his family, was an outstanding athlete at St. John's Lyceum High School in Pittsburgh and in semipro ball. The hard-nosed player with many tools signed with Boston after graduation and spent his rookie year, 1950, with the Radford Rockets in the Blue Ridge League. From 1951 to 1953 he worked his way up the minor league ladder, before serving in the military in 1954–1955.

When he returned in 1956, Boston sent him to the Seals, where he appeared in 89 games and established himself as one of the speediest catchers in San Francisco history. In 1957 he appeared in 108 games, including nine at second base and six at shortstop after Chip Aspromonte was

Eddie Sadowski (Mark Macrae Collection).

recalled to Boston, and though his .245 batting average didn't reflect it, he punched many clutch hits that helped the team win and regularly landed his name in the hero column in the sports pages. The fans loved his style of play and he was extremely popular.

He remained in the Boston system with the AAA Minneapolis Millers in 1958–1959. Ten years after his rookie season, at age 29, he broke into the major leagues in 1960 and spent five seasons with the Red Sox, Angels, and Braves as backup catcher to Russ Nixon, Earl Averill, Bob Rodgers and Joe Torre. After he hung it up in 1966, he was a minor league manager, coach, and pitching coach with Montreal before he left the game in 1971 and became a physical education teacher in southern California. He played 217 major league games, got exactly 100 hits and logged a deceptive .202 career batting average.

Smith, Robert W. "Riverboat" (1928–2003), LHP from Clarence, Missouri, had

Robert "RW" Smith (Mark Macrae Collection).

a slow Southern drawl and colorful expressions enjoyed by all. After high school graduation he pitched for the University of Missouri Tigers from 1948 to 1950, where many scouts were interested in his talents. He signed with Boston and spent his first season with the Scranton Red Sox, where his teammates included Ken Aspromonte and Bob DiPietro. He pitched a no-hit game at Class B Roanoke the following year before he spent 1956–1957 with the San Francisco Seals, mostly as a starter. In 1957 he led the team in innings pitched (190⅔) and strikeouts (120). He also led the Coast League in shutouts with six.

During that season local sportswriter Bob Stevens christened him "Riverboat," describing his slow, confident gait and the way he stared down batters one pitch at a time as that of a riverboat gambler. Smith told author Brent Kelley he then started calling the short, stocky writer "Tugboat," and it stuck. The 1957 Seals Yearbook said, "Bob is a man who may never make the major leagues, but he should be a winning minor leaguer for years to come." He briefly defied that prediction in 1958 at age 30, when he pitched 66⅔ innings with Boston and logged a 4–3 record, then returned to AAA ball with the Minneapolis Millers, and helped them win the 1958 Junior World Series.

After retiring in 1963, Smith continued farming in Clarence, where he also owned and operated Bob Smith Feed Lot Systems from 1969 to 1999, and remained involved in regional baseball programs and youth activities for the rest of his life.

Spring, Jack (1933–), LHP, was signed out of Lewis and Clark High School in Spokane, Washington, by the Phillies and played on their farm clubs from 1952 to 1956. With the AAA Miami Marlins in 1956, he enjoyed the stories and pitching tips of his oldest teammate, Satchel Paige. At the end of the season, following winter ball in Venezuela, he was selected by Boston in the Rule 5 Draft in December. After spring training with the Red Sox in Sarasota, Florida, he was sent to the 1957 Seals as a starter. He pitched 169⅓ innings in 28 games and posted an 11–9 record with a 3.19 ERA.

From 1958 until his retirement in 1965 he was involved in a variety of deals that took him to five major league teams: Washington Senators, Los Angeles Angels, Chicago Cubs, St. Louis Cardinals, and Cleveland Indians. Earlier he had pitched for the Phillies and Red Sox. He felt the biggest break in his career came when he was selected by Los Angeles in the 1961 Expansion Draft and manager Bill Rigney used him as a short reliever. His hard work to master the demands of being "on call" paid off and he loved it. He had great success and wished he could have gone that route years earlier in his career. In May 1964, he was sold to the Chicago Cubs, and a month later he was part of a six-player deal that took him with Lou Brock to the St. Louis Cardinals.

After retirement as a player he taught school briefly, managed in the minor leagues, then worked with his son's flooring business. In 2005 Jack Spring was inducted into the Inland Northwest Sports Hall of Fame.

Sullivan, Haywood "Sully" (1930–2003), a catcher born in Donalsonville, Georgia, and raised in Dothan, Alabama, was always known as an athlete. In 1950–1951 he was a star quarterback and outstanding catcher for the University of Florida Gators, and was courted in both sports. He chose baseball, signed with Boston for an $80,000 bonus before the 1952 season, and went to the Albany Senators to play pro baseball.

He lost 1953–1954 to the military, caught 128 games with the Louisville Colonels in 1955, made his big league debut on September 20, 1955, and caught just two games for the Red Sox, who had plans for him in San Francisco.

With the Seals in 1956 he shared duties with Eddie Sadowski, another top-notch prospect. Their somewhat friendly rivalry

Jack Spring (Mark Macrae Collection).

Haywood Sullivan (Ray Saraceni Collection).

continued through 1957. After back surgery cost him the 1958 season, Sullivan spent 1959–1963 at the major and AAA levels with Boston and Kansas City. He retired in 1963 after appearing in 312 major league games, posting a disappointing .226 career batting average. He then managed the Vancouver Mounties (AAA) in the Kansas City Athletics system in 1965 until owner Charlie Finley hired him to manage the big league club. At 34 he was the youngest manager in the majors. After one season he was recruited by the Red Sox to work in the front office, was appointed General Manager in 1977, and later bought a one-third interest in the club. His years there were tumultuous and unsatisfactory.

He was posthumously inducted into the Boston Red Sox Hall of Fame in 2004.

Tanner, Joe (1931–) a third baseman from Mississippi, always had a love of baseball. He was a youngster with a ton of talent and no fear of hard work, and there was no doubt he would play in the majors one day. He was seen by scouts when he starred

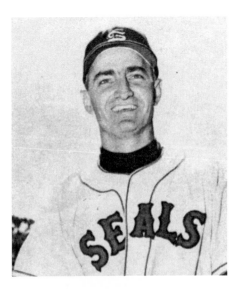

Joe Tanner (Mark Macrae Collection).

with the University of Texas Longhorns and was named All-Southwest Conference plus Collegiate All American, third team.

In 1953, at 21, he was signed by Boston and immediately went to the AAA Louisville Colonels for the last 25 games of the season, then remained with them through 1955. He was sent to the PCL in 1956 and appeared in 82 games and batted .281, but suffered back stress which affected his mechanics at the plate. He became inconsistent, his batting average slumped, and Joe Gordon sent him to AA Oklahoma City as a mini-rehab program in hopes the warmer climate would help him get things back together. He completed the season there, the first time he had played below the AAA level.

Back with the Seals in 1957, he had an outstanding spring training and started the season with a bang. However, while he batted .333 with sparkling defense through 30 games, the back problems flared up again and he was lost for the season. In 1958 he was reunited with many former Seals teammates who played for Boston's new AAA club, the Minneapolis Millers, but his old form was absent and he appeared in only 12 games.

Although he never regained his earlier level of play, he persevered and remained in the game through 1961, when he retired as a player without reaching the majors. He then coached collegiate and minor league baseball for many years.

Taormina, Sal (1922–1979), an outfielder, was a career minor leaguer from San Jose, California, who became a fan favorite everyplace he put on a uniform. In addition to his good eye at the plate and powerful swing that made him a respected batsman, the tenacious competitor with a chew of tobacco clearly visible in his cheek was a hard-nosed player who always found ways to beat the opposition.

Affectionately dubbed "The San Jose Milkman" by the fans and writers because he managed a milk company in the off-season, he rejoined the Seals in 1946 after military service in World War II when the squad defeated Oakland for the PCL pennant. He remained with the team in 1947, then hit the road in 1948 and played for five different teams all over the baseball map until 1952 before he returned to the Seals from 1952 to 1957. Happily, in 1956, he was one of three veteran Seals retained by Boston when they purchased the franchise.

Following the 1957 campaign he spent three seasons with the Giants' AAA affiliates in Phoenix and Tacoma, then retired after playing in 1,761 games with a career average of .278. His next stop was as a Giants minor league coach and mentor. Willie McCovey said he owes his career to Sal Taormina's help. He managed the Fresno Giants in 1961–1962, then returned to coaching until he left the pro ranks and accepted the position as head baseball coach at the University of Santa Clara, from 1965 to 1979. During those 15 years under his leadership, the Broncos won six league titles and never had a losing season. The players he mentored loved him.

Thiel, Maynard "Bert" (1926–), RHP from Wisconsin, called "the man of many deliveries, deceptions, and determinations," was the last pitcher to win a game for the San Francisco Seals (September 14, 1957), and had credentials as a pitcher, manager, and scout.

Following military service, in 1947 he signed with the Boston Braves, and by 1951 he had pitched no-hit games at the class A and class AAA levels. After recurring arm problems that were surgically corrected, he broke into the big leagues with the Braves in 1952 at age 25. In seven innings pitched in four games he logged a 1–1 record with a 7.71 ERA, and that was the sum total of his major league experience. He returned to AAA ball in the American Association until 1956, when he had his best year since 1948 in the AA Texas League with the Dallas Eagles: 249 innings pitched and an 18–11 record that got him named Texas League Pitcher of the Year. He assumed his role as a starter was secure.

Sal Taormina (Mark Macrae Collection).

Maynard "Bert" Thiel (Mark Macrae Collection).

Boston drafted him in 1957 and sent him to the Seals. Expecting a starting role, he was initially disappointed when he was used in relief. But he quelled many "uprisings" in 41 appearances (109⅔ innings) and logged a 5–4 record with a 2.79 ERA. He spent the last four years of his playing career, 1958–1961, in the minors in Minneapolis, Corpus Christi, New Orleans, and Pocatello where he was player-manager with the Bannocks. In 14 minor league seasons, he logged a 145–108 record with a 3.77 ERA. The Wisconsin lumberjack then scouted for the Senators, White Sox, and Braves, and managed for three seasons in the AA Midwest League through 1974, when he retired.

Tornay, Anthony "Nini" (1929–), catcher, was a San Francisco native described as a high school phenom on the diamond at Galileo High School, where his name is on the list of Notable Alumni, Class of 1947. Everyone expected him to make the major leagues.

After three years in the lower minor leagues he jumped to the Seals full-time in 1951 and handled the primary catching duties through 1955. "The laughing Spaniard," as he was known by many, was one of only three Seals veterans kept by Boston in 1956. He explained that although he was a good defensive catcher, the main reason Boston kept him was to use his experience to help with the young pitchers.

Although he generally batted in the .240–.260 range, his bat sizzled in the Veracruz Winter League between the 1956–1957 seasons, then continued through spring training and into the season. There was talk that it might be his ticket to the majors. But talk and his hopes faded as appearances dwindled and he shared catching duties with younger Boston prospects. Eventually he was sidelined by injury and relegated to bullpen catcher. Tornay appeared in 44 games and got 32 hits for the year. When coach Cap

Anthony "Nini" Tornay (Mark Macrae Collection).

Wright became ill, Tornay took over his duties.

He spent 1958–59 with the Portland Beavers and the last year of his career with the AAA Columbus Jets in 1960. This opera-loving, tuba-playing man spent his entire career, 13 seasons, in the minor leagues where he appeared in 942 games and posted a career .264 batting average. After he retired he was a regular participant at old timers' games and numerous other baseball events.

Umphlett, Tom "Tommy" (1930–2012) a lifetime North Carolinian who excelled at basketball and baseball at Ahoskie High School, has been described as a "thoroughly mediocre player," probably by those who never saw him play. Throughout his career it was said that nobody ran like him in the field or was as smart on the bases. Walter Mails touted him as the greatest Seals fielding acquisition since DiMaggio. Umphlett loved the comparison.

The tall, lean, low-key player signed a contract with Boston scout Mace Brown and played with four minor league teams

Tommy Umphlett (Mark Macrae Collection).

until he broke into the big leagues with Boston at age 22 in 1953, following in the footsteps of former Seals star and fellow center fielder Dom DiMaggio. He batted .283 in 137 games before he was traded after the season to the Washington Senators. He spent 1954–1955 with the Senators, then was traded back to Boston so they could send him to San Francisco in 1956, where he batted .285 in 120 games. He returned in 1957 and never went back to the major leagues, where he had appeared in 361 games and batted .246.

In 1957, he felt Gordon was mad because he thought Umphlett took his "slow, sweet time" driving from Florida cross-country to spring training, and limited his playing time that resulted in his batting average dropping to a dismal .233 though his fielding percentage improved to .995. He always felt unappreciated in San Francisco. After that season he played ten more years in the minors before he retired in 1967. He had appeared in 1,756 games with a career .274 batting average and a fielding percentage of .989. He then returned to Ahoskie and worked for many years for a company that sold farm equipment used in growing and harvesting tobacco and peanuts. And he finally had enough time for hunting and fishing.

The Seals by the Numbers

The following information includes the final 1957 team standings and individual leaders. This is put into perspective by an historical record of the San Francisco Seals, 1903–1957; and a record of all 18 Seals managers.

1957 Pacific Coast League Final Standings

Reference: http://www. Baseball-reference.com/bullpen/1957_Pacific_ Coast_League season

Team	Record	GB	Manager	Affiliation
San Francisco Seals	101–67		Joe Gordon	Boston
Vancouver Mounties	97–70	3.5	Charlie Metro	Baltimore
Hollywood Stars	94–74	7	Clyde King	Pittsburgh
San Diego Padres	89–79	12	Bob Elliott/	
			George Metkovich	Cleveland
Seattle Rainiers	87–80	13.5	Lefty O'Doul	Cincinnati
Los Angeles Angels	80–88	21	Clay Bryant	Brooklyn
Sacramento Solons	63–105	38	Tommy Heath	none
Portland Beavers	60–108	41	Bill Sweeney/Frank	
			Carswell/Bill Posedel	Chicago Cubs

1957 League Leaders

References: *The Early Coast League Statistical Record, 1903–1957*, Baseball Press Books, San Diego.

1957 MVP
Steve Bilko

TEAM LEADERS
Batting Average: San Francisco, .278
Runs Scored Per Game: San Francisco, 4.7
Home Runs: Los Angeles, 167

Individual Leaders by Category

BATTING

At Bats: Jim Marshall, Vancouver, 661
Hits: Jim Marshall, Vancouver, 188
Singles: Sparky Anderson, Los Angeles, 144
Doubles: Bobby Balcena, Seattle, 40
Triples: Albie Pearson, San Francisco, 11
Home runs: Steve Bilko, Los Angeles, 56
Batting Average: Ken Aspromonte, San Francisco, .334
RBI: Steve Bilko, Los Angeles, 140
Runs scored: Steve Bilko, Los Angeles, 111
Bases on Balls: Steve Bilko, Los Angeles, 108
Strikeouts: Steve Bilko, Los Angeles, 150
Stolen Bases: Solly Drake, Portland, 36

PITCHING

Games Pitched: Chuck Churn, Hollywood, 67
Wins: Leo Kiely, San Francisco, 21
Losses: Jack Carmichael, San Diego/Seattle; Portland, 18
Games Started: Charlie Rabe, Bennie Daniels, Hollywood, 31
Complete Games: Jim "Mudcat" Grant, San Diego, 18
Shutouts: Bob "Riverboat" Smith, San Francisco; George Witt, Hollywood, 6
Bases on Balls: Bennie Daniels, Hollywood, 121
Strikeouts: Jim "Mudcat" Grant, San Diego, 178
Earned Runs Allowed: Marshall Bridges, Sacramento, 104
ERA: Morrie Martin, Vancouver, 1.90

San Francisco Seals: 1903–1957

References: *The Early Coast League Statistical Record, 1903–1957*, Baseball Press Books, San Diego. Snelling, Dennis. *The Pacific Coast League: A Statistical History, 1903–1957*, McFarland, http://baseball-reference.com.

Year	Manager	Stats	Finish
1903	Charles Irwin	107–110	4th
1904	Charles Irwin	101–117	5th
1905	Parke Wilson	125–100	2nd
1906*	Parke Wilson	92–81	3rd
1907	Kid Mohler/Charlie Irwin/Kid Mohler	104–99	2nd
1908	Kid Mohler	100–104	3rd
1909	**Kid Mohler**	**130–80**	**1st**
1910	Kid Mohler	115–106	3rd
1911	Kid Mohler	95–112	5th
1912	Kid Mohler/Del Howard	89–115	5th
1913	Del Howard	104–103	4th
1914	Del Howard	115–96	3rd
1915	**Harry Wolverton/Roy Corhan/**		
	Harry Wolverton	**115–89**	**1st**

Year	Manager	Stats	Finish
1916	Harry Wolverton	104–102	4th
1917	**Harry Wolverton/Danny Long/ Jerry Downs**	**119–93**	**1st**
1918	Jerry Downs/Charlie Graham**	51–52	5th
1919	Charlie Graham**	84–94	6th
1920	Charlie Graham**	103–96	4th
1921	Charlie Graham**	106–82	3rd
1922	**Dots Miller**	**127–72**	**1st**
1923	**Dots Miller/Bert Ellison**	**124–77**	**1st**
1924	Bert Ellison	108–93	3rd
1925	**Bert Ellison**	**128–71**	**1st**
1926	Bert Ellison/Doc Strub**/ Nick Williams	84–116	8th
1927	Nick Williams	106–90	2nd
1928	**Nick Williams**	**120–71**	**1st**
1929	Nick Williams	114–87	2nd
1930	Nick Williams	101–98	4th
1931	**Nick Williams**	**107–80**	**1st**
1932	Ike Caveney	96–90	4th
1933	Ike Caveney	81–106	6th
1934	Ike Caveney	93–95	4th
1935	**Lefty O'Doul**	**103–70**	**1st**
1936	Lefty O'Doul	83–93	7th
1937	Lefty O'Doul	98–80	2nd
1938	Lefty O'Doul	93–82	4th
1939	Lefty O'Doul	97–78	2nd
1940	Lefty O'Doul	81–97	7th
1941	Lefty O'Doul	81–95	5th
1942	Lefty O'Doul	88–90	5th
1943	Lefty O'Doul	89–66	2nd
1944	Lefty O'Doul	86–83	3rd
1945	Lefty O'Doul	96–87	4th
1946	**Lefty O'Doul**	**115–68**	**1st**
1947	Lefty O'Doul	105–82	2nd
1948	Lefty O'Doul	112–76	2nd
1949	Lefty O'Doul	84–103	7th
1950	Lefty O'Doul	100–100	5th
1951	Lefty O'Doul	74–93	8th
1952	Tommy Heath	78–102	8th
1953	Tommy Heath	91–89	5th
1954	Tommy Heath	84–84	4th
1955	Tommy Heath	80–92	6th
1956	Eddie Joost/Joe Gordon	77–88	6th
1957	**Joe Gordon**	**101–67**	**1st**

*1906 season shortened due to San Francisco Earthquake on April 18, 1906; **Charlie Graham and Doc Strub were part owners of the team when they managed.

Seals' All-Time Individual Season Records

References: *Encyclopedia of Minor League Baseball*, Lloyd Johnson & Miles Wolff, editors. *The Early Coast League Statistical Record, 1903–1957*, Carlos Bauer, editor.

BATTING

Games: Irv Waldron, 225 (1904)
At-bats: Irv Waldron, 888 (1904)
Batting Average: Smead Jolley, .404 (1928)
Hits: Smead Jolley, 314 (1929)
Doubles: Paul Waner, 75 (1925)
Triples: Brooks Holder, 24 (1939)
Home Runs: Gus Suhr, 51 (1929)
Runs Batted In: Smead Jolley, 188 (1928)
Total Bases: Smead Jolley, 516 (1928)
Runs: Gus Suhr, 196 (1929)
Hitting Streak: Joe DiMaggio, 61 games (1933)
Stolen Bases: James Johnston, 124 (1913)
Walks: Ferris Fain, 129 (1946)
Strikeouts: Roy Nicely, 97 (1949)
Hit by Pitches: Charles Irwin, 23 (1903)

PITCHING

Games: Jimmy Walen, 64 (1905)
Complete Games: Cack Henley, 47 (1910)
Victories: Cack Henley, 35 (1910)
Losses: Jimmy Whalen (1904), Oscar Jones (1908), 26
Winning Percentage: Sam Gibson, 22–4, .846 (1935)
ERA: Larry Jansen, 1.57 (1946)
Innings Pitched: Jimmy Whalen, 510 (1904)
Consecutive Wins: Frank Browning, 16 (1909)
Shutouts: Curt Davis (1932), Sam Gibson (1942), 9
Strikeouts: Harry Sutor, 339 (1911)
Walks: Eric Erickson, 153 (1917)
Saves: Bob Muncrief, 23 (1952)

Bibliography

Interviews

Ken Aspromonte (2011)
Bob DiPietro (2008)
Grady Hatton (2011)
Gary Hughes (2010)
Marty Keough (2011)
Don Klein (2007)
Albie Pearson (2011)
Bill Renna (2011)
Jack Spring (2011)
Bert Thiel (2011)
Tommy Umphlett (2011)

Periodicals

Brooklyn Daily Eagle
Fresno Bee
Fresno Daily Republican
Los Angeles Herald
Los Angeles Times
Modesto Bee
New York Herald-Telegraph
New York Times
Oakland Tribune
Orange County Register
Pasadena Star News
Portland Press-Herald
Sacramento Bee
Salt Lake City Tribune
San Francisco Call
San Diego Evening Tribune
San Francisco Chronicle
San Francisco Examiner
San Francisco Morning Call
San Francisco Seals Yearbook, 1957
Seattle Times
Stockton Record
Sporting News

Articles

Barney, Chuck. "PCL's Seals, Oaks: Bitter Enemies for Half a Century." *Contra Costa Times,* 2 July 1997, p. 11.

_____, and Bob Hoie, eds. *The Minor League Baseball Research Journal, Volume 1.* Cleveland, OH: The Society of American of American Baseball Research, 1996.

Berger, Ralph. "Ping Bodie." SABR Baseball Biography Project; http://sabr.org/bioproject.

Between Innings. *Baseball Digest* 15, no. 8 (September 1956): 20.

Burbridge, John. "The Brooklyn Dodgers in Jersey City." *The Baseball Research Journal* 39, no. 1 (Summer 2010): 18–26.

Claire, Fred. "Make Way for the Coast League." *Baseball Magazine* 84, no. 4 (July 1955): pp. ?.

Daniel, Dan. "DiMaggio." *Baseball Digest* 12, no. 2 (February 1953): 86–87.

Dolgan, Bob. "Claxton Was Really First." *Cleveland Plain Dealer,* 15 September 1997.

"Eddie Joost Fired as Seals Manager." *Sarasota Herald Tribune,* 9 July 1956, p. 6.

Ellsworth, Peter. "The Brooklyn Dodgers' Move to Los Angeles," *NINE* 14, no. 1 (Fall 2005): 19–40.

Evans, Tim. "The San Francisco Seals Goodwill Baseball Tour of Japan, 1949." Online write-up for 2009–2010 exhibition at the Society of California Pioneers, San Francisco, California. www.californiapioneers.org/sanfran_seals.html.

Johnson, Charles D. "The Little Corporation: Professional Baseball in San Francisco, 1953–1955." *The Baseball Research Journal* 38, no. 1 (summer 2010): 106–116.

Larwin, Tom. "The 1907 Pacific Coast League Championship Series." *The National Pastime* 20 (2000): 112–121.

Leizer, Bill. "For Fans It's Year of the Seal." As Bill Leizer Sees It. *San Francisco Chronicle*, 6 February 1957, p. 3H.

_____. As Bill Leizer Sees It. *San Francisco Chronicle*, 12 February 1957, p. 1H.

Leutzinger, Richard. "Lefty O'Doul and the Development of Japanese Baseball." *The National Pastime* 12 (1992): 30–34.

Lukas, Paul. Sports Fan Fare. *Reading Eagle*, 29 July 1964, p. 41.

"Pard Ballou Saves Many Seal Games." *Spokane Daily Chronicle*, 7 June 1938, page not legible.

Price, Jim. "Devastating Crash Reverberates 60 Years Later." *Rain Check: Baseball in the Pacific Northwest*, edited by Mark Armour. Cleveland, OH: The Society for American Baseball Research, 2006.

Ritter, Collett. "Did Black Sox Throw 1920 Flag, Too?" Reprinted article from *Dayton Journal Herald*. *Baseball Digest* 22, no. 1 (February 1963): 43–44.

Samuelson, Rube. "O'Malley Wants Cold Facts." *Pasadena Star News*, 6 May 1957, page number not legible.

Shapiro, Michael. "Forgiving the Demon of the Dodgers." *The New York Times*, 16 March 2003, p. 12.

Sheldon, Harold. "He Was In On Two Unassisted Triple Plays." *Baseball Digest*, May, 1964, p. 39.

"PCL Cry for Independence." *Time Magazine*, 18 December 1944, p. 27.

Tramel, Berry. "There Was Much More to MLB Player Frank Kellert Than Photo Shows." Website of the *Oklahoman*; http://newsok.com. Accessed May 5, 2009.

Treder, Steve. "Open Classification: The Pacific Coast League's Drive to Turn Major." *NINE*, 15, no. 1 (Fall 2006): 88–109.

White, Gaylon H. "When the Peanut Was Banned from Baseball." *The National Pastime* 16 (1996): 21–22.

Wilson, Darreell. "S.F. Missed Franchise by Two Votes in 1955." *The San Francisco Chronicle*," February 10, 1957, pp 1H & 3H.

Books

Barrow, Edward Grant, with James M. Kahn. *My Fifty Years in Baseball*. New York: Coward-McCann, 1951.

Bauer, Carlos. *The Early Coast League Statistical Record, 1903–1957*. San Diego, CA: Baseball Press, 2004.

Beverage, Richard. *The Angels: Los Angeles in the Pacific Coast League, 1919–1957*, Placentia, CA: Deacon Press, 1981.

_____. *The Early Coast League Statistical Record, 1903–1957*. San Diego, CA: Baseball Press, 2004.

_____. *The Hollywood Stars, Baseball in Movieland, 1926–1957*. Placentia, CA: Deacon Press, 1984.

_____. *The Los Angeles Angels of the Pacific Coast League: A History, 1903–1957*. Jefferson, NC: McFarland, 2011.

Bitker, Steve. *The Original San Francisco Giants: The Giants of '58*. Champaign, IL: Sports Publishing, 2001.

Carlson, Kip, and Paul Anderson. *The Portland Beavers*. Charleston, SC: Arcadia, 2004.

Creamer, Robert W. *Stengel: His Life and Times*. New York: Simon & Schuster, 1984.

Dobbins, Dick. *The Grand Minor League: An Oral History of the Old Pacific Coast League*. Emeryville, CA: Woodford Press, 1999.

_____, and Jon Twitchell. *Nuggets on the Diamond*. Emeryville, CA: Woodford Press, 1994.

Dragseth, P.J. *Eye for Talent*. Jefferson, NC: McFarland, 2010.

_____. *Major League Baseball Scouts: A Biographical Dictionary*. Jefferson, NC: McFarland, 2011.

Erskine, Carl. *Tales from the Dodgers Dugout: Extra Innings*. Champaign, IL: Sports Publishing, 2004.

Jacobs, Martin, and Jack McGuire. *San Francisco Seals*. Charleston, SC: Arcadia, 2005.

James, Bill. *The New Bill James Historical Baseball Abstract.* New York: Free Press, 2001.

Kelley, Brent P. *The San Francisco Seals, 1946–1957.* Jefferson, NC: McFarland, 2002.

Kraus, Rebecca S. *Minor League Baseball: Community Building Through Hometown Sports.* Binghamton, NY: Haworth, 2003.

Lane, F.C. *Batting.* Reprinted with a foreword by Fred Ivor-Campbell. Cleveland, OH: The Society for American Baseball Research, 2001.

Leutzinger, Richard. *Lefty O'Doul: The Legend Baseball Nearly Forgot.* Carmel, CA: Carmel Bay, 1997.

Lowenfish, Lee. *Branch Rickey: Baseball's Ferocious Gentleman.* Lincoln: University of Nebraska Press, 2007.

Luke, Bob. *Dean of Umpires: A Biography of Bill McGowan.* Jefferson, NC: McFarland, 2005.

Mackey, R. Scott. *Barbary Baseball: The Pacific Coast League of the 1920s.* Jefferson, NC: McFarland, 1995.

Mickleson, Ed. *Out of the Park: Memoir of a Minor League Baseball All-Star.* Jefferson, NC: McFarland, 2007.

Neft, David S., Richard M. Cohen, and Michael L. Neft. *Sports Encyclopedia: Baseball.* New York: St. Martin's Press, 2004.

Nelson, Kevin. *The Golden Game: The Story of California Baseball.* San Francisco: California Historical Society, 2004.

Nemec, David. *The Great American Baseball Team Book.* New York: Plume Books, 1992.

O'Neal, Bill. *The Pacific Coast League 1903–1988.* Austin, TX: Eakin Press, 1990.

Rader, Benjamin. *Baseball: A History of America's Game.* Urbana: University of Illinois Press, 2002.

Reidenbaugh, Lowell. *Take Me Out to the Old Ball Park,* rev. ed. St. Louis: The Sporting News Publishing, 1987.

_____. *Baseball Book, Vol. 38.* Cleveland, OH: The Society for American Baseball Research, 2000.

Riley, James A., ed. *The Biographical Encyclopedia of the Negro Baseball Leagues.* New York: Carroll & Graff, 2002.

Silvey, George. *Fifty Years in the Bushes, Baseball That Is.* Florissant, MO: Hardbound (self-published), 1999.

Smith, Ron. *The Ballpark Book.* St. Louis, MO: Sporting News Books, 2003.

Snelling, Dennis. *The Greatest Minor League: A History of the Pacific Coast League, 1903–1957.* Jefferson, NC: McFarland, 2012.

_____, *The Pacific Coast League: A Statistical History 1903–1957.* Jefferson, NC: McFarland, 1995.

Sullivan, Neil. *The Dodgers Move West.* New York: Oxford University Press, 1987.

_____. *The Minors: The Struggles and the Triumph of Baseball's Poor Relation from 1876 to the Present.* New York: St. Martin's Press, 1990.

Swank, Bill. *Echoes from Lane Field: A History of the San Diego Padres, 1926–1957.* Nashville, TN: Turner, 1997.

Ward, Geoffrey, and Ken Burns. *Baseball: An Illustrated History.* New York: Alfred A. Knopf, 1994.

Weiss, William J. (PCL statistician). *Pacific Coast League Record Book 1903–1969.* San Francisco: Pacific Coast League, 1969.

Wells, Donald R. *The Race for the Governor's Cup: The Pacific Coast League Playoffs, 1936–1954.* Jefferson, NC: McFarland, 2000.

Zimbalist, Andrew. *Baseball and Billions: A Probing Look Inside the Big Business of Our National Pastime.* New York: Basic Books, 1994.

Zingg, Paul J. *Harry Hooper: An American Baseball Life.* Urbana: University of Illinois Press, 2004.

Zingg, Paul J., and Mark D. Maderios. *Runs, Hits, and an Era: The Pacific Coast League 1903–1958.* Urbana: University of Illinois Press, 1994.

Online Sources

http://www.baseball-almanac.com
http://www.baseball-reference.com
http://bioproj.sabr.org
http://www.triple-a-baseball.com

http://www.baseballlibrary.com
http://www.oregonencyclopedia.org
http://sabrpedia.org
http://www3.telus.net
http://www.findagame.com
http://www.sportscyclopedia.com
http://www.worldlingo.com
http://burritojustice.com/2010
http://www.thisgreatgame.com/1918.html
http://www.timelinesdb.com
http://www.timelinelad.com
http://www.sportshollywood.com/venon tigers.html
http://www.coe.Ksu.edu
http://www.baseballoakland.com
http://research.sabr.org/journals/
http://www.usfamily.net
http://www.buzzle.com/articles/brooklyn-dodgers-move-tolos-angeles-califor nia.html
http://urbanshocker.wordpress.com/2007/09/21/duane/pillette
http://groups.google.com/group/alt.obit uaries
http://www.baseballhappenings.net/2011/05/duane-pillette
http://www.historicbaseball.com/players
http://minorleagu,researcher.blogspot.com
http://sfgate.com
http://bioproj.sabr.org

http://mopupduty.com/index
http://wwwbaseballinwartime.com
http://thedeadballera.com
http://webcache.googleusercontent.com
http://mlb.mlb.com
http://www.texas-league.com
http://baseballwalloffame.org
http://www.sportshollywood.com
http://minors.sabrwebs.com
http://research.sabr.org/journals/last-hur rah-for-the-seals
http://senior-spectrum.com
http://www.sportshollywood.com/lawrigley.html
http://www.timelinesdb.com
http://www.tdlk.com/-thawley/seals.htm
http://www.baseball-statistics.com
http://sportsillustrated.cnn.com/vault
http://www.hawkeegn.com/Seals
Http://www.outsidelands.org/ewing-field.php
http://oaklandoaks.tripod.com
http://losangeles.dodgers.mlb.com
http://ebbets-fieldmemories
http://www.andrewclem.com/Baseball/Seals Stadium.html
http://misc.baseball.wordpress.com
http://www.19cbaseball.com
http://www.greggsports.com
http://baseball-fever.com

Index